How
to Get
Over
Being
Young

Charlotte Bauer is a prize-winning journalist and Nieman Fellow at Harvard University. UK-born, she and her family moved to South Africa in the 1970s. She lives between Johannesburg and south-west France.

How to Get Over Being Young

A Rough Guide to Midlife

Charlotte Bauer

Atlantic Books
London

Published in hardback and trade paperback in Great Britain in 2021 by
Atlantic Books, an imprint of Atlantic Books Ltd.

This paperback edition published in Great Britain in 2022 by
Atlantic Books, an imprint of Atlantic Books Ltd.

10 9 8 7 6 5 4 3 2 1

A CIP catalogue record for this book is available from the British Library.

Paperback ISBN: 978 1 183895 200 6
E-book ISBN: 978 1 183895 199 3

Printed and bound by CPI Group (UK) Ltd, Croydon, CR0 4YY

Atlantic Books
An imprint of Atlantic Books Ltd
Ormond House
26–27 Boswell Street
London
WC1N 3JZ

www.atlantic-books.co.uk

For Clive Cope, who never let go of my hand.

In ever loving memory of Vicki Wright, my country gal.
November 28 1952 – May 7 2019

Contents

Preface

The bulk of this book was written BC – Before Covid.

Reading through the final draft a year after the pandemic flipped our world upside down, I could see how certain themes might now appear utterly beside the point. How could I care about what was happening to my *face* in the shadow of far graver events? Never mind my flailing hormones and flagging influence, my quest to find the meaning of life after youth, unrealised dreams and restless ambitions, and hovering fears about how I'd handle being really old – *ancient* old. Growing old suddenly seemed a priceless gift, one that not all of us would get. Would my loved ones survive? Would I ever get to hug my mother again? In less noble but no less anxious moments I'd wonder whether I'd ever see my hairdresser again.

Yet even as priorities shifted with the ground beneath our feet and choices I'd assumed were mine to make fell away, I knew that the questions I set out to explore in this book remained real and legitimate: life goes on, relationships go on, changes to our hearts and minds and bodies do not come to a grinding halt, regardless of earth-shattering events beyond our control. It stands to human nature, if not to reason, that we will carry on arguing and laughing and loving and renewing our vows to mad diets and age-defying elixirs as our big fat funny scary odyssey through the unchartered territory of midlife continues.

One day at a time, by any means necessary.

Charlotte Bauer, April 2021

Fifty

'Looking fifty is great if you're sixty.'

— JOAN RIVERS

'There is only one question to be answered in this room,' said the couples counsellor. 'Do you want this marriage or not?'

We'd heard he was a fast worker.

'Either way,' he continued, 'I can help.'

The counsellor's consulting room was in a tree-house-like extension at the bottom of his garden. It perched on top of a steep and perilous flight of steps, and I wondered if they'd been made that way on purpose.

Now that he had our full attention, the counsellor said we were going to start off with a quiz. This sounded more fun.

'Ready? Here goes. When you attend a social function do you:

a. stick together;
b. split up and do your own thing?'

'Split up and do our own thing!' we shouted in unison.

'OK,' said the counsellor, 'if there was a buffet at this function would you:

a. help yourselves;
b. find your partner and offer to fetch them a plate of food?'

'Help ourselves!'
This was almost disappointingly easy.
'Right,' said the counsellor, 'last question. If one of you wanted to leave the function early and the other one wanted to stay, would you:

a. agree on a time and leave together;
b. tell the one who wanted to leave to call a cab?'

Our hands shot up. 'B!'
Husband and I looked at each other and grinned. It had been a while since we'd agreed on anything much, let alone three things in a row.
The counsellor took off his glasses and pinched his eyes. 'You're both what we'd call Selfish A-Types. Now, let's talk about why you're here, shall we?'
A less entertaining hour-and-a-half later, we gingerly descended the steep and perilous steps.
'Be careful going down,' the counsellor called after us. 'They're slippery after the rain.'
As we got into our separate cars to go back to work, Husband said, 'I always knew you were a Selfish A-Type.'
We'd made it out of the tree-house, but we weren't out of the woods.

Fifty

*

Around the time I turned fifty, I got the feeling the universe was trying to tell me something: certain changes I'd started to notice with mild concern seemed to be taking on a life of their own.

Being the oldest person in meetings told me so, the way my grown-up children bossed me around told me so, my moods told everybody.

Relationships that had been good suddenly soured and my once rock-solid marriage seemed to be cracking faster than my face.

I was hot, but not in the way I used to be: the only men who looked at me *that way* any more had hair coming out of their ears or were young enough to be dismissed as perverts.

At first these changes were subtle, erratic and wily enough to make me shake my head and think I'd imagined them. It was like being in a scene in one of those crime thrillers where the woman comes home late at night, alone, and notices the bedroom window she locked that morning is open and the curtain is gently swaying – except there is no breeze. Every tingling bone in her body is telling her to grab the nearest heavy object and get the hell out of there. But when, a moment later, the cat jumps out from behind the curtain, she chides herself for being silly and takes off her make-up instead. *We* know something bad is about to happen, but despite all the alarm bells going off, she can't seem to see it coming.

I didn't see middle age coming. Who does? The indignation! The outrage! The *disbelief*. It began with a series of little jolts and surface wounds, before it got into its stride. The big jolt came when I realised, not so much that I wasn't young any more, but that as far as the rest of the world was concerned, I was old. I had to face facts: youth was a passing phase and I'd passed it.

On a scale of One to Dead, I'd reached the tipping point. There must be things I could do to stop it. It was time for action.

I made an appointment to see Dr Z, to check if I had any hormones left.

Dr Z was French and had a sense of humour that had won him fans and ex-patients alike. He'd told a friend (honestly, a *friend*) who went to see him because she'd gone off sex that his wife had the same problem. Another time he told me when he came flying into the surgery late for our appointment that he was sorry, but he'd overslept and had a hangover.

I trusted Dr Z with my life.

He looked at the results of my blood tests and tutted that I needed an emergency infusion of oestrogen and pro-gesterone. When I asked him to talk me through the pros and cons of hormone replacement therapy, he said there weren't any cons. When I asked about the increased risk of breast cancer, he made a sound like blowing into a paper bag and said that's why we have mammograms.

Dr Z put his elbows on the desk and laced his fingers. 'Do you know Jen Funda?'

'Excuse me?'

He made two air balloons over his jumper. '*Barbarella*?'

Ah, Jane Fonda.

None the wiser as to where this was headed, I nodded.

'She is *eighty* and still *very attractive*.' He gave one of those big French shrugs. 'OK, she is also doing some exercises, but how do you think she got to look like that at her age?'

Apparently not just by doing some exercises.

'Are you saying if I take hormone replacements I'll look like Jane Fonda?'

'Let me put it another way,' said Dr Z. 'When you are a young woman, your body is producing a lot of hormones to make you look a certain way, to attract a mate to make babies with. The hormones keep coming – very good for the baby when you are pregnant and also during breastfeeding.'

Dr Z clamped an air-baby on his left balloon.

'The hormones keep coming while your children are growing up, until you are too old to make babies any more. After that, they start to disappear, and then, one day, they will be finished. Kaput!'

His voice dropped to a dramatic whisper. 'And do you know why?'

I held my breath. He waggled his biro.

'Because your job is finished! *You can die now!*'

He slumped back in his swivel chair, seemingly exhausted by his performance.

By this primal biological clock, I'd be popping out kids at twelve years old and have reached my sell-by date by, what, thirty-six? My life's purpose would be served and there'd be nothing left to look forward to except being clubbed to death by my favourite son as a mark of the esteem in which I'd been held by the tribe after producing fourteen live children before my uterus fell out.

I hastily agreed to take every patch and pill Dr Z recommended and wobbled to my feet.

'One more thing,' he said, handing me the script. 'You might inflate.'

'Excuse me?'

Dr Z put down his biro and made the Jane Fonda balloons. 'If you don't like them, come back and we'll try a different dose. But many women, they are happy when this happens, *very happy*!'

And that, to the best of my fraying short-term memory, was when it officially began: my big fat funny scary odyssey through the dark comedy of midlife.

Striking out through terra incognita, I stumbled on a quest: I would search for the meaning of life after youth. Youth, after all, is fleeting, and by the time most of us notice we've got it, it's gone. Then there's the rest of our lives. The rest of my life had arrived, and deep down I knew there had to be more to look forward to than the children confiscating my car keys.

In truth, I didn't precisely know what the definition of an existential crisis was, but I felt sure I must be having one – or turning into one of those raging, weeping case studies that menopause gurus with suspiciously white teeth write runaway bestsellers about.

Big questions I hadn't known existed started clamouring for my attention – questions every woman seeks answers to as they transition to an older female, answers we hope will lead to, well, more … hope.

How would I know when I'd arrived safely on the other side? Who said we'd get wiser as we got older? What if I found myself and wished I hadn't?

Fifty

In a world obsessed with youth, how was I going to get over being young?

In pursuit of this question, if not the answer, I'd start conversations with my equally destabilised girlfriends as we lost influence, equilibrium and teeth. I would accost colleagues and strangers at parties and pump them for information about their experiences, doubts and desires on the journey into our older selves. Looking ahead to proper old age, I would stalk my mother and aunt and see that the next stage wasn't necessarily going to be all about bed baths and baby food. Mum and Auntie were happy to talk on the record about sex and death and their cosmetic surgeries: my mother gaily shared the details of her own sex life after sixty – a double-edged gift for me – and Auntie still wore thongs. I warned them that everything they said could be taken down and used against them, and kept the voice-recorder rolling.

As the clock ticked, I would track the changes that were happening to me, changes whose significance I had perhaps not yet fully grasped, and others I couldn't yet imagine but which surely lurked in the wings. I resolved to do this as honestly, as unflinchingly, as I could without embarrassing my children any more than I'd have to. My observations would be wholly unscientific and probably deeply flawed, but they would be faithful to my experiences and whatever I learned along the way. Or didn't learn. It would be my truth.

It was time for a reboot; time to unearth buried passions, discover new purpose, make new connections and find a different way to engage with a world that was starting to engage somewhat differently with me.

Whatever the challenges – ugh, I hated that word – that lay ahead, this much I knew: if I didn't make my story now, I might never.

Like every woman old enough to be ageless, I would need to cut my losses and look to my gains – keeping an open mind to the possibility that there *would* be any gains. I was going to have to get comfortable in my skin, the skin that no longer fit quite like a glove.

By any means necessary.

Mental!

'Sometimes it's just better to lie on the floor and
do nothing.'

— ANON

To celebrate her eightieth birthday, Sister Four and I took
Mum on holiday to Nice. One broiling afternoon, siesta
time for the sane, we caught a bus to Monte Carlo, that
ritzy Riviera playpen of high rollers, minor royalty and
good-looking rich people who somehow managed not to
look stupid in boat shoes. Yachts and helicopters were the
main form of transport in Monte Carlo – nobody who was
anybody would be caught dead on a bus; buses were for
day trippers and flunkeys, the busy little elves who swabbed
decks, mixed drinks and generally maintained the life of
luxury that billionaires seemed to believe they deserved.

The bus – I must say it was a very nice bus – wound
up the charming cobbled streets, depositing us high above
the fairy-tale city from where we could see the glittering
harbour bobbing with super yachts. We licked our pista-
chio gelatos and admired the view. Sister Four took selfies.
The sun beat down. Mum said it was the best birthday
treat ever. But once we'd been suitably dazzled by how the

one-per-centers lived, there wasn't a lot to do and it was too hot to walk very far, so we headed back to the bus stop.

There was only one other person waiting, a middle-aged woman with whom Mum immediately struck up a conversation in pidgin French: it emerged from this conversation that the woman was a cleaner, originally from Mali, who was on her way into town to work the night shift at one of the fancy casino hotels. She and Mum, who'd been a hotel cleaner on and off for years, compared notes on how the richest clients were usually the ones who made the most disgusting mess, left the meanest tips and stole the bathrobes. By the time the bus arrived, the queue had swelled to about thirty people, and as the doors hissed open, order collapsed in a savage jostle to board. Everyone surged forward as if it was the last helicopter out of Saigon, elbowing past us and knocking my mother's new friend out of pole position. For a moment Mum was too stunned to move – the British are the world champions of queueing and my mother is no exception. Knowing your place in the line was part of her national heritage, a hat-doffing dance of *after you*. She never thought she'd live to see the day when grown men shoved women and children aside to get on a bus. Her sense of fair play had been violated, and there would be consequences. I recognised the signs: her flame-red hair practically combusting, she pressed her palms against her new friend's substantial bottom and launched her up the steps, shouting, 'Excuse me, this lady was first!' In English, which had absolutely no effect. Having made it onto the bus, my mother's new friend was now peering anxiously through the window, waving at her encouragingly.

But it was too late.

'I'm not getting on this fucking bus!' Mum screamed, attempting to land a slap on the last of the passengers still squeezing on. Sister Four and I definitely weren't getting on the bus: as our mother ramped up, we scuttled behind a lamp post and pretended we didn't know her.

As the bus pulled away from the kerb, Mum shook her fist and yelled, 'You're all cunts!'

I could have told her French people don't do queues.

In the end we took a taxi back to Nice after Mum beat the driver down to a price she considered *fair*. As her hair was still on fire, the driver had rapidly dropped his saw-you-coming-tourist smirk and agreed.

Back at our modest hotel, I put the kettle on while Mum cooled off in the shower.

Later that night, she said she regretted her behaviour, but it wasn't her fault – she'd forgotten to bring her oestrogen on holiday. On top of this terrible news, she told us she'd also had a steroid shot for her arthritis before we left.

'Thank you, my darlings,' she said sleepily as we tucked her up with a bottle of Rescue Remedy. 'I'm sure those French people didn't understand what *cunts* meant.'

Once she was softly snoring away, Sister Four and I got stuck into the minibar and reviewed the day's events. We had to admire her spunk. At eighty there was still fire in her belly; her sparks still flew. She was never going to shut up and subside into an armchair with a Bourbon biscuit or stop standing up for what she believed to be right, even when she went about it all wrong. She was still our Tiger Mum. She was holding the line.

*

The female side of my family has always been excitable.

I'd certainly done my share of door slamming and huffing out of restaurants, but I didn't think it was my fault: the tantrum gene must have gone back several generations, as unaccountable and unavoidable as our blue eyes and fear of clowns. It just couldn't be helped, and anyhow, our lightning tempers usually passed as quickly as they came. We didn't hold grudges and we always said sorry. We were amazed when outsiders – i.e. anyone who got caught in the crossfire – seemed to take longer to recover their good humour than we did. After an indecently short interval, all but our most shameful episodes (we buried those) could be spun into comedy gold, providing hours of entertainment for the whole family – victims, perpetrators and helpless bystanders alike.

There was the time my sisters and I drove from Washington DC to New York City on an eagerly anticipated road trip reunion. It would be the first time I'd seen my sisters in more than two years, and, almost as excitingly, it would be my first visit to the US. It was a shame that Sister Three couldn't be there to complete the circle – I no longer remember why – but the rest of us were in a tizzy of excitement at the prospect of being together again, and in such exotic surroundings. Plans were laid, pennies were saved. I was counting down the sleeps.

Around this time, we were all leading very different lives on a variety of different continents. Sister Four, the youngest, was living in Maryland, Virginia, with her brand-new American husband. Sister Three was couch-surfing around France with her artist friends, and Sister Two had recently moved to Wales, where she acquired a job with prospects and a moulting sheepdog. I had no idea if they were happy. I was the oldest (hence Sister One status) and had settled in South Africa – the furthest away from anyone. In the dark ages before mobile phones and Skype calls, or even affordable air travel for the masses, this meant I was always the last to know anything about anyone. No one exactly *hopped* on a plane to South Africa – in those days it took two flights and eighteen hours to reach London from Johannesburg. Passengers used to change into their *pyjamas*.

I missed my sisters terribly. We hadn't all lived under the same roof, or even in the same country, since our parents' marriage fell apart while we were living in South Africa. We'd emigrated from England several years earlier when our South African father had announced that, after years of having to wear a raincoat to the beach, he was homesick for the sunny land of his birth, which also happened to be the universally reviled home of apartheid. But to my thirteen-year-old eyes, already clouded by misery at having been torn away from my home and school friends and beloved grandmother, South Africa mostly just struck me as a deeply weird backwater, stuck in a time warp – they didn't even have *television* – an end-of-the-earth kind of place into which I had been abruptly, unjustly dumped. It was not a happy move.

I was eighteen and Sister Four was five years old when our parents got divorced, an event that dramatically changed the course of all our lives in ways we could not yet begin to imagine. Like all divorces where children are involved, when a couple breaks up a family breaks up, and no one escapes unscathed. Our father moved to the other side of the country to start his new life with New Wife. Not long afterwards, my mother scooped up my younger sisters and moved back to the UK to be closer to *her* mother and extended family.

Having recently flunked out of journalism school (apparently you had to attend classes in order to graduate), I was all set to move back with them. But then I hit the jackpot: in the space of a single day, I found a job and a boyfriend with prospects.

I chose to stay.

Decades went by in an energetic blur of husbands, children and friends, and a career in journalism that overcame its pathetic beginnings. I missed my English family – my mother and sisters, my grandmother, aunts and cousins. I missed them being around to see my children grow up, to trade the everyday news and gossip, the shared experiences and internecine bitching we reserve exclusively for those nearest and dearest to us, offset by fierce loyalty and unbending support when the chips were down. All the wonderful, terrible things that make families go round: Christmases and birthdays, school plays and holidays and heartaches. Memories I had excluded myself from making with the rest of my big, boisterous clan.

Still, we seized every chance to be together, which in the early years when everyone was hard up took serious effort. When Daughter was born, my mother moved to Johannesburg for a year to help me out, paying her way by getting a job in a bar in a seedy downtown hotel, with room and board. A few years later, on a dark and stormy night when I was heavily pregnant with Son and couldn't sleep, the doorbell rang, giving me such a fright I almost went into labour. Gingerly tiptoeing up to the spyhole, I saw Sister Three standing outside, dripping wet and carrying only a backpack. *From London.* She wanted it to be a surprise, she said. There were many times when I felt alone and bereft, but at times like these, I knew that I was blessed.

1990 was a good year, not only because of my sister reunion road trip: it was the year Son was born, Nelson Mandela was released from jail, and I had just turned thirty – a nice round number, I thought. And now, here we were, Sisters Two and Four and I, bowling along the Interstate 95 from Maryland to Manhattan, passing signs to places whose names we recognised from movies and TV that turned out to actually exist. Baltimore! Philadelphia! New Jersey! We were having so much fun we overshot the New Jersey Turnpike and were soon lost in a maze of grubby streets sagging with car washes, pawn shops and betting joints. New Jersey: stomping ground of the Sopranos. I kept a lookout for bulky men with bouffant hair chewing toothpicks, while Sister Two (who was navigating) and Sister Four (who was driving) tried to get us out of there. After an hour or so, the temperature in the car had risen significantly, despite the air-con blasting away. Sister Four started blaming Sister Two for not being able to read a map; Sister Two blamed Sister Four for shit driving. I sat – blamelessly for once – in the backseat, wondering if the man with the bulging jacket who'd been hovering around giving us funny looks was packing or just had big love handles. Suddenly, Sister Four leaned across the backseat grabbed Sister Two's new camera – the one she was going to use to stalk Robert de Niro when we got to Manhattan – and threw it out of the window. After a moment's shocked silence, Sister Two got out of the car, calmly walked around to the driver's side and picked up the camera, which, thankfully, was still in one piece. Then, in a lightning move, she reached in through the window, grabbed Sister Four by the hair and proceeded to bang her head against the frame. As I sat sniffling in the backseat, begging them to stop, I noticed that the man with the bulging jacket had vanished.

No one in New Jersey ever saw anything.

The thing is, by the time we saw the Manhattan skyline, everyone was friends again. Once we'd checked into our midtown hotel, we were even making jokes about it, all adding our tuppence to the story, polishing it up for future airings.

Menopause only exacerbated our natural inclination to violence.

*

Auntie was forty-eight when she hit Uncle over the head with a frying pan. Uncle was a gentleman of the old school; he wrote books on cricket and wore cravats and a pinkie ring. Hearing he'd been hit on the head by Auntie with a frying pan was like hearing Lord Grantham was going to be in *EastEnders*.

That, said Auntie, was when she knew she needed help. The very next day she went to the doctor and was informed that she'd embarked on the perimenopausal stage of the female life cycle. In Auntie's defence, perimenopause feels a bit like being hit over the head with a frying pan. It comes as a terrible shock to the system, flagging the onset of multiple undesirable losses – fertility, sleep, teeth – and multiple undesirable gains – hot flushes, night sweats and a growing feeling that you've left yourself somewhere, like an umbrella on a bus, except you can't remember which bus. Perimenopause is a *nightmare*.

Luckily, Auntie got on the HRT wagon and never looked back, and Uncle was not a man to hold a grudge.

I was agog to discover that both Mum and Auntie were *still* on HRT. I'd imagined that one of the upsides of being old (if indeed there were any) would be that the symptoms of menopause – the furies, the sweats, the swings – would go away. Yet here they were, Mum at eighty and Auntie four years younger, still knocking back the oestrogen.

My mother went into menopause at fifty-one after a hysterectomy. Everything instantly changed for the worse: she felt awful, she felt *old*. Eventually someone said, 'Try HRT.'

'Darling, it was like the sun coming out.'

She'd been taking it ever since and had never even had a mammogram. 'Why go looking for trouble?' she reasoned.

In her seventies, my mother's doctor had insisted she stop the treatments and refused to renew her script – the cancer risks outweighed the benefits of feeling like Jane Fonda, et cetera et cetera.

My mother was having none of it. 'I went absolutely *mad* after he took me off HRT. I went back and told him, "Now listen here, I know my body better than you do, and at my age I frankly don't care about getting cancer so just give me back my hormones!"

'How could he possibly know what I felt like? He was a *man*.' This, said Mum, who had enthusiastically taken to her role as my menopause mentor, was a good example of one of the upsides of getting old: not giving a fuck what anyone else thought.

Auntie's doctor – also a *man* – had tried the same stunt, so Auntie picked up her frying pan and walked, replacing him with a 'nice lady doctor' who was more sympathetic and gave her a lifetime prescription for Evorel.

HRT, Mum and Auntie agreed, made them feel normal and prevented them from having homicidal thoughts. Well, enough of the time to give their victims a fighting chance, anyway.

As I began to lose equilibrium and general *esprit*, I pondered whether my own increasingly erratic behaviour could be blamed on the onset of menopause or just flammable genes.

Could I help it? Did I need to *own* it?

The hormones Dr Z prescribed seemed a wise investment in the future, but I couldn't honestly say they made me feel fantastic. Though the hot flushes and night sweats had subsided, there were other factors at play. Neurological evidence pointed to the fact that the brain cells of women my age were drying up faster than my fairy. I ricocheted between bouts of self-pity interspersed with stabs of self-loathing and a rumbling, nameless fear that could not be pinned down and would not abate. I had also fallen out of love with the country I'd lived in for most of my adult life: a country that, actually, I doubted I'd ever been much in love with in the first place.

South Africa remained a place of extremes that in some

ways had changed little since the end of apartheid. Racism, homophobia, sexism ... these things were no longer institutionalised, but breeding them out of our hearts and minds was going to take more than a dazzling new constitution. Johannesburg, my home town, was a simmering cauldron of poverty and wealth, glitter and decay, fun and murder. Always on the verge of some or other catastrophe, always just managing to pull back from the brink of chaos. In Johannesburg we partied like there was no tomorrow, because sometimes there wasn't. I felt guilty – for being white, for having chosen to live there even during the years when my race gave me opportunities and privileges I took without thinking twice (actually, sometimes I had thought twice, and I still took them). I was scared – of getting hurt, of someone I loved getting hurt, in what was still one of the most violent cities on earth.

I put on blinkers and shrank my world view to a size I found manageable. It was easier to look away, clap my hands over my ears, protect myself from the knowledge of things I was powerless to change. I felt my moral centre slipping.

When the news didn't depress me, it irritated me: the cult of wellness, billionaire boy racers and their rockets to the moon, celebrity butt implants. The most piffling hiccups in my day would leave me feeling overwhelmed and resentful – last-minute guests, someone being late for a meeting, me being late for a meeting; anything that didn't go according to plan and the lists I made that gave me a slippery sense of control. When I achieved something that hadn't been on my list – tidying the cutlery drawer, remembering to call pest control – I'd write it down and cross it off afterwards. Bewildered, befuddled, I felt, as one friend had described her own state of mind, like a little old lady on the side of a main road wondering, 'Shall I cross? When should I cross?'

I picked fights with Husband, who refused to fight back: arguing with him was like kicking the tyre when the car wouldn't start – pointless and painful. With infuriating calm, he would say I was being irrational, impractical, that I'd lost perspective; that I would come around to seeing things his way if I thought logically for a moment. Then he'd sit back and simply wait for me to blow over. Gaslighting hadn't been invented yet, but sometimes it felt like that was what he was doing. Somehow, he was always right, which I knew couldn't always be right, but they who kept a firm rein on their temper invariably won most arguments in the end. Unlike me, Husband never shouted: he just persisted like the tortoise who beat the hare.

'Mum's kicking off again,' Son would sigh, and I would slide another notch down the family totem pole.

As I drifted further and further away from the people and things I cared about, I saw my family through a scrim of cheesecloth; I strained to hear them. The further away I floated, the smaller they got. Soon I'd be a little speck in the sky and surely it would only be a matter of time before I burst in a small fart of shrivelled rubber. If I wasn't careful, I'd become a self-fulfilling prophecy.

As my fuse got shorter, curiously, my memory seemed to be going the other way. I could remember the dress I'd worn to my tenth birthday party but I forgot my wedding anniversary.

I was out of town on a work trip when I checked my messages in the tea break and saw two from Husband.

The first one said, 'Happy Anniversary!!!!'

The second one said, 'Happy Anniversary????'

Later, I would wonder if this had been a Freudian slip on my part.

*

Being the eldest of my four sisters, I was curious to see how they were coping with the M-word. Half-Sister Five was still too young to merit a seat on the midlife-crisis roller-coaster, but the rest of them were definitely on the verge.

Sister Two was the Dr Doolittle of the family; she and I couldn't have been more different. She tinkered with cars, talked back to horses and let dogs lick her face. She'd watched *Jaws* fifty-three times. In her forties, Sister Two had retreated from society-at-large and moved to the countryside, where she spent happy hours in conversation with her pet chameleon who, she said, made more sense than most people.

But recently I'd noticed that she too had become more … strident in her view that humans needed to be phased out, men first, and the planet returned to its rightful rulers in the animal kingdom. The only sensible solution, she proposed, was mass sterilisation, failing which the government would need to implement a one-child policy while working with all possible speed towards banning children altogether. Sister Two had a remarkably cheerful disposition for someone who believed humanity would end in her lifetime and the stragglers be picked off by lions stalking the aisles in Boots. She could not have been a more affectionate, more thoughtful, more fun aunt to her nieces and nephew, but if they hadn't existed, it's doubtful she would have missed them.

Hmmm, I thought as she banged on about overpopulation and dug up her apocalypse-sized potatoes. But I thought this quietly to myself, eyeing the rifle she used to shoot the rats that had invaded her garden to scavenge from the bird feeders, strung like lanterns in the trees, to save the birds – which, thanks to climate change, apparently had fewer menu options – from starvation. Rats were among the few four-legged creatures that would not inherit the earth if she had anything to do with it. Sister Two had no truck with menopause – she just wasn't having it. Anyhow, her diary was already full. I envied her in a way; unlike me, she didn't seem to be in any doubt about who she was and what she was for, not only what she was against.

Sister Three was the artist and activist of the family, a sort of cross between Marina Abramović and the Baader–Meinhof Gang: she was born stylish and could paint, sculpt, write, compose brilliant music and agitate all at the same time. People still talked about the night she gatecrashed a black-tie dinner in a spangled flying-trapeze onesie; she always stood out from the crowd, often in the lace thrift-store wedding dress she wore to nightclubs. Sister Three tirelessly plotted the overthrow of the rich, the royals and anyone who shopped at Tesco. As she entered the perimenopausal twilight zone, her beliefs seemed to intensify, her readiness to agree to disagree with anyone who disagreed with her less ... ready. She was restless, she chased change – in her life, not only in the wider society. I understood perfectly – I was feeling increasingly like bolting myself. Sister Three and I had always been close; we'd shared friends and gone to the same parties. I wondered if her train was about to leave the station too.

Sister Four was the Shirley Temple of the family, skipping through life in imaginary tap shoes and dimples, keeping everyone entertained. She even had ringlets, though these got straightened out in adulthood with hot irons. But from the far shores of my fifties – a significant twelve years ahead of her – I detected that even she, the consummate people-pleaser, the one who went out of her way to make sure everyone was happy, was starting to go off like a Nokia ringtone.

Sister Four and I had many heart-to-hearts about our dodgy state and status at our respective points on the crisis continuum. We compared notes and timelines and reviewed the empirical evidence.

'It's bewildering,' she told me during one raging, weeping phone call, 'I just don't recognise myself any more.'

Innocently, inescapably, she was about to tap-dance smack into a lamp post, otherwise known as perimenopause. My sweet-tempered sister, the funny girl, was turning into a human hand grenade. She called her explosions the *red mist*. And when the red mist rolled in, it felt as if she was having an out-of-body experience.

'You look down at yourself and you see the fire and scorched earth and people running for cover all around you, *but you can't stop.*'

I didn't like to tell Sister Four it was probably going to get worse before it got better. She tried HRT for a while but put on seven pounds and decided she'd rather be miserable for the rest of her life than get fat. Ditching the hormone replacements, she resorted to other methods – dabbling in yoga, bathing in camomile tea and rubbing yams on her thighs.

We swopped inspirational self-help literature, which, occasionally, I read all the way to the end. There was certainly no shortage of advice being peddled out there: science and pseudo-science, academic tomes, ageless goddesses, wellness gurus, preachers, teachers and flakes of every stripe. There was upbeat literature that made middle age sound like an exclusive club that women had to put their names down for at birth (Mindful Members Only). There were pally in-jokes on greeting cards ('Miranda could no longer stand the sight of her husband and wondered what was wrong with him'); there were the Flat Earthers ('age is just a number'), the Middle Earthers ('magnesium can be found in clay deposits') and the Conspiracy Theorists ('they put it in the water'). Everyone had their little catchphrases, their USPs, but the messaging was essentially the same: we would emerge from the chrysalis of crisis like beautiful butterflies, with brilliant wings, wisdom and inner radiance (outer radiance no longer being possible, whatever it said on the jar). Jolts on the Trans-Menopause Express that might send us stumbling into the wrong carriage and mystery detours en route were only to be expected. The rewards at the end of the journey would make it all worthwhile, as long as we embraced the ride and didn't lean too far out of the window between stations.

One thing the scientists and shamans all agreed on was that a carefully curated approach to health was key to our transition from young to ageless. Mind, body and spirit were symbiotically linked. Like triplets, they could never be truly happy apart. This holistic trinity was called self-care and could be achieved by taking up a brisk physical activity, following your dreams and doing crossword puzzles to ward off early-onset dementia.

I pictured myself running down the road with knickers on my head.

Yes, dementia would definitely need to be warded off, though I was startled to hear how much effort this mission would require on my part, even though menopause wasn't my fault! Apparently, I was the only person who could change things, flip the tables, rearrange the stack on a loaded deck. Being the best new version of myself I could be was *entirely my responsibility*, which didn't seem quite fair. I stopped reading self-help books; there was too much self-help involved.

Perhaps I was depressed?

Mum and Auntie didn't believe in depression. In the war it had all been stiffened spines and sing-a-longs in air-raid shelters. Everyone just *got on with it*. 'Your grandmother didn't have time to be depressed,' said my mother. 'She was too busy picking glass out of the dining-room table and trying to excavate Auntie from her cot after the ceiling fell in on it.'

Going on HRT had helped to alleviate some of the physical symptoms of menopause, but they didn't seem to have brought Jane Fonda and me much closer together.

A multipronged approach was called for. I booked appointments with a GP, a gynaecologist, a menopause-management consultant, a cognitive therapist and a psychiatrist. Then I booked second opinions. Perhaps I could medicate my way through menopause and have someone wake me up when it was over.

Dr R, our family doctor, was a tonic all by himself. He sat on the same side of the desk as his patients, settling into his chair as if he had all the time in the world and that syringing your ear wax was the high point of his day. Twenty minutes with Dr R could bring down my blood pressure and I almost looked forward to getting sick just so I could make another appointment to check my vital signs.

But today the troubles I tipped on his desk were all in my head: the moods, the generalised anxiety, the broken nights during which I'd imagine terrible things happening to my children that I was helpless to prevent.

I wanted it to stop. I wanted the sun to come out. I wanted drugs.

Instead of pulling out his script pad, Dr R put down his pen and said, yes, this was a difficult time of life – confusing, confounding and not always a pretty sight. He tapped a deep crease running the length of his cheek. 'This isn't a wrinkle,' he laughed, 'it's a *crevasse*. But you know,' he went on, 'there just isn't a pill for everything, and anyway, we shouldn't try to numb our feelings, even painful ones – especially painful ones – because it won't help in the end.'

We all had to grope our way through the same tunnel with its unexpected twists and hair-raising turns. We would need to stay sharp, keep our wits about us as we prepared to meet whatever awaited us on the other side, over the hill no longer so far away.

Dr R was somewhere in his fifties too, but until then I hadn't imagined that men had midlife crises, at least not such thoughtful ones.

At the end of this conversation he suggested that I see a psychiatrist: being in touch with our painful, if potentially cathartic, feelings was one thing, but being in pain was another. Sometimes, we needed to get by with a little help from our allopathic friends. 'Let me know how it goes,' he said, throwing in a mercy pack of diazepam and a lollipop.

Dr S, the psychiatrist, was of Eastern European origin and had an old-country feel about her – china-white skin unblemished by direct sunlight, a thrilling accent and a faintly melancholic air that made me think of Cold War era socialism and samizdat books stuffed into overcoats. It made her seem older and wiser, though she had only just turned forty (I asked her). Dr S still had menopause to look forward to.

She asked me lots of questions that I tried to answer as honestly as I could. Did I have violent dreams? Problems at home? Problems with relationships? How much did I drink? How well did I sleep? Had I ever had a panic attack?

Two hours later she said she didn't think my anxiety issues were related to menopause or that I was clinically depressed; she prescribed a medication shown to be extremely effective in the treatment of bipolar patients. Not, she added, seeing my face, that she thought I was bipolar – she just didn't want me to get a fright when I read the insert. Dr S decided I had a mood-destabilising disorder and that I must have caused myself and my family *much misery* that could have been avoided if only I'd come to see her sooner. Echoing Dr R, she warned me that there wasn't a pill for everything and recommended that I see a cognitive therapist.

I'd never been in therapy before, unlike a friend who'd been dragged there by her mother when she was fifteen and diagnosed with acute adolescence. Once, when we were waiting outside the school gate for her mother to fetch her for an appointment, she said, 'Have you had any interesting dreams lately? I've run out.'

My friend said therapy was a lot of pressure: having to look smarter than the therapist, entertaining the therapist, bullshitting the therapist. I wondered if it would feel grown-up and glamorous saying things like 'My therapist said' or merely self-absorbed and pretentious.

Dr E was another brilliant younger woman with whom I felt instantly at home. She made us mugs of tea and steered me to an armchair in her office sliced with late-afternoon sunlight. I couldn't see a fainting couch, but there was a box of what used to be called man-size tissues on the coffee table, which men were only ever supposed to use to blow their nose. We talked about my childhood. We talked about my children's childhood. We talked about Husband and me. We talked about me and me. I unravelled so fast, gave up classified information so quickly, I knew I'd never stand up under torture. I dribbled and leaked, I blurted and blabbed and begged.

Dr E said she thought I had anger issues. She said that when I was done being angry, I'd be sad, and when I was done being sad I'd start to feel better about myself, more optimistic about the future. And that slowly, many tissues later, I would begin to *feel*.

Leaving no chia seed unturned on the path to wellness (a new word in my vocabulary and one I would never get fully comfortable with), my final call was to a self-styled menopause-management consultant who, despite having suspiciously white teeth, came highly recommended. The MMC made me get on a scale. The last time I'd stood on one of these ghastly instruments was at my six-week check-up after Son was born. I shed three grams worth of shoes and closed my eyes, but I could practically hear the digits climbing. This immediately set me against her. She spoke about bioidenticals – apparently a plant-based alternative to old-fashioned HRT with a squirt of pregnant horse urine thrown in. Considering what was in the Botox and fillers I had, the thought of ingesting a bit of horse pee didn't bother me unduly. The MMC printed out a long list of vitamins and mineral supplements. She raised the delicate subject of diet and exercise. I left clutching my report card and assured her that I would give up sugar and walk further than the fridge: once emptied of everything worth eating, it would, hopefully, be easier to walk past.

The MMC said, 'When you feel you're about to lose your cool, take a deep breath and count to ten.' She said it would take practice.

*

One Saturday afternoon, Mum and I were on a bargain hunt in TK Maxx when I got an opportunity to practise the count-to-ten anti-meltdown method. She had followed me into the change room under a pile of clothes. I wasn't sure I wanted her there: I hadn't taken my clothes off in front of anyone since 2009. In any case, TK Maxx's famous end-of-line designer-range bargains had been made to fit dainty Spanish women and tended to get stuck over my head and leave my arms flailing helplessly in the air like Winnie-the-Pooh trapped half-in half-out of Rabbit's front door after a honey binge. This was the change-room surrender position and the reason I preferred to go clothes shopping alone these days. I told Mum she could wait outside and I'd call her if I got into difficulties.

'Don't be so silly, darling,' she said. 'Trust me, I'm your mother.'

I took off my top.

'Goodness!' she gasped. 'That French doctor was right – your boobs *have* got bigger since you went on the HRT!'

Since going to see Dr Z and Dr R and Dr S and Dr E and the MMC, I can't tell you how much more hopeful I was feeling about the future – more in control of my emotions, more tolerant; *tethered*. No more hot flushes, no more drenched nights. The holistic trinity of my body, mind and spirit seemed to be coming together nicely.

I took a deep breath and managed to count to two-and-a-half.

'If you don't turn around and face the wall right now, you can just *get out*!'

Without another word, my mother obediently turned to face the wall. I checked on her in the mirror before trying on the next top. She looked so small standing in the corner with her arms meekly at her sides. Her rowdy red hair had gone very quiet. In a contrite little voice, she said, 'I think your boobs look nice bigger.'

Afterwards, I felt deeply ashamed.

Sister Two, who'd claimed to be breezing through an asymptomatic menopause, said that lately she'd started to feel strange and unsettled, not only because the end of the world hadn't happened yet. She spoke of a sort of brain fog that would leave her staring at her laptop, wondering what she was supposed to be doing; she had road rage and terrible dreams; she'd even gone off overpopulation, her favourite subject.

She and Boyfriend, who was in the direct line of fire, decided they needed a safe word – a code they could use before minor disagreements reached boiling point, while there was still time to turn off the gas. Apparently, he'd suggested 'Calm down, dear'. Luckily Sister Two hadn't yet lost her sense of humour and chose to take this as a joke. Their safe word, she said, had been 78.9 per cent effective. She suggested that Husband and I get one for ourselves.

'Make it something silly,' she advised, 'a word that'll defuse the situation and make you both laugh – a private couple's in-joke.' Sister Two revealed that her and Boyfriend's safe word was 'emu'.

'That's ridiculous,' I said.

'That's the point,' she said.

Husband and I played around with safe words and finally settled on a safe phrase, which was 'nice knowing you'. There would come a time when our safe words wouldn't seem quite so hilarious, and we would find ourselves having to make far-reaching decisions about our future.

But not before I'd kicked a few more tyres.

Understanding the basic mechanics of how the menopause machine worked, all the little cogs and wheels that had to click together before the engine turned over, was one thing, but learning to drive it was going to take a very different set of skills as the rubber hit the road.

Well, there was no time like the present.

Indeed, it was beginning to dawn on me, there was no time *but* the present.

Mortal!

'Listen, the best advice on ageing is this: What's the alternative? The alternative is death. And that's a lot of shit to deal with.'

— WHOOPI GOLDBERG

I couldn't believe it – apparently I was going to die one day. Mortality – or, at least, my own – was not something I gave much thought to when I was young enough not to mind other people using my toothbrush.

It wasn't normal to think about death when you were about to burst into fully formed adult life, that luxuriously self-regulating state I'd dreamed about in the throes of spotty adolescence, wondering if real life – the one where no one would tell me to tidy my room or be nice to my sisters – would ever begin.

As far as I was concerned, anyone older than forty who breathed their last had lived a rich and full life. Incontinent pets were put down; ancient aunts and uncles went up in a puff of talcum powder and pipe smoke. Such losses were sad, especially the pets, but they were not tragedies, and I didn't see what they had to do with me.

Recently, my mother said, 'I know a lot of dead people.' As if they might pop round for a coffee or use their influence to fast-track her through the NHS.

Despite being in good health and high spirits, she had started to talk about euthanasia as if it were a prize she could win in a raffle. She'd already compiled her funeral playlist, though she had left off one of her favourite tunes, 'Every Time We Say Goodbye' sung by Ella Fitzgerald, because she said it would be too sad. Unless, of course, she'd become such a *burden* on her daughters when the time came that it *wouldn't* be too sad. She said she'd leave it up to us.

My mother played the euthanasia card for laughs – she'd always wanted to visit Switzerland et cetera – but behind the jokiness, I sensed that she was preparing for the inevitable, doing mental warm-ups, getting herself used to the idea that she wouldn't last forever. And, really, who wouldn't fear facing up to the end before the end? The not-so-distant day when you'd start being more and more dependent on the kindness of others, having to swallow the small humiliations of asking for help with the most basic of needs.

Marginal, inconvenient. Jam sandwiches for supper.

When you tripped over the pavement, no one would say you fell over, they'd say you'd *had a fall*. And that would be the beginning of the end.

I'd known my mother all my life and knew how upset she'd be just about not being able to wield a mascara wand without risking putting an eye out. She applied fresh make-up and put on a bra before going to bed in case there was a fire and she had to be rescued by strapping firefighters. Considering she smoked in bed, this wasn't such a far-fetched scenario. She was a health-and-safety hazard on a mattress. My sisters and I warned her that if she went up in smoke she'd never get to see the Alps. We asked her, 'Was this the end you had in mind when you said you wanted to be cremated?'

*

It was only in my fifties that it first occurred to me I might not be immortal, that I was actually going to die one day. I don't remember what triggered this visceral knowledge, but it made me go all watery, not unlike the feeling I'd had when I was eight months pregnant and realised the baby would have to come out.

I knew a few dead people too, beautiful young people I couldn't bring myself to delete from my contacts. A close friend had succumbed to Aids; there was a car crash, an overdose. These were tragedies. But I never thought, 'This could happen to me.'

But these days I knew people, beautiful older people, who were getting cancer, a disease that, for all but the unluckiest young ones, was depressingly common in middle age. The big C was no longer the illness that could barely speak its name; in my circle we spoke of it a lot. Conversations began to include words like oncologist and white cells. There were lumpectomies and mastectomies, colonoscopies and biopsies. I learned how to pronounce metastasize. I thought, 'This could happen to me.'

A friend survived for seven years after being diagnosed with colon cancer. Seven years of chemotherapy, seven years of keeping the bad days to herself and living the good ones with gusto and gratitude, though happily not of the saint-like variety: to the end, we gossiped about people we knew behind their backs; we got drunk and danced like old rock chicks, singing along with our air mics. She never stopped caring about the joys and troubles of her family and friends, always wanting to know how *you* were, how things were going in *your* life, endlessly interested in hearing about the stories and people who made the world go around. She was determined, she said, not to become a 'cancer bore'.

When the doctors said there was nothing more they could do, she called to tell me. It was the only time I would ever hear her cry. A little while later she called back to apologise for 'making a fuss'. She made a bucket list, she and her husband threw wild parties, she ditched the wig and tramped off to deserts and jungles with her children. She was making memories for them.

'I love you,' she said as we stood in her driveway and hugged goodbye for what I think we both knew was the last time. And for seven years I'd almost managed to convince myself that the only thing making her sick was the chemo.

I was afraid. Afraid that I'd wasted too much time already on things that didn't really matter, taken myself too seriously, not taken myself seriously enough; neglected to pay sufficient attention to things that *did* really matter, like making the people around me happy while I still had people who wanted to be around me. Saying 'I love you'.

Could it be time to forgive my father? Had I held tightly enough to my own children? Was I careless with my marriage to the only man I'd ever truly loved? Was I trying hard enough to be the best damn ... whoever I could be?

*

When my father left home I went through a phase of wishing he was dead because it would have been easier than believing he'd abandoned us.

Estranged was too strong a word to describe our relationship after he left, but since he'd moved away with New Wife when Sister Four was still in nursery school, we'd not been in close contact. New Wife was only six or seven years older than me, so you can imagine how much I appreciated *her* coming along and stealing our father. He'd been a wonderful dad – playful, patient, kind; he made my Easter hat for the school parade; he took me to the Royal Festival Hall to hear my first classical concert when I was ten; he bought the *Jungle Book* LP and my sisters and I would march around the living room behind him, in order of age and height, while he did his Colonel Hathi impersonation. He was a dentist and came home from work smelling faintly antiseptic. To this day I love the smell of pink mouthwash.

Then he was gone. We seldom saw him after that: *she* wanted him all to herself; *she* wanted her own family. Well, that's what we told ourselves: it was easier to blame her for being possessive than him for being a coward. He sent gifts. He kept his visits short. He said he loved us. But we needed him to love us more.

Over the years my sisters and I had cried a river of bitter tears, revisiting the devastating consequences of his departure, the way in which our lives changed – abruptly, irrevocably and not, for a very long time, for the better. Even as a grown woman I'd seek his attention, often to berate him when I got it, to punish him for what he never quite seemed to grasp he'd done. When would he acknowledge the pain he'd caused us? When would he say sorry?

My mother and sisters had long ago decamped back to the UK, but Dad and I both lived in South Africa – he in Cape Town, me in Johannesburg. The cities were a thousand miles apart, but you could hop on a plane after breakfast and be there by lunchtime. Thanks to my work at the time, I flew to Cape Town quite often. Dad and New Wife always made me feel welcome in their home, would lay on a spread and break out a bottle of Prosecco when they knew I was coming, but I would never have simply popped in unannounced and I seldom stayed the night.

He was good company, my dad, full of beans and stories and boundless curiosity about the lives of others. He was a sentimental man who could well up at the first sign of raindrops on roses and whiskers on kittens. He still smelled faintly, reassuringly, of pink mouthwash. As the years went by, we seemed to have struck an unspoken peace accord of sorts. After all, I was now a middle-aged woman whose own children were almost grown up. How much longer could I go on nursing the wounds of childhood? How much more could I flog a dead past? Anyhow, if I tried to raise anything uncomfortable, remind my father that our upbringing hadn't all been whiskers on kittens in spite of the misty-eyed narrative he'd constructed, he would simply beam fondly and say, 'But look at how wonderfully you and your sisters have turned out – I'm so proud of you all.'

I could never stay angry at him for long. He was my dad, and we all made up our own stories: we had to make the most of the now, the time we had left. Which turned out to be less time than we'd thought.

In his early seventies my father was diagnosed with cancer. Seventy-three no longer seemed very old. A few weeks before he died I went to stay with him. New Wife, a teacher, had to work until the end of term, and he could no longer drive or be left on his own. She called me and asked would I come. I took leave and I went.

Dad was still having the treatments, though I'm not sure why he put himself through them. He wasn't in pain, but he wasn't going to be cured either. He slept in the day time; he needed help making a sandwich; he needed me.

He was still a big, huggy bear and so pleased that I'd come, so … sweet. He was mostly lucid, though there were random moments of odd behaviour, caused, no doubt, by the deadly tumour now pressing on his brain. One afternoon he sat on a kitchen stool watching me make a trifle with a topping of whipped cream that shot out of the aerosol can like shaving foam. Suddenly he lunged forward and grabbed the can and squirted the cream straight from the nozzle into his mouth.

It can't hurt him, I thought, *he's dying.*

New Wife and I had drawn closer over the years; we had a lot in common besides my father, like menopause. We compared symptoms and traded anti-ageing skin-care tips while ruefully agreeing that anti-ageing was an oxymoron. She told me where to get the best one-piece swimsuits – modest, but not too matronly. We marvelled at the striking physical resemblance between our daughters.

When all was said and done, we were family. Under the circumstances, the rest was just water flowing pretty fast under the bridge.

When New Wife went to work, my father and I would pore over family photo albums and take drives to Fish Hoek beach where, until almost the end, he swam every morning with his Breakfast Club, a jolly band of retirees whose numbers were shrinking by the year: heart attacks, strokes, falls from which they never recovered, cancer and more cancer – the predictable wages of age and death. But no one could have predicted the grisly end that one of their members would come to. Early one morning, the retired doctor in her eighties who swam every day, whatever the weather, whatever the safety flags said, was carried off by a great white shark. All that remained was her red rubber swimming cap, bobbing in the waves. The Breakfast Clubbers gawped helplessly from the beach as the shark breached and flipped her up in the air before snapping its jaws around her rag-doll body and plunging back beneath the surface, now blooming with blood. It only took a few seconds, my father said. 'We'd begged her not to swim so far out, but she wouldn't listen. She said it wouldn't be such a bad way to end, doing what she loved, doing what she loved *and could still do*. She said she wasn't afraid.'

I don't know if my father was afraid to die. I never asked him. I never asked him if he'd been happy, if he'd done the things he wanted to do, if he had any regrets.

In the afternoons I read to him from William Boyd's *Any Human Heart* – one of the finest novels ever written about a life. 'What a marvellous story,' he'd say, and, after a while, 'Sorry, I must have nodded off – could you read that bit again?'

Years later I found the bookmark tucked between pages 54 and 55, the page that would never be turned. We never did have *that* conversation: in the end we didn't need to. The only thing left between us was love.

I wondered if New Wife and I would stay in touch, whether there would be much reason to now that the person who'd bound us together was gone. To my initial surprise, in the following years our bonds strengthened. We have laughed and cried together, we are ageing together, we are family. It is never too late to love.

*

There is a growing trend that encourages you to prepare for your own funeral as if you're going to be there in person, or at least be the party-planner-in-chief. You can choose what to wear for the occasion – from your favourite cocktail dress to a range of biodegradable shrouds that help facilitate your transformation into compost. You can decide on the menu and leave instructions about the seating arrangements: revenge can be a dish served very cold indeed. With forward planning you can even video your own eulogy, remembering to leave your login details to a surviving loved one. Passing on your social media usernames and passwords is critical unless you wish to wander ghost-like among your RIP messages on Facebook, never making any new friends and having annual alerts pop up reminding everyone to wish you happy birthday. Secret WhatsApp liaisons and malicious gossip that might upset the bereaved and dent your legacy would obviously need to be deleted while you still had any say in the matter.

There are numerous ways to break taboos around dying and show consideration for the living. You could relieve them of the burden of cleaning out your closets, the kitchen drawers crammed with congealed cough sweets and dry-cleaning stubs from 2007. You could let things go, have a good clear-out before you leave, formulate a neat exit strategy. Apparently, this can be tremendously cathartic, and if there were a Picasso buried under all that crap in the attic, you'd find it first.

Brawls over the will can be avoided too by leaving scrupulous instructions regarding the distribution of your worldly goods. In my family, this wasn't necessary because my sisters and I busied ourselves scrapping over the spoils while Mum was still in the building. Not having the kind of money that caused blood feuds, we contented ourselves with dividing up her furniture. The idea was to stick a Post-it with your name on it under a table or a trinket you fancied while the others weren't looking.

The next time I visited Mum I wrote down my name on two Post-its and went to stick them on a handsome pair of spoon-back chairs my parents had bought on honeymoon and which had moved with my mother to every home she'd lived in since. Stapled to the hessian underside of each chair I found two Post-its with another sister's name written on them and the words 'Don't even think about it'. I am not going to say which sister because it's still not funny – not to me anyway.

'You know I've always loved those chairs!' I whined to my mother.

'Well, you and she can have one each.'

'But they're a pair!'

'You girls really must learn to share.'

Mum held all the power cards, and sowing division and making side deals while she was still around was infinitely preferable to missing all the fun when the gloves came off in the crematorium car park.

Beyond this fun-for-the-whole-family game, Mum showed little interest in curating her own death, and having refused to engage with the digital world, we wouldn't have to worry about capturing her passwords or finding out she'd been carrying on with strange men on WhatsApp. To be fair, she'd been an enthusiastic early adopter of computers in the days when they were the size of the guest loo and you could have any colour you liked as long as it was grey. She used to 'send' me emails when MIT scientists were still struggling to launch the internet, then call to ask why I hadn't replied. When she found out that email hadn't yet caught up with the Royal Mail, she gave up.

'Oh, fuck this, life's too short.' There was no arguing with that.

After that, she refused to even try using the mobile phone Sister Two had given her for emergencies. 'Meet me under the clock at Paddington station at 2 p.m. next Thursday,' she'd say, sending me into a flat panic about what would happen if my train was late or her train was late or they'd moved the clock.

'Don't be ridiculous,' she'd say. 'How do you think people made arrangements before mobile phones?'

At least I knew her last words wouldn't be Zxy5&rt3Lc.

By stark contrast, Mother-in-Law, who would soon be ninety, was the Mark Zuckerberg of her retirement village. She did her banking online, played Scrabble with people all over the world and was a regular contributor to the family WhatsApp group.

One of her hobbies back in the days when newspapers still ran classified adverts for second-hand cars, never-used wedding gowns and funerals was reading the death notices. I wouldn't say Mother-in-Law exactly relished finding out that someone she knew had died, but she often clicked her tongue in the same way as when she got a seven-letter word on a triple corner. The deceased – Phyllis or Doris or Babs – was not a close enough friend for her to have heard the news of their passing in person, which made hearing it less of a shock and more like learning of the death of an old movie star whose films had been part of your youth: it gave you a little jolt, brought long-forgotten memories to the surface and added a bit of drama to the day – an opportunity to ring up whichever Phyllis or Doris or Babs was still alive and share the news, 'Did you hear about …?'

But as time went by and the trickle of Mother-in-Law's late acquaintances became a steady stream of late friends and both her sisters, she seemed to lose interest in reading the death notices. Perhaps doing so felt too close to home or was just plain depressing. In Mother-in-Law's close-knit Jewish community, everyone went to everyone's funeral. The protocol never varied: the rabbi came, the deceased was buried within twenty-four hours, the same prayers were said over every grave. Afterwards, everyone repaired to the family home where more prayers were said and the bereaved family made sure there was too much food. A year later, a headstone would be unveiled in a ceremony to mark the end of the official mourning period.

After the death of her husband, Mother-in-Law stopped going to funerals.

My mother said this was perfectly understandable. She said she felt the same way – losing more and more of the people you'd shared your life with, laughed till you cried with, filled photo albums with was awful. They'd been at your wedding; you'd been at their *children's* weddings. But now these friends were fading to sepia, and soon you might be the only one left who remembered. It could get you down if you dwelt on it. Best to turn your face to the light, to the living, to the now.

Having been raised on compulsory church services twice on Sundays, Mum and Auntie despised organised religion. This meant that there would be no religious or community rituals to fall back on when it was their turn, no automatic rites to manage the immediate shock of the lonelier grieving to come. Mum and Auntie's options were open, which, in a way, made things more complicated. I sat them down and asked them how they'd like to be laid to rest when the time came.

My mother said the only service she'd countenance was a humanist one and that no one in a dog collar should be allowed to attend, except for her dog. Auntie said we could bury her in cardboard for all she cared, as long as it was painted red, her favourite colour, and perhaps we could throw in a couple of Mars bars.

She already had a plot reserved in the cemetery on top of Uncle's.

'He always liked me on top,' said Auntie, which set her and my mother off giggling like a pair of drunk schoolgirls.

I reminded them that this was a serious business and that one of their last duties on earth would be to make things easier for their surviving loved ones.

Hang on, they protested, 'We're not dead yet!'

It was hard getting them to take being dead seriously, but I persevered until my mother told me something I hadn't known before: when she was forty she'd had a near-death experience. She was undergoing emergency surgery a few weeks after a botched procedure, when suddenly she saw her late father standing at the far end of a brilliantly lit garden in his bank-manager suit, beckoning her to follow him through an archway. She felt, she said, utterly euphoric. But before she could reach him, she felt herself being tugged back. The brilliant light receded; her father turned and walked through the arch. My mother was brought back to life on the theatre table. What gave this story credibility was that it sounded like everyone else's near-death experience I'd ever heard about – the light, the euphoria, the familiar figure beckoning them forward. My mother was an accomplished storyteller and I knew she would have made up a more original near-death experience if she'd been lying.

I remembered that night: I'd had a starring role in the school play. I got an award for it, the only prize I'd ever won or would ever win during my school years, which largely passed in a haze of contempt and cigarette smoke behind the netball courts. It was only after the show that I'd realised Mum hadn't been there, that my father had come alone. Mum had been too ill to get out of bed for weeks, but I'd thought she was getting better: she'd said she'd try to come. Like most fifteen-year-olds, I was blithely uninterested in anyone else's problems, least of all my parents'. I didn't know how ill she was, I just remember thinking how *selfish* of her to pick that night of all nights – my one shining moment in the spotlight – to not make the effort. Then Dad told me she'd been rushed to hospital. Though my parents' marriage was limping towards the end by then, he looked pretty shaken. He kept his voice light, said he was going to drop me at home and get back to the hospital. No one ever said that by the time the doctors got her into theatre they thought she was likely to die, which, as one of the attending nurses told Mum the next day, technically, she had.

For a long moment after Mum finished telling us about her near-death experience, Auntie and I sat in unusually silent contemplation – of the fine line that exists between life and death, of how very close we had come to losing her and, in my case, of how callous youth could be.

Mum put the kettle on. 'Being old,' she said, 'is much more challenging than being dead.'

Auntie hadn't had a near-death experience herself, unless you counted the time she almost got trampled by a rogue police horse at the Changing of the Guard. She agreed with Mum that there was no point being scared of death, even if you weren't sure anyone you actually wanted to see would be waiting for you on the other side with a large vodka tonic. Auntie confided that she was afraid that my mother would go before her; that she was far more afraid of the idea that she might live long enough to lose her independence and be unable to take care of herself, to do her own housework, to drive Sugar Babe.

Auntie loved Sugar Babe, her tarmac-hugging white Honda that I already struggled to climb in and out of. But even Sugar Babe's body was starting to rust. Instead of having the car resprayed – Auntie said she needed to hang on to her pennies for future repairs on her own rusty bits – she bought a bottle of white nail polish at Boots and touched it up herself. Cousin and I went over to inspect her handiwork: the car now looked like a bad French manicure, but Auntie was so pleased with it we didn't have the heart to suggest it was probably time to get her eyes tested.

Auntie was already on beta blockers and blood thinners for an irregular heartbeat; she got out of breath walking up the single flight of stairs to her flat, which, she said, had nothing to do with smoking. Sometimes she had trouble with her feet, which, she said, had nothing to do with the fact she still wore heels and wouldn't be caught dead shuffling along in 'old lady trainers'. Alright, she no longer had quite the same physical stamina she'd once had, the Duracell Bunny energy. But these were minor things, things you got used to.

'If push comes to shove,' said Auntie, 'I'm not going to be put to bed in a home at 6 p.m. without my ciggies and vodka. I'll spend my money on round-the-clock home care if I have to. I'd *hate* to go into a retirement village. Ugh, even the word is repellent. I'd rather go to an orphanage.'

'What do you mean an *orphanage*, Auntie?'

'Well, darling, I *like* children.'

Sometimes Auntie's nonsense made complete sense.

Picking up on this theme, Mum said she knew what Auntie meant: she tried to steer clear of *certain types* of old people, the ones whose world had shrunk to a pinpoint of self-absorption, the ones who'd lost interest in anything besides the minutiae of their own lives – what they'd eaten for lunch, a running commentary on the weather, the roadworks, what the doctor said.

Nothing, said Mum, made her feel old as much as being around other old people who banged on about their aches and pains. It could be hard enough liking them when they didn't.

'Ask them how they are and they actually *tell* you,' she spluttered. 'No, darling, I will only hang out with old people who don't grizzle and moan.' She admitted this could be the reason why she had only a modest handful of good friends, including Auntie, of course.

'Finding people I like and admire, people who are still interested in other people, *amusing* people, is getting harder, because there aren't so many to choose from any more.'

Age prejudice, she said, wasn't always the fault of the beholder. Let's say you'd been a dull, self-centred twit when you were young: chances were that you'd still be a dull, self-centred twit when you were old, plus by then your children would have emigrated to the Australian Outback where they'd be hard to track down.

*

For as long as we had a living parent, there would always be a part of us that would be the child. Until the roles were thrown into reverse.

Several of my friends were increasingly caught up in the care of their frail parents who, thanks to medical advances, were living longer than Galapagos tortoises.

My sisters and I hadn't had to take care of our father, so there'd never been any need for upsetting decisions about whether it was time for him to go into a home, or rotate him among us, or how we'd divvy up the costs of his care. He died after a relatively short illness, in his own bed, years before decrepitude set in, and was attended to by a wife who remained steadfast and was young and strong enough to do the heavy lifting.

Sometimes I'd see my friend M lugging shopping bags up the hill en route to visit her parents. M's mother was in her late eighties, her father in his early nineties. M herself was sixty-two: she joked that she'd barely noticed her midlife crisis because it had been upstaged by her parents.

M's parents were lucky: they lived in a big bright flat and could afford to pay for day care. They still had each other. They had a loving family living practically next door. But luck was a strong word when you needed help getting washed and dressed and thought Prince Charles was your best mate.

M had never got on well with her mother, and old age hadn't made their relationship any easier. Dealing with her mother's moods, said M, required a special kind of patience. By contrast, M adored her father, but now that he'd become so friendly with the royal family, he wasn't around much. He dithered about which tie to wear to Buckingham Palace and said he couldn't come to dinner because Harry and Meghan were about to arrive with little Archie and he had to babysit.

Their car keys had long ago been confiscated, curtailing their daily excursions to the shopping mall to while away an hour or two drinking coffee, window-shopping for things they no longer wanted, staving off the boredom and buying cake in case Charles and Camilla popped round unannounced. These little outings were the reason M's mother still put on make-up and a nice frock in the morning.

I remembered accompanying my mother (who was her mother's carer until she – my mother! – was in her seventies) to fetch Grandmother from the care home and drive her around the village, stopping at scenic spots overlooking the sea. Getting her ready for the outing, getting her into the car and getting her out of the car, practically took up more time than the outing itself. My mother visited Grandmother every single day until the end, watching her beloved mother become an empty shell of the bouncy, giggly, busy woman she'd once been. Yes, said M, that was the hardest part for her, being forced to watch her father 'slowly dissolve, until he was barely there at all'.

While M and I were talking about all this, her mother called to say that she – M – had forgotten to buy Listerine and bananas, so she – M – would need to run back to the shops before they closed. 'Right, bananas and Listerine,' said M. 'Sure, Mum, no problem.' After hanging up she said, 'I just say yes to everything, but I don't necessarily do anything because I have to ration my own energies.'

M had recently quit her dream job in Cape Town, a two-hour plane shuttle from the family home in Johannesburg – a flat in the same street as her parents – where M's husband and student daughters lived. In the beginning, M commuted between the two cities every three weeks. As her parents' health deteriorated, she arranged with her boss to fly home every two weeks; eventually M was coming home every weekend. She worried that she'd be in the wrong city when her parents died; she felt bad about leaving her husband and daughters to care for them – rotating the night shift, calling out the electrician, ferrying them to the doctor, bundling them up and driving them to their favourite coffee shop to break the tedium of their days.

The day came when M made the decision to hand in her notice and come home for good.

'Though my husband and daughters never implied that I was absconding in the years when I worked away from home, it seemed terribly unfair to shift the burden of care onto them, and as my parents needed more and more attention and became more demanding, I felt as if I was outsourcing my responsibilities.

'The day I wrote my letter of resignation I just cried and cried and cried. But I don't regret it, because you can't outsource being present; you can't outsource love.'

Being there for aged parents when you yourself were ageing and had only recently recovered from teenaged children demanded a powerful degree of unrequited effort.

A few weeks later, I bumped into M at the shops. I told her that what she'd said in our conversation about love and duty had moved me deeply. I told her how much I appreciated her sharing her story. M snorted and said she'd like to retract her statement. She'd just spent two hours in the bank bickering with her mother about whether to move their money from Savings to Current while her father sat in his wheelchair, straining to remember where he'd left his invitation to Prince Harry's birthday party. It had been a bad day.

Thank God Mum and Auntie were ambulant, continent and had most of their marbles. They were still capable of making their own decisions; they still had *agency*. Of course, my sisters and I talked about their little quirks behind their backs (as they doubtless talked about ours), but we did not talk about them as if they'd left the building.

I noticed that my mother was becoming more ... reflective. It wasn't that she didn't have things to look forward to, she said, only that, there being more of her life behind her than in front of her, the most exciting things had already happened: riding pillion on a motorbike through Spain with a little black dress in her knapsack for when they got to Madrid; falling in love; buying a first home; fluffing up the nest with babies ... being at the pumping heart of life, making things happen.

Often these days she reminisced about the past – the war, her childhood, our childhood, her parents and grandparents; the people and events stitched into the rich tapestry of her formative self. She mostly stuck to the happy memories, or made them happier than perhaps they'd been at the time. Regaling us with these stories – many of which I'd heard before but was always ready to hear again – seemed to bring her comfort. Apart from being glimpses into our family history, these were fascinating social histories, bringing to life a bygone age of rag-and-bone men, horse-drawn milk carts and standing up for the national anthem; the Great Smog of London in '52 that cloaked the city in perpetual night and turned her white gloves black. Long-dead relatives rose before my eyes with fob watches and taffeta dresses, drinking sherry from tiny crystal glasses and gathering around the radio for Winston Churchill's every pronouncement. There were darker stories too: a secret love child, the cousin who 'fiddled' but got his comeuppance at Delville Wood. My mother's past returned to nuzzle up against her present: she was a living archive. Now I was old enough to appreciate that this was how clan memory was preserved, how the DNA links connecting one generation to another passed along the human chain: this was our legacy. I would pass these stories on to my children and they would tell their children fireside tales about the olden days, when vast ice mountains rose from the ocean, when trolls roamed the internet, and their grandparents went on holiday to places called Airbnbs.

But Mum and Auntie weren't consigned to the vaults of history yet, and there were plenty of things they still wanted to do. They were making the necessary adjustments, discovering new purpose and pleasures in their smaller world.

Auntie got three papers a day and did the Sudoku in all of them. She volunteered at the local hospice and took up art classes where she unearthed a real talent for figure drawing. Spurred on by her success, she threatened to finish an unfinished study of two goose girls by Augustus John that Uncle had bought many years ago, *for a song*, that now hung temptingly on her red living-room wall.

Mum still threw an occasional dinner party and looked forward to her weekly coffee morning with her small circle of non-moaning friends, including Poor Iris, who, Mum said, had a wicked bitch of a daughter and lived with her centenarian father. If anyone had a right to moan it was Iris, but she never did.

Mum got voted on to the body corporate of her block of flats and developed a taste for grass-roots politics, taking up a post in the peanut gallery at council meetings and exercising her democratic right to heckle. Her big moment came when she and her boon companion, Mr B, fomented an uprising against the sudden appearance of a pay station at the free car park above the dog walkers' section of the beach. Mr B made placards and they were interviewed by a local TV station, after which they triumphantly repaired to the Tiggy Winkle Tea Shoppe for a round of clotted cream scones.

But by far and away my mother's biggest life-changing new hobby arrived in the form of a miniature apricot-coloured poodle. She and Dog looked uncannily alike and had the same hair. The question of getting a pet in old age was a litmus test for the balance of power that see-sawed between middle-aged children and their parents. It was the first time my sisters and I had made our mother consult before coming to a decision. What if she couldn't cope with the physical demands of having a dog? What if the dog got lost or Mum got lost? Who would take responsibility for the dog in the event of ...? A friend who'd recently been through the same scenario with her elderly mother had finally relented: her mother could get a dog, but they'd both have to be chipped.

The parent was becoming the child, a child begging for a puppy for Christmas and being lectured about responsibility. It wasn't nice, but it was kind of inevitable if you insisted on getting old enough to be infantilised.

At a family round table we laid out the pros and cons, and my mother made her pitch. Having a dog would keep her on her toes, it would be lovely to have a helpless creature to look after, a dog would be good company – as long as it didn't bitch about its problems – and she promised faithfully to walk it every day and not take it on protest marches. Mum wound up her pitch:

'Anyhow, I'm not going to subside in a heap of dust just because I'm old and I will *not* just do what anyone tells me to do. I will be *seen* and *heard*, so hear this, daughters: I'M GETTING A DOG.'

Mum doted on Dog, though she pretended not to, speaking to it in a snappy tone that didn't fool Dog for a moment. Dog got hand-chopped best-butcher's liver for lunch, which I could vouch for because I ate some when I found it in a pan on the stove and thought it was for us. Whatever the weather, Dog got walked four times a day because it didn't like 'doing its business' on the convenient patch of grass outside the back door, preferring instead to lead my mother a merry dance through the Burrows, along the beach, past the shops and round the kiddies' play park. After lunch Mum and Dog snoozed on the best seat in the house, an orange wingback chair roughly the same colour as them. Mum lost half a stone and fit back into her skinny jeans. She was thrilled with Dog, with her new waistline, with life in general. She announced that she was changing her will and leaving the wingback chair to Dog, who refused to sleep anywhere else.

Mum and Auntie were never bored, which meant they were never boring. They were still writing their story, even if it was a short one. I learned a lot by observing them: making light of the inevitable while being mindful of its approach; ending phone calls and visits with *I love you*. Except on Saturday nights when they went all out to kill each other at canasta.

I couldn't be at Auntie's surprise eightieth birthday party, so I sent her a French lace thong to add to her everyday underwear collection. The next time I saw Auntie, I asked her how she felt about being eighty. Did she feel any different? But Auntie simply looked confused for a moment and said, 'No, no different from when I turned forty or fifty. Why would I?' It wasn't easy getting Mum and Auntie to take old age seriously, but I came to think of this as one of the secrets of their success. They laughed a lot and surrounded themselves with positive people and thoughts. They felt lucky – lucky to have each other, lucky to have children who still wanted to be around them, lucky, said Auntie, 'to have warmth and food and money and family'.

'I don't think there's anything more I want,' she said. 'Does that sound silly, darling?'

'No, Auntie, I don't think it sounds silly at all.'

*

Under Sister Two's supervision, Mum eventually replaced her car that had no heater and doors that opened at whim with a nippy red hatchback with racing stripes. Sister Two sent me a photo of her beaming from the driver's seat in a jaunty headscarf with Dog leaning out of the window. When I called to congratulate her, she didn't sound as pleased as I thought she'd be.

'Oh, darling, I think I left your grandmother in the old car.'

My grandmother had been dead since 2006. I had no idea what she was talking about.

'She was in the boot – I forgot to take her out.'

This was how I found out my mother had been keeping my grandmother's ashes in a Lidl bag in the boot of her car.

When I asked her why, her voice wobbled. 'So she'd always be with me.'

Sister Two went back to the garage to ask if they'd seen our grandmother, only to be told by a stunned mechanic that the car had already been sent to landfill.

One day I'd have to let my mother go too, and Auntie, and perhaps others I could not bear to think about. Life was so precious, so fragile, so random; and still it was impossible to be grateful for it all the time. I pictured Mum and Auntie going out like Thelma and Louise, holding hands as Sugar Babe flew over the cliff and soared above a sunlit canyon.

And they would always be together.

Face Time

> 'One's chronological age is usually obvious.
> [...] Nobody who is asked the question "How
> old do you think I am?" ever answers the question
> honestly. The question that is answered is, "How
> old do you think I think you think I am?"'
>
> — GERMAINE GREER

Once, I could no sooner imagine being middle-aged
than believe I'd die one day. But lately I was starting to
look better from the back than the front and I couldn't
tell where my lipstick should end. It was all very upsetting and I wondered if being upset made me a vain and
shallow person.

But as the first shadows fell across my body, how could
I not wish them gone?

Who wouldn't be tempted to make deals with the devil?

It wasn't vanity, it was panic.

These changes to my body stirred up powerful feelings
because I knew that they were mere marker flags to places
where still darker changes lay just beneath the surface.

Show me the woman who doesn't feel a stab of despair
as her youthful looks are lowered into the ground,

irrevocably, unreachably, forever. But without a ceremonial pause, a wistful salute as the flag comes down, how can we move on, face up to new realities? How will we recognise the gains if we don't first acknowledge the losses? How will we get over it?

A decent mourning period is essential if we are to accept that the girl we've taken for granted all these years has gone, and that it is time to turn around and greet the strange woman sneaking up behind us.

But look how we cling to the clichés and maxims of faux youth as we grow older: *age is just a number, you're as young as you feel, I'm young at heart.* Young people don't go around saying they feel young; only old people speak like that. Youth is the gold standard against which we continue to measure ourselves, refusing to accept that our hearts are as old as we are, that the chronology is on the wall.

The paradox of the age-is-just-a-number brigade is that they actually love playing the numbers game. At fifty my grandmother looked sixty. Now sixty is the new fifty and fifty is the new forty. With scrupulous self-care and attention to detail, sixty could even be the new forty-five and fifty the new thirty-five. Unfortunately, there is no quibbling with the fact that twelve is the new twenty and, for those of us still harbouring a millennial in the back bedroom, twenty-five is the new ten.

Auntie was a paid-up member of the age-is-just-a-number club.

When her granddaughter once asked her how old she was going to be on her next birthday, Auntie replied carefully, 'Well, darling, I could be *seventy-five* or I could be *fifty-seven.*'

Granddaughter, who was eight going on twenty-four at the time, thought about this for a moment. 'But, Nonna, you can't be fifty-seven – Mum's fifty-six.'

Auntie's fantasy age could be calculated in dog years, backwards.

Even Gloria Steinem, the grandmother of sexy feminism, played the numbers game in her own way. She had a great party trick I'd once witnessed first-hand at a conference. Gloria was the star turn. She came on stage dressed from honey mane to booted toe in New York black – turtleneck sweater, slender belt brushing slender hips and a flat stomach which practically got a standing ovation all of its own. 'This is what seventy looks like!' she whooped, punching the air. The crowd went wild. I heard she'd done it again when she was eighty, and would do it again if she was still around at ninety. As ninety was the new seventy and Gloria was in very good nick, this would likely come to pass.

Any old way you cut the maths, the Age of Agelessness was upon us, and I was now plainly old enough to be ageless. This terrible word came into vogue thanks to a raft of celebrity menopause gurus who were obviously feeling their age. What being ageless actually means is flinging everything we still have or can buy, barring time, into looking younger. Never mind (for a moment) the fact that our bottom is falling out of the desirability market, looking younger enhances our currency everywhere: we get better work opportunities, babies let us kiss them, shop assistants see us.

How could we have known then that youth was the gift that wouldn't keep on giving?

Pretending my face wasn't at war with itself wouldn't make a jot of difference to time, which would march all over it anyway. My rational brain knew this; my primal brain was harder to convince. Perhaps, said Primal Brain to Rational Brain, we should give it a whirl, put our ageless heart and aching back into transitioning with flair and self-care – self-care, a term I'd only recently heard of, meant doing things that were good for you, healthy things that would lull your petals into thinking they weren't about to go brown and drop off one by one.

I remained deeply sceptical of anti-ageing cult-speak, but equally of the more Confucian school of thought that urged us to love our wrinkles and embrace our battle lines because they embody the sum of our rich experiences and attest to how much laughter there's been in our lives – at least up to now. Hahaha.

If the Confucian school aimed to help us go forward gracefully, the outer extremes of the ageless crowd clawed at the doors of desperation.

And I was desperate.

*

I think I'll get Botox, I announced to Husband while he was watching a penalty shoot-out.

You don't need Botox, he said, flapping me away from the TV screen. True, nobody needed Botox, like nobody needed upper arms like Michelle Obama and seventeen pairs of sandals. But the whole point of Botox and fillers (and a plethora of other non-surgical procedures catering to our desire to look younger) was that it was meant to look as if you hadn't had any.

I did my homework: I pored over the what-went-wrong

pictures; I learned that aesthetics doctors weren't all born equal and that the ones who spend too much time with their own heads in the Restylane cabinet are to be avoided. I knew that if I came out looking like Donatella Versace I'd have only myself to blame.

The clinic's reception area was arranged with pale velvet sofas and orchids in beaten pewter bowls. Glossy young assistants glided about in white jumpsuits serving herbal teas in little china pots. The assistants all had very high foreheads, though I supposed they couldn't all be intellectually gifted. It was nothing like any doctor's waiting room I'd ever been in, cluttered with chewed up magazines, kiddies' corners and plastic chairs.

'Dr B will see you now,' said one of the shiny assistants with a creaseless smile.

It was impossible to tell Dr B's age; he'd had so much work he looked like a ventriloquist's dummy. Opening his trapdoor mouth, he said, 'Ageing is a disease and it's my job to cure it.'

I know, I should've run, but it had taken so long to get an appointment.

'Um, I don't think of it as a *disease*,' I said, looking around in case there really was someone with a hand up Dr B's jacket. 'I just want to look more like me – you know, realistically speaking.'

But there was nothing realistically speaking about Dr B. His awful maw seemed to move on invisible hinges. Despite these clear warnings, Primal Brain got the better of Rational Brain and agreed to a few other minor adjustments at the same time. Snapping on latex gloves, Dr B handed me a condom full of ice and told me to put it on my head. 'Forehead,' he said, seeing my confusion, 'to numb the area I'm going to inject.'

Twenty minutes later I walked out looking like Dr B's secret sister, the one the family kept locked in the basement.

If we lived somewhere civilised like Hollywood, I sniffled to Sister Four, I'd sue him. If we lived in Hollywood, said Sister Four, there'd be a police unit dedicated to fighting cosmetics crimes.

Of all my sisters, Sister Four and I had the most in common when it came to pulling out all the try-me-buy-me beauty stops. We puzzled over mixed messages in women's magazines (*Love yourself the way you are! Lose 7lbs by Saturday!*) and kept abreast of new technologies. We fought the enemy on the beaches and in the salons. We were the beauty equivalent of the Bletchley Park decoders: racing against the clock, honing our methods, performing experiments with hyaluronic acid, Dead Sea serums, fat burners, pore shrinkers, collagen infusions and mood-altering oils. Sister Four teamed up with her doctor and threw Botox parties with mojitos and group discounts. She made microblading sound like a daring new sport. She showed me how to use an epilator that pulled out leg hair by the roots and felt like being run over by a lawnmower. She gave me second-degree burns with a chemical peel she found on the Dark Web.

TV makeover shows that warned viewers not to try this at home only spurred Sister Four on. Her apartment was a red zone of electrical wires, laser guns and hot wax. She bought an infrared sleeping bag which she planned to take on a camping trip before remembering it had to be plugged in.

Sister Four believed in covering all the bases: when she wasn't weeping under a collagen lamp, she was mixing up home remedies – turmeric face masks that made her look like a Dorito for a week and whitening toothpaste with bicarbonate of soda that caused her to foam at the mouth. The toothpaste turned out to be excellent for stubborn carpet stains.

Those of us who weren't embracing our wrinkles were embracing the propaganda that decay could be stopped in its tracks with a personal trainer and a jar of exorbitantly expensive moisturiser. What the cosmetics houses and media laughably called *premature* ageing could be shown the door; there were secrets and spells which could be cast to keep the Wicked Queen away from our mirror. Not all of us bought into it, but Sister Four and I were leaving nothing to chance.

'It's the patriarchy's fault,' said Sister Four, snuggling into her infrared sleeping bag one night and plumping the silk pillow that promised to prevent new wrinkles from developing overnight. What, *all* of it? I wasn't so sure. Were men alone guilty of insisting we remain decorative or get off the stage, or did we also pile on the pressure, make judgements, covertly observe other women to see how we were measuring up – or down – by comparison? Why was 'You look younger' the highest compliment a woman over forty could pay another woman after 'You've lost weight'? I didn't know any woman who didn't love receiving such compliments – including the thin ones. I didn't know anyone who aspired to being old and fat. If there were no men left, say they simply vanished off the face of the earth like the dinosaurs, what would we look like? Would we care about thread veins and getting our roots touched up? Would we still bother plucking? Would there be nail bars? The patriarchy may have got the first kick of the ball on an unlevel playing field, but hadn't we too been programmed from birth to discriminate in favour of youth and beauty?

As far as I was concerned, we were all complicit, all involved.

But never mind where it had all begun, my biggest worry was where it would all end.

Fifty-four, fifty-five, fifty-six, tick tock ... Propping everything up was getting harder and more expensive. Maintaining a face was like renovating a house: you started with the kitchen, which made the other rooms look tired by comparison, but you couldn't afford to do everything at once, and by the time you got around to the bathroom, the kitchen needed doing again.

There were many ways to approach a relationship with midlife, but there were only two types of relationship you could have with Botox (read: any youth-enhancing non-surgical procedure): it was either 'I can't wait to take you home to meet my folks' or 'no one must ever know about us'.

I was the first type. I told everybody. Not because I was proud of it, but because I didn't see the point of keeping it a secret – pretending I wasn't doing it would somehow feel more pathetic than craving the needle. I didn't go around saying, 'My name is Charlotte, I've had work', but if it came up in conversation I was happy to share. Even if I hadn't shared, my high shiny forehead was a dead give-away because it looked ten years younger than the rest of me and I didn't have the excuse of being a genius. The French philosopher and feminist Simone de Beauvoir was a genius, and even she'd hated the way she looked as she got older. Apparently, she had a recurring nightmare about how middle age made her feel.

'Often in my sleep I dream that in a dream I'm fifty-four, I wake and find I'm only thirty. "What a terrible nightmare I had!" says the young woman who thinks she's awake.'

Germaine Greer quoted this dream in *The Change*, her book on ageing published decades ago when she was still a Grumpy Middle-Aged Woman who called meno-pause the *climacteric*, which made it sound like an orgasm gone wrong. It might not come as a surprise to learn that Germaine scoffed at Simone's age angst: it made her no better than 'an empty-headed beauty queen' she argued. Which struck me as a pretty cheeky way for one feminist giant to describe another; not exactly sisterly. Then again, Judge Germaine, who boldly lives her contradictions to the full, was not insensitive to the anti-magnetic effects of her own ageing. In the opening chapter of *The Change* Greer had just turned fifty. She and a friend were sitting in a Paris café, trying to catch the waiter's eye.

'The unkind sunlight showed every sag, every pucker, every bluish shadow, every mole, every freckle in our fifty-year-old faces. When we beckoned to the waiter he seemed not to see us, and when he had taken our order he seemed to forget it and we had been obliged to remind him.'

Aside from her croissant, what did Germaine want if not the modest-enough vanity of being seen?

If Germaine didn't approve of Simone de Beauvoir having dreams she couldn't help about her unhappiness with the side effects of ageing (Simone would definitely have had Botox if it had been invented in her day), what chance did the rest of us stand? Germaine didn't even approve of older women wearing make-up: if a face was becoming something to be looked *out of* rather than looked *at*, she argued, it didn't need to be painted. I took her point, but I also knew that women like my mother and Auntie would never give up their right to wield the Pan Stik. The day before she died at ninety-six, a friend's mother – an architect who had designed and managed the build of her own house when she was in her eighties – sat up in bed and demanded her make-up bag. 'How do I look?' she asked her daughters once she had her face on. These were practically her last words.

I admired Germaine Greer, clumping about putting her foot in it; 'old, fat and busy', as she had once put it when asked to describe herself in three words in a radio interview. In a media-led world obsessed with twelve-year-old internet influencers, how many eighty-year-old women commanded her kind of airtime? You didn't have to like Germaine to acknowledge she had clout, that she was still making herself seen and heard, whether you agreed with her or were outraged by her. Even Mum, whose fantasy persona was more Kris Jenner than Germaine Greer, admired Germaine's refusal to shut up: 'I say, you go, girl!'

*

My sisters and I used to laugh at our mother when she said that if she won the lottery she'd have everything done – face-lift, bum-hike, boob-hoick – the *lot*. She'd have been in her forties then. It wasn't that we thought her vain, but from the smooth shoreline of our youth, we couldn't see the point. Why would someone who was already old bother?

When she turned seventy-eight and still hadn't won the lottery, Sister Four bought her a Botox voucher. Mum was excited, more excited than she was about Sister Two's birthday present which was an ice-skating lesson. It seems Mum had once mentioned in passing to Sister Two that she had wanted to be an ice skater when she grew up: she could see herself twirling round the rink in one of those little skirts that flipped over your head in the triple jump. Not wishing to look Sister Two's limb-threatening gift in the mouth, Mum sportingly agreed to the lesson and spent an hour wobbling round the rink, clutching the instructor with her teeth chattering while Sister Two sat on the sidelines with a mug of cocoa and egged her on. I was furious with Sister Two: Mum could have had a fall and broken a hip and got pneumonia and *died*, which was what happened to old people just going around Lidl in lace-ups, never mind carving up the ice in boots with blades like samurai swords on the bottom.

'But it was her dream,' said Sister Two.

'So? You wanted to be a racing driver when you grew up and I wanted to be Sandie Shaw. We were *seven*.'

Luckily, Mum still had Sister Four's Botox voucher to look forward to.

But when the Botox doctor saw her she said she was sorry, but Mum was really too old for Botox and it would be a waste of Sister Four's money.

Too *old* for Botox?

Mum wasn't as disappointed as I thought she'd be.

'It was just a bit of fun, darling. I made peace with my wrinkles when I turned seventy. These days, I'm just grateful for small mercies, like not breaking my legs ice skating.

'Anyhow,' she said, 'I'll always have my nose.'

My mother loved her nose. It was called the California Button and she'd bought it with a modest inheritance from her grandfather when she was nineteen. In the 1950s plastic surgery was in its elective infancy, reserved mostly for burns victims and war heroes who'd returned from the front minus their noses.

Leaving the Harley Street clinic after her procedure, my mother splurged on a black cab home: she didn't want anyone to know, especially her father, who was already livid that she'd spent the other half of her inheritance on a fur coat. The driver took one look at Mum's battered, bandaged face in the rear-view mirror and goggled. My mother told him her boyfriend had beaten her up.

'It was the fifties, darling,' she said when my jaw dropped. 'It was far more acceptable to get beaten up by your boyfriend than to have a nose job.'

I took a closer look at her nose: it was like a miniature ski jump with a little turn-up at the end. Being the only nose on my mother's face I'd ever known, it looked real enough to me.

'Mum, what did your nose look like before?'

Busying herself with mugs and tea-bags and a plate of French Fancies, she didn't quite look me in the eye when she said, 'A bit like yours, but with a conk.

'But your nose suits you perfectly, darling,' she quickly added.

My mother was the George Washington of the family; she couldn't tell a lie, even when it was in her own best interests to do so.

Having recovered from her fleeting disappointment about the Botox, Mum reverted to her age-old beauty regimen: soap and water and a blob of toothpaste on blemishes. She had lovely skin and didn't look her age. Oops, did I just say she looked good *for her age* instead of just saying she looked good? These were the little age-discrimination traps we would need to avoid in future if we wanted to shake up the status quo and feel more empowered as we grew older: the language had to change before hearts and minds followed.

After Uncle died, Auntie, who also looked good – for any age – had a full face-lift. She was fifty-nine and nowhere near ready to don widow's weeds and grow a moustache.

'It was lucky he went then,' she mused, 'because I still looked good naked.' She didn't mean it that way – she'd adored Uncle – but as so often with Auntie's more startling pronouncements, I knew what she meant.

'Luckily it was only my face that needed freshening up – pouches like kangaroos under my eyes, darling.'

With her firm new chin held high, Auntie was ready to begin a new chapter.

*

Recently, I'd heard about a freshening-up treatment that could be more accurately described as a freshening down. Trying to distract myself from the agony of having fillers injected into my upper lip lines during a needlework session with my trusty new aesthetics doctor one day, I asked her which was her bestselling treatment.

Dr N didn't even have to think about it. 'Definitely genital makeovers. In the trade we call it *vajuvenation*.'

I could no longer feel the pain in my lip.

Dr N explained that you could get your fairy tightened, brightened, winched and cinched. Lost G-spots could be found and libidos relit from the dying embers. It cost more than putting in a conservatory and sounded absolute torture, but Dr N said her clients were thrilled with the results: imagine, a fully renovated fairy with the grip of an octopus! Dallying with my crow's feet suddenly seemed faintly Victorian.

Vajuvenation was especially sought after by older clients – middle-aged divorcees and singletons who were getting back into the dating game.

'Let's just say,' said Dr N, 'that you've been married for a long time. Well, to put it delicately, you and your partner have *grown older together*. But if you're on the market again, you need to feel as ... confident as you can.'

It was mind-boggling to think of how much money I'd saved by growing older with Husband and it was an incentive to redouble my efforts to make our marriage work so that I never had to go back on the dating game.

*

My passport photo, taken when I was forty-nine, would shortly be due for renewal. At passport control in Paris after a sleepless flight from Johannesburg, the official looked at my photo then looked at me then looked at the photo then looked at me again: evidently a lot had happened in the intervening nine-and-a-half years and ten hours on a plane in traveller class. I knew what the passport official was thinking, and it wasn't that I could be on a terrorist watchlist.

'I look older now,' I said, cringing at myself for saying it.

'*C'est la vie*,' he shrugged, waving me through.

I'd yet to meet the woman who believed her looks improved with every passing year, who didn't sigh when she saw an old photograph of herself in a bikini and wish she hadn't been so hard on herself, so dissatisfied with her body, so self-conscious.

Everyone had their limits, and I drew the line at a surgical face-lift: it was too expensive and I was scared of coming out looking like someone else. When my friend B turned fifty she'd had everything done – eye-lift, face-lift, boob job; she got dental veneers and virgin hair extensions and would probably have got her fairy done too if she'd known about vajuvenation. Seven years after the face-lift she said her ears no longer felt like part of her body, her cheeks were still numb in places and the boobs needed doing again after gravity eventually got its way. She said she'd never have had the surgeries if she'd thought about the whole undertaking in a more sober light. But there you go: midlife is not a more sober light. It's the less catchy B-side of adolescence, with a credit card.

When I was a sulky teenager barricaded behind my bedroom door, adulthood had seemed an impossibly long way off. Would I ever get away from my annoying family, earn my own money, be in charge of my own life? When

I was a grown-up – God, it was taking forever – I'd never clean my room or do the washing-up; I'd lounge about with cucumbers on my eyes and practise flirting.

Until then, I'd just have to stick it out, squeezing pimples and wondering why my best friend had a boyfriend and I didn't and how come I could never find anything to wear in the heap of clothes on the floor.

Then miraculously, one day, I emerged from my musty cave with clear skin and straight teeth. I learned to drive and earned my own money. I moved into a flat with my new best friend from work and we never cleaned it. An odd-looking boy spied me across a smoky dance floor and took me home for bad sex.

It was a start.

Now, here I was, forty years later, playing out the interior drama of adolescence all over again, only this time I wasn't going to come bursting out of my room orthodontically poised to take on the world; this time I was going to come out slowly with my hands up and hope for the best.

If eyes are the windows of the soul, teeth are the pain in its butt. And they always act their age. In infancy they have to tunnel their way out, causing sleepless nights and nappy rash. Six years later they all fall out and leave you looking like a miniature cage fighter. Eventually they grow back again – crookedly this time – and require the wearing of ugly braces, which is why teenagers never smile. After a dazzling but all too brief respite in your twenties, they go yellow and start falling out again. Crowns, bridges, more braces, implants, dentures … and before you know it, you're sleeping next to them.

The maxillofacial surgeon who'd just hammered a metal post for an implant into the gap where a back molar once lived looked up from my file and smiled with big white teeth that looked like Chiclets. I could tell he was proud of them and I wondered if they were real.

'Ah, I see it's been two years since we had that nasty abscess.'

Why do doctors and dentists always say *we*?

In an unexpected change of subject, Dr T suddenly said, 'Do I look younger?'

'Excuse me?'

'Do you think I look younger than the last time you were here?'

Had I missed something?

'Go on,' he grinned, tapping his Chiclets, 'have a guess – how old do you think I am?'

I was starting to understand why he always ran late.

'Mid-fifties?' I lied.

He beamed. 'Sixty-five!'

Which was exactly what I'd thought.

'OK,' he said, rubbing his hands, 'I'm going to guess you're in your mid-forties?'

I knew he was lying but I couldn't help myself. 'Oh *thank* you,' I simpered. 'Fifty-five!'

He acted suitably astounded. 'Well,' he said, 'you certainly don't need Botox.'

Well, I thought, *that's because I've had it.*

After receiving the maxillofacial surgeon's bill for the implant, I took out dental insurance. Unfortunately, teeth weren't something you saved up for, like Botox or a boob job; they weren't optional extras.

*

Without naming names, let's just say I was one of *very few* women in my family who hadn't had a boob job. But now my once mighty breasts were starting to fall like the Roman Empire, and I toyed with the idea of getting them done before the Visigoths finished them off. But in the end I admitted defeat and simply got a better bra.

What is vanity anyhow? Bleaching your teeth? Wearing contact lenses? An eyebrow tint? Who defines it – who decides where grooming ends and vanity begins? Still, the fear has to stop somewhere.

Of course, I didn't want to get old – who does? At forty I thought fifty was old. At fifty I thought sixty was old. Now I was about to turn sixty – and sixty was officially old. But whether we go kicking and raking our nails against the closing door or sailing across the threshold in something white and billowy, we're all going.

And we will keep on coming of age until there is no age left to come of.

Step by baby step, I would learn to appreciate what I had and let go of what I would never have again. But for now, I was in transit; midway between clinging to the woman I'd been while warily watching another woman materialise in my mirror like ectoplasm at a seance, a woman who looked oddly familiar but whose identity I couldn't quite put my finger on. We certainly weren't yet on first-name terms.

Oh my God, was that *grey* in her hair?

Hair Is Not for Sissies

'A woman who cuts her hair is about to change her life.'

— COCO CHANEL

If you added it up, by this point I'd probably spent more time crying over my hair than raising my children.

Every woman I know has issues with her hair – too much, not enough, too curly, too straight, falling out, frizzing up, limping along. I can't think why the Met Office bothers with satellites when they could just plant a woman outside with an aerial on her head and get an accurate forecast – humid, dry, wet, windy et cetera.

I've inherited my father's hair. It is thick and grows faster than bamboo, mostly sideways. It refuses to be pacified with hot irons and vats of boiling Moroccan oil; in humidity it goes off like a cluster bomb.

Examining old photos of the younger me, I squirmed through a montage of celebrity copy-cat hairdos – Bonnie Tyler, Boy George, Princess Diana, Prince Valiant, *Friends*. Flipping through the albums, I watched, mesmerised, as my natural hair colour – the same shade of mushroom everyone painted their dining room in the eighties – got blonder and blonder as the decades went by.

Yet my hair was the envy of family and friends. 'It's so lovely and thick,' they exclaimed. 'You'll never go bald.' Ah, the consolations.

Hair is so personal. Hair is so political. Once, I was arrested after getting caught up in a student protest march. I spent the night in a prison cell full of ideologically aroused women singing freedom songs at the top of their voices. We slept – if you could call it that – under smelly horse blankets and drank from a communal tin can of tepid water into which a tea-bag may or may not have been dipped. The most upsetting part was that I'd missed my hair appointment with Raoul, who was harder to get than bail. Sadly, during that sleepless night, I realised I'd never be a genuine activist for as long as my roots meant more to me than my grass roots. I hugely admire women who manage to combine both.

The history of powerful women who've artfully employed their hair in the service of their message is long and chequered. There is first-lady hair (Michelle Obama's 'White House hair strategy'); leadership hair (Margaret Thatcher's flinty set and wave, rivalled only by the Queen's); radical hair (the Angela Davis mega 'fro). There is fuck-you hair (Vivian Westwood and Sinead O'Connor, brave and shaved) and fuck-me hair (Botticelli's Venus, her floor-length beach waves directing the viewer's gaze to her coyly draped fairy). Then there is the former prime minister of Ukraine's mighty golden rope, which could tug warships out to sea. It is said that Yulia Tymoshenko contrived her signature coronet braid to make her look folksy and patriotic. *Forbes* magazine and the *New York Times* wrote articles about her hair. There were YouTube videos demonstrating how to get the look at home. The new kid on the global power block is a braider too. Greta Thunberg, the teenage climate change activist, wears her Pippi Longstocking pigtails so tightly plaited they look as pained as the planet she has set about saving. At the same time, the pigtails emphasise her youth, *the* youth, our children and grandchildren who will reap the apocalypse we've sown if they don't overthrow us. It is absolutely genius messaging.

Of all the statement hairdos through the ages, it's the bob that intrigues me the most. Historians credited Joan of Arc with being the first woman to wear it – warrior style, easy to maintain in the heat of battle. As we know, things didn't go well for Joan in the end, but her appropriation of the knight's hairstyle *du jour* survived, re-emerging in the twentieth century as a symbol of the modern young woman's resistance to the patriarchal status quo and hairpins: striking for independence, fighting for the vote, demanding the right to dance alone in nightclubs. As Nietzsche didn't say but might have, by the 1920s, Venus was pretty much dead.

Older-women leaders of contemporary times – Angela Merkel, Hillary Clinton – adopted their own versions of the bob: short, sexless, practical hairstyles that said *don't look at me, look at my policies*. (Interesting to note that around the same time male leaders like Donald Trump and Boris Johnson were cultivating bouffs that said *don't look at my policies, look at me!*)

In the world of fashion and pop culture the bob never really died. Hollywood screenwriters are always finding excuses to include a scene where the lead actress chops off her hair with the kitchen scissors. The chop signals that our heroine has reached the limits of her forbearance – with men, with her mother, with aliens, whoever – and is gearing up to fight back. Miraculously, in the next scene her home hack job has turned into a perfect, razor-sharp bob, making her look as if she's just walked out of Vidal Sassoon.

Cutting off your hair is cathartic. Or at least, it always seems like a good idea at the time. Who hasn't rushed to the hairdresser after finding out their boyfriend is the wrong gender or putting on ten pounds between Christmas and New Year, in the mad conviction that a new hairstyle will make everything better? 'Do whatever you like,' we tell the trainee stylist, the only one available at 9 a.m. on 2 Jan. 'Cut it all off!' The funny thing is, it actually does make you feel better because the haircut instantly becomes the worst thing that has ever happened to you. It's like referred pain.

A woman's hair can say more about looming disasters than a thousand words. Who could forget the scene in *Bridget Jones* where Renée Zellweger and Hugh Grant are bowling along in an open-top sports car, en route to their romantic mini-break in the country, when her Grace Kelly headscarf suddenly flies off into a hedgerow and she arrives at the hotel with a haystack on her head? Right there, you know the weekend isn't going to go according to plan.

Having lived through forty years of Farrah Fawcett flicks, lunatic fringes and shags that made me look as though I'd been tasered, I still wasn't exactly sure what my hair was trying to say. What I did know was that, like everything else about me, its temper was not improving with age – brittle, moody, sneaking up on me unawares – and it really didn't care about my problems.

I was not alone.

In her forties, a friend's hair went white overnight after a traumatic event. Another's Titian waves were receding like the tide; the friend who still couldn't feel her cheeks after the face-lift had hair extensions, one of which fell out in an art exhibition on top of a video installation where it lay, coiled like a viper, on top of Pasolini's crucifixion scene. Apparently, there was a smattering of applause.

Comic, tragic, compliant, ungovernable; at different times of our lives our hair will be all of these things, but even the baddest of bad hair days is nothing compared to not having any hair. Cancer is a roulette game, and even if you don't get the bullet, there's no question your hair will die under the toxic drip of the drugs that, if you're lucky, will let you live. By my fifties, several people I knew had had cancer – mostly women, mostly breast cancer. Losing their hair, they said, was one of the hardest parts.

A girlfriend who'd just had her second round of chemotherapy had been warned what to expect: after the second round, it fell out, no exceptions. She asked me to go hat shopping with her.

Her beautiful shoulder-length hair was still in perfect condition, but she wanted to be prepared. Perhaps it wouldn't fall out; perhaps she'd be the one who got away. It all seemed a bit of a lark – going into the department store to try on hats, giggling at the fascinators. Suddenly, as she tugged off an unflattering beret – 'Definitely not that one!' – I noticed that a glossy strand of hair had come away with it. She hadn't seen it yet. I froze. She lifted her hands to smooth her hair, ready for the next hat, and more strands fell out. Now she noticed. She shook the long hairs off her fingers as if they were spiders and with barely contained hysteria began pulling out chunks. Soon, I could see her scalp.

I don't know how long we stood there staring at her hair as it floated to the floor before one of us said, 'Let's get out of here.' We stood outside on the pavement, we didn't really have a plan. She was shaking. She said, 'I want it all off, *now.*'

We walked into the first salon we saw. It was a Saturday and the place was heaving, but when the receptionist saw that this really was a hair emergency, she went over and whispered to one of the stylists, who hurried over and settled my friend in a chair, draping her in the last hair-dresser's cape she would need for a long time. As the clippers buzzed we held hands and sniffled a bit. My friend kept her eyes on the mirror. The rest of the clientele tried not to stare. We pretended that being bald really suited her; that she should have done it years ago.

'There's no charge,' said the receptionist. 'Good luck.'

'Well, that's that,' said my friend, running her hand over her shockingly smooth pate.

In the end she decided not to get a hat after all, or a wig or a scarf. 'I'm not going into hiding,' she said bravely. 'This is me. For now, anyway.'

Two years later she was declared cancer free. It took ages for her hair to grow back, and when it did, it was different. It had been straight, now it was curly; it was a shade or two darker.

It really did suit her.

*

I'd once heard the difference between black hair and white hair described as sculptural versus painterly. In Chimamanda Ngozi Adichie's novel *Americanah*, I had been intrigued by the opening pages describing a scene in a hair salon, a subtly hilarious account of how identity politics are encrypted into every braid and weave. I wanted to know more about the relationship between black women and their hair and compare who had it worse. But not wishing to put my big white foot in it, I hadn't found the nerve to ask a black woman for the gory details. Then one evening while having a drink with my neighbour and her cousin – black, single and a generation younger than me – I worked up some Dutch courage and asked them. The truth was even more complicated than I'd thought.

'White women have no idea,' said Neighbour after our first bottle of Prosecco.

'No idea,' echoed her cousin.

Whereupon they plunged into a long and intricate tale involving whipping and stretching and twisting and lubricating.

It sounded more strenuous than sex.

'Definitely more time-consuming,' hiccupped Neighbour, 'and don't be fooled by the relax in relaxant.'

Between them and the second bottle of Prosecco, the gory details emerged: just getting your hair ready for bed could take an hour with all the detangling and hydrating you have to do before wrapping it in a silk scarf and going to sleep on a satin pillow so it doesn't get messed up and then the scarf falls off in the night and it gets messed up anyway so you have to do it all over again in the morning, and we're not even talking about the woman-hours lost, the time you'll never get back, because braids can take up to twelve hours to put in – you practically have to take leave – and let's not even get into the maintenance involved in going 'natural', because if a girl wants a career *and* a serious relationship *and* a chance to do the grocery shopping in between hair care, she has to invest in an emergency standby wig, which costs a month's salary unless you don't mind a cheap synthetic one likely to combust if it gets too near the stove, and really, when all's said and done, the only lasting solution to black hair is to shave it all off and take tranquillisers.

I was glad I hadn't mentioned that I'd thought black women woke up in the morning with neat little cornrows.

Neighbour refreshed our glasses. 'So, what are *your* hair issues?'

It was a contest I couldn't win. 'Oh, you know, fly-aways and, um, nothing much, really ...'

Neighbour and her cousin were in their early thirties. I wondered, did black hair change as it grew older? Would it become even more high-maintenance? Hmm, they said, this wasn't something they'd had to think about yet. They'd ask their mothers and aunts and get back to me. But I saw the fear in their eyes: how much harder could things possibly get?

*

My mother said she couldn't afford to *fanny about* with her hair. Once upon a time she'd been a happy housewife, but in her early forties she found herself divorced, just scraping by, with no professional qualifications and four children to fend for. For the next thirty years she worked cash-in-hand jobs. She never spent more than a tenner on a haircut and, as she got older and her natural flame-coloured hair started to fade, she fired it back up to Ronald McDonald red from a box in the bathroom. She was in her seventies before she finally allowed herself the luxury of going to a proper salon where they didn't expect the clientele to arrive with their hair wet.

She loved her new choppy bob and started to use words like *texturise* in everyday conversation.

My mother had hated her hair as a child because, surprise, surprise, the other kids called her Ginger. But as a young woman she discovered there was a world of men out there who adored Rita Hayworth and she finally owned the wow factor. Redheads had a reputation for being fiery and passionate, she boasted. 'We've always been portrayed as wicked, powerful, fascinating,' she told me. 'Mary Magdalene was a redhead, you know.'

I didn't know that, and I wondered how she knew that. But considering Christian kids accepted that Jesus had beach waves, I was happy to believe that the Bible's scarlet woman had red hair.

In her seventies, my mother developed a coin-sized bald patch. It was barely visible to the naked eye but she was obsessed with it. 'Is my bald spot showing?' she'd hiss in the supermarket. She began to snub anyone taller than her and wore headscarves knotted under her chin like the Queen on holiday at Sandringham. Wind was the enemy. She and Auntie would call each other: are we still going out for coffee? Ooh, no darling, there's *wind*.

*

Mum began to let some of her greys grow out. Now that she got her hair professionally coloured it was softer, subtler and silvery strands framed her face; now when she went out she arranged her headscarf with the knot at the back, which made her look more Grace, Princess of Monaco, than the Queen on a hunting trip.

To grow or not to grow out our greys was the subject of much debate among my fifty-something peers. My generation being predicted to live to at least a hundred, we were too young to ignore the prospect of having grey hair for another half a century. Most men I knew didn't seem as bothered about going grey as my women friends did. Was this another example of how they got away with things because they cared more about how *we* looked than about how *they* looked and we allowed it? On the other hand, as one girlfriend said, 'Would you trust a man who dyed his hair?'

I kept a watching brief: my sister-in-law had started tinting her hair zany My Little Pony colours: she could go from green to purple to pink in the space of a week and matched her outfits accordingly. A friend who'd started going grey in her forties decided to just keep going. But most of the women I knew were worried that letting nature take its course would make them look like a pot scourer rather than like Emmylou Harris.

Nora Ephron didn't even wash her own hair but had it done twice a week at a fancy salon. She basically argued that not having to worry about our hair any more would give us something to look forward to when we were dead. The late, great Nora who died in 2012 aged seventy-one (an age that now seemed quite tender to me) also declared that the reason women in their fifties and sixties looked younger than their mothers at the same age had nothing to do with feminism or omega-3s: it was thanks to hair dye.

But times had changed, and grey hair had made a spectacular comeback. The catwalks shimmered with platinum-maned supermodels; grey-haired girls swished along the high street; Helen Mirren, the ultimate poster girl for how good the future could look if we just put our backs into it, looked better and better the whiter and whiter her hair went. She must have had a little help from the bottle to make it look *that* good.

When I heard I was going to be a grandmother, I decided that dyeing my fake blonde hair fake grey would be a fun way to mark the happy event, signal my readiness to step up to the part and celebrate my new identity. Here was my chance to embrace the next phase of life rather than simply brace for it – a timely moment to stop moping in front of the mirror. The best part was, I'd still be in fashion.

It crossed my mind that going granny grey when you actually *were* a granny might not produce quite the same effect as going granny grey when you were a sixteen-year-old Victoria's Secret model. There was the risk that my fake grey hair would end up looking like real grey hair and result in an embarrassing reversal of the situation where you run into someone from your school days, draw a blank and conclude that she must be one of your mother's friends; if you were lucky she'd give you clues: 'I used to wear braces? Second netball team? *Darren's* girlfriend!'

Oops, we were the same age. Did I look as old as she did? I decided to go ahead and take a chance on my grey colour experiment with the conviction that, as long as I picked the hottest stylist in town and parted with enough money, the risks would be minimal.

My mother couldn't believe I was going to pay someone to make my hair grey.

I've always had complicated relationships with hairdressers – they can make or break your day, your *whole life*. They can also be exciting, imaginative partners who know exactly how to please a woman. I've consummated crushes on many stylists over the years; all men, for some reason – gay, straight, bi and, in one disastrous case, high. But love is only blind until the day you come out looking like Donald Trump and realise they're still going to make you pay.

Still, I never gave up hope that someday I'd find my prince, the perfect match, a man who really understood me. He didn't need to have a sense of humour or cook or like children: he just had to be The One who'd make my hair want to commit.

Gilbert threw rock-star tantrums and had an Instagram following. He treated me like groupie scum but he was hot, and I never knew what I was going to get till I got it, by which time it was too late.

Gilbert did all the It girls and society matrons. He regularly popped up in the 'Seen Around' section of fashion magazines, got up in outfits so bizarre there could be no doubting his A-list status: skirts with socks, scrubs and espadrilles.

I had to have him.

The first time I tried to get an appointment with Gilbert I got one, which was a bit disappointing. But I perked up when I arrived and saw half a dozen other women draped expectantly around the salon in various stages of undress, waiting for their turn with him. I joined the queue. Every so often Gilbert would sweep through the adoring throng, dispensing outrageous compliments, chemicals and hot fashion tips from Italy, from where he always seemed to have just returned.

Gilbert would do the business with anyone as long as you weren't the clingy type and didn't mind a quickie. When it was my turn, I'd speak to him slowly and clearly: Gilbert worked the line like Edward Scissorhands and you could never be entirely sure that *he* was entirely sure whose hair he was busy with at any given moment.

Still, a year and several quickies into our relationship, I felt ready to trust Gilbert with my latest hair fantasy. I told him I wanted to go grey – *platinum* grey, I emphasised, not old-underwear grey.

'No problemo!' he said, turning his best side to pose for a selfie with another satisfied customer. He mussed my hair around a bit and said he'd put in some platinum highlights but keep the blonde too, so it would look more natural.

I didn't like to think about how much money I'd spent making my hair look more natural over the years.

Of course, Gilbert didn't listen to a word I'd said: after four hours with tin foil on my head, my hair came out the colour of I-can't-believe-it's-margarine. I could barely believe it myself. It was so yellow people started asking if I had jaundice.

On a good day Gilbert made dreams I didn't know I had come true. But lately he hadn't had many good days. He'd left me little choice: it was time to visit his rival for my affections.

Philippe was cool, classically trained and French; he called me Madame. He could be relied on to give me the same cut, colour and blow-dry every time, which was a bit like bringing a girl red roses every Wednesday – exciting at first, but could get yawny after a while, which was why I wasn't prepared to stop cheating on him with Gilbert. Philippe never quite took my breath away, never made me feel like smoking a cigarette afterwards, but he was a safe pair of hands.

Philippe worked at one of those walk-in salons that don't take appointments; it was beginner's luck that he was free the day I wandered in. That first time, we had pored over the Big Book of Fabulous Hair and he'd stared into my eyes while fondling my tresses. 'I adore your hair,' he said.

But a few months later, in the aftermath of the margarine incident with Gilbert, even Philippe couldn't think of anything polite to say.

'Who did this to you?' he gasped. 'It's *yellow*.'

Philippe fetched down the Big Book of Fabulous Hair and pointed to a picture of a model with platinum locks and said, 'Is this the colour you want?' I practically swooned.

It could be done, he said, but it would take time and patience. First, the hair would need to be stripped of all colour with industrial-strength bleach. Then, if it hadn't died of fright, new layers of colour could be built up, with breaks in between to check for signs of life.

And so it began, with a few modest silver strands and a bottle of purple shampoo.

'Next time,' Philippe promised, 'if your hair hasn't fallen out, we'll do more.'

Next time he wasn't there.

'It's Philippe's day off,' said the receptionist. 'Would you like to see someone else?'

'That's OK,' I said. 'I'll come back. Will he be in on Wednesday?'

'Every day except today,' she said, with a touch of frost.

I went back on Wednesday; he wasn't there.

'Philippe's on training,' said the receptionist. 'He'll be here on Friday.'

Now I was annoyed. 'What time?'

'Nine a.m.,' she said, narrowing her eyes, as if anyone ever started work at any other time.

By Friday my hair was so big I had to put it on the passenger seat. I arrived at the salon at 8.55 a.m. to be sure to be first in line.

At 9 a.m. the salon doors swung open. Philippe wasn't there.

'His shift starts at noon,' said the receptionist.

I wanted to stab her with the thinning scissors.

I went back at 11.58 a.m.

Philippe was waiting for me. 'Shall we look at the Big Book of Fabulous Hair?'

'Oh, *Philippe*,' I sighed, 'let's!'

Going Grey Step Two was declared a success. 'Come back in three weeks,' said Philippe, 'and we'll take the final step.'

I went back in three weeks. Philippe wasn't there.

'He's off sick,' said the receptionist.

'When will he be back?'

'I really can't say.'

I pictured her lying on the floor bleeding.

A pasty youth with frosted hair sidled over. 'Philippe's left,' he whispered. 'He's not coming back.'

'Ever?'

'Never.'

The frosted youth beckoned me deeper into the salon and told me his name was Valentine.

Valentine? *Valentine?*

I felt the old familiar flutter as he led me to the washbasin.

Four hours later I walked out with gorgeous grey locks, posted a picture on my Facebook page and waited for the Likes. While I was waiting – it seemed to be taking an awfully long time for my friends to find the thumbs-up emoji – I WhatsApped a picture to Husband.

He texted back straight away. 'You look like a granny.'

Nobody said it was going to be easy.

*

It was known in the trade as *unwanted facial hair*, though I didn't personally know any woman who wanted facial hair (eyelashes don't count).

What had hitherto been peachy face fuzz was start-ing to prickle. I carried my Tweezerman around like an asthma pump. I bought a vibrator-like appliance that promised to kill hair at the root and was absolutely useless, unless I'd got my appliances mixed up. I had laser treatments and was variously waxed, threaded and plucked. At the salon one day I bumped into a friend's aunt who I knew had recently celebrated her ninetieth birthday. Sixty years after fleeing her homeland and

Hitler, she still had a strong German accent. She was here for her monthly vax, she said.

'Vax?' I repeated dumbly. 'Vhere?'

'Lip and chin, darlink,' she said, giving me a watery wink.

Until that moment I'd imagined unwanted facial hair to be a side effect of menopause that would be over before I was too old and weak to get a good grip on the tweezers.

'Ah no, *liebchen*, it keeps on growing until you are dead. Like noses.'

One day I spotted a strange new addition to my already quite crowded face – a hair trying to make its escape from my left nostril. I sped to the salon to get a professional to clear the area, during the course of which she managed to plug up both nostrils with wax. I breathed through my mouth and tried not to panic. Failing to dislodge the waxy corks with tweezers, she hurried off to fetch a colleague – a merciless Russian who put her knee on my chest and ripped them out with her thumb and forefinger. Stripped of cilia, my nose ran unchecked for a week.

Facial hair was scary, it was humiliating, like being a fuzzy-legged thirteen-year-old again and walking past a group of boys in the playground and hearing one of them snicker, 'Hasn't she heard of Nair?' That was when I realised I would have to act fast if I was ever going to get thrown down on the backseat of a car and ravaged, which, in my virgin fantasies, meant getting a love bite and respect from the netball team at school the next day.

That night I went home and made a bloodbath with my father's razor. Afterwards, I knew I'd undergone an important rite of passage that would stand me in good stead for woman life. Mum bought me a pack of pink disposables and showed me how to achieve a clean leg shave without needing a transfusion. I handed down this knowledge to my son.

On the hair front, the gender doors were revolving in a most interesting way.

Men of my generation didn't bother attending to their surplus body hair. Indeed, they seemed proud of their furry legs and tufty shoulders, chests you could rappel down.

In the 1970s hard core feminists and female hippies had tried to level the playing field: if men weren't ashamed of their body hair, why should we be? Who decided women weren't allowed to have body hair? Real women had hair *everywhere*, so let 'em have it, sisters! Mercifully, this craze died out with CB radio and pet rocks.

But wait, what if things were the other way around? What if men aspired to be like us instead of us trying to be like them?

As the third millennium dawned, this miracle came to pass. Enter a third generation of fine young men, marching alongside us with their heads held high, climbing on the wax wagon, demanding their rights to silky legs and separate eyebrows, spurning the traditions of their shaggy fathers and following in the footsteps of their mothers.

The day Son asked if he could try my epilator, I was so proud of him. In a triumphant reversal of my father's morning roar in the general direction of his daughters – 'WHO'S TAKEN MY RAZOR?!' – I would bang on Son's door yelling, 'WHERE'S MY EPILADY?!'

From top to bottom and head to toe, men were demanding equality.

Before long, even greater parity was achieved when hairdressers realised that well-groomed men were prepared to pay the same price for a decent cut and blow-dry as women. Some of them got highlights; some even went all the way, because hair dye had evolved and no longer made men look as if they'd been rubbed in shoe polish. The bald saved up for transplants; the brave submitted to the wax. Men were no longer an exotic sight at my local beauty spot but would vanish into the treatment rooms to deal with their unmentionables, biting the sheet to stop from screaming, just as their mothers had before them.

In my day, taking care of the unmentionables meant getting a bikini wax before the summer holidays. These days, there are entire topiaries to choose from. There's the Brazilian, a sort of labial landing strip, and the Bermuda Triangle, named after a mysteriously magnetic patch of the Atlantic where light aircraft go down, never to be seen again. Most controversially, there's the Hollywood – a clean sweep. My mother, who had a thing or two to say on most subjects, certainly had a thing or two to say about the Hollywood. 'It's *disgusting*,' she said, 'designed to please the kind of *rats* who want women to look like pre-pubescent children. Women who have the Hollywood,' she huffed, 'are nothing more than *enablers*.'

For once, I agreed with her.

However, recently internet influencers and the unimpeachable *Vogue* magazine had announced that body hair was back. Models at London and New York fashion weeks were striding down the runways with hairy legs sticking out of Dolce & Gabbana petticoats; a campaign called #hairypits was gaining ground on social networks.

Apparently the Brazilian and the Hollywood were OUT; tidy triangles were IN.

Hair history was being revised – again. God, it was exhausting.

According to media reports the trend had something to do with gender fluidity: as far as I could make out this meant that boys would be girls, girls would be boys and that boys and girls *per se* no longer existed. The child of a friend demanded that from now on their parents refer to them as *they*. A non-binary person I read an interview with said they waxed their legs four times a year in order to 'enjoy a spectrum of presentation'. For the rest of the year they let their hair grow into a full-length shag in order to trigger 'gender confusion and anxiety'. I had no idea what this person was talking about. Why would they want to spread confusion and anxiety? What would their mother say? It was one of those moments, occurring more and more frequently, when it came home to me that I was getting old: too old to 'get' the zeitgeist, the doings, desires and aspirations of the young.

I mentally clicked my tongue when I saw boys hobbling about in jeans yanked so low you could see their underpants; I was mystified as to why young people never used the phone part of the phones from which they were never parted. But then, I supposed that was the point: if anyone over thirty understood how the youth thought or what they wanted, there'd be little point in them thinking it or wanting it. It was a wake-up call, of sorts, though in youth-speak, I was too far gone to be *woke*.

Still, I was encouraged by the news that the Hollywood was out and the clipped hedgerow was coming back – in this respect, at least, I'd be part of the avant-garde.

'Darling,' said my mother, 'let me tell you how things were down there in my day.'

God, Mum, do you have to?

'When I was young and having relations with a certain gentleman' – *please, Lord, let it not be my father* – 'he explained why it was necessary to have good coverage down there.'

'Mum, I don't want to talk about it.'

She wasn't finished.

'Anyway, according to this gentleman, it's to avoid friction burns.'

As a dedicated follower of the Kardashians, Mum was right up to date with the zeitgeist – celebrity brats, trans dads, rapper chic. It was she who introduced me to another v-word I'd never heard of – *vajazzle,* which sounded like a Las Vegas tribute show to Liberace.

She set me straight. 'No, darling, it's getting your fairy studded with rhinestones.'

Surely friction burns would be preferable to scraping away against a gem-encrusted fairy, which I imagined might feel more like running aground on the Great Barrier Reef? But not wanting to egg my mother on, I kept this theory to myself.

'And on the subject of colour trends in the nether regions,' she continued, not that we were on the subject, 'Auntie dyed hers with boot polish the night before her first wedding.'

Somebody up there had to stop her.

But now I had to know, *what colour?*

'Oh, I can't remember, darling – you'll have to ask her.'

Auntie, who, as far as I could see, was a natural blonde,

was no prude, but I wasn't sure she'd appreciate me asking her this, even if she could remember the answer. Perhaps I'd put it in a delicate, Jane Austen-y way: *was it something blue?*

The next time I saw Auntie I forgot all about going down her memory lane when she revealed that she'd stopped washing her hair (on her head) since reading that the chemicals in shampoo stripped it of natural oils. I thought it was a bit late for her to go *that* natural, but her gamine crop looked as healthy as ever and passed the sniff test. Auntie was more concerned about *my* hair. 'Don't go grey before your time, sweetie – your time will come soon enough.'

Having grey hair had been fun for a while, but much as I pretended otherwise, it wasn't really working for me. I didn't look like a fey artist or one of those Brussels Eurocrats *à la* Christine Lagarde: I looked like wallpaper paste.

Working life was becoming more challenging, too. I'd already doctored my resumé to show less experience: five to ten years looked solid on a CV; fifteen to twenty was top of the tree; twenty-five to thirty sounded more like a life sentence handed down by a judge – it wouldn't even get you on the shortlist. It was one thing being the oldest person in meetings, it was quite another *looking* like the oldest person in meetings.

I slunk back to Gilbert and begged him to make me yellow again.

Drugs Used to Be Fun

'I used to do drugs, but don't tell anyone – it'll ruin my reputation.'

— COURTNEY LOVE

My dealer was an elderly woman with frizzy grey hair under a squashed felt hat. While she waited for customers in her battered Ford Fiesta, she knitted things for her church group. Scoring from her made me feel like a Good Deed. She looked like a granny, she very possibly was a granny, but when you were handing over cash for contraband through the window of a car, it was best not to hang about making small talk.

By the time I was in my fifties, it was so long since I'd called that good Christian woman, she'd probably retired. After all those years risking her own liberty in the service of others, I liked to think of her putting her feet up with a pot of tea and toast, knitting needles clacking away on the next batch of toilet roll covers for the church fête.

I'd never taken a fun drug until I was in my thirties: I certainly didn't mix in the kind of sophisticated circles where everyone had their own spoon. By the time I caught on, even the stuff that was sixty per cent Ariel cost too much to be consumed in anything but furtive little groups in bathrooms at parties with people who'd paid their share upfront. Cocaine was a greedy drug – it always demanded more. Why did I do it? Because it made me feel like the most fascinating person in the room for up to ten minutes. It made me talk and talk and talk until the person whose ear I was bending with my profound insights fell asleep. It turned dull events into sparkly occasions. It made me want to dance. It made me want to stay. Anxieties melted away to be replaced by a sense of wellbeing that made everything feel right with the world.

On top of all that, it was a highly effective appetite suppressant. Once, I was at a dinner party where the host was so busy passing round lines of coke like olives, she forgot to cook the dinner. No one was hungry anyway. What was not to like about a drug that made you feel fascinating *and* thin?

Occasionally, I had flirted with MDMA and its little cousin, Ecstasy, too. Like piano lessons, playing their tune required practice. Take too much and you'd be pinioned to a sofa for six hours speaking in tongues and praying for it to be over. But if you took just a nibble, you'd be transported to a plane it took Buddhist monks a lifetime of praying and fasting to glimpse. Like Alice going down the rabbit hole, you had to play around with the Drink Me bottle and adjust the dosage accordingly. But when you got it just right, you could dance all night to terrible trance music with a bottle of water and think you were having the best time of your life.

At a certain point, there were a lot of drugs going around in my social circles. It was a popular middle-class professional pastime – an indulgence that made us feel that we were living dangerously without really being in danger – we had good, steady jobs and families, we were highly functional, and we were still young enough not to know better.

I steered clear of what I considered to be the really hard drugs: I never tried LSD – I was far too scared of running into the Queen of Hearts and being turned into a croquet mallet or discovering that I *was* the Queen of Hearts, stomping around chopping off people's heads, that *she* was the alter ego lurking in the dim recesses of my subconscious. I never took heroin either – too scared of it being the one drug so indescribably fantastic (as it had once been described to me) that I'd go out so far I might never come back. Heroin was not a drug to be dabbled in, and I had seen the walking wounded, the syringe-skinny ghosts who lived only for the next fix – if they survived, which not everyone I knew did.

I've never had a moral problem with drugs, but what goes up must come down, and the downs no longer seemed worth the ups.

Everything was changing, and it was high time to accept that I was on a journey not a trip, and that my physical and mental health was no longer an optional extra.

These days my drugs came in blister packs instead of baggies: anti-inflammatories, anxiety pills, sleeping pills and an oestrogen gel I had to rub into my thighs every night that was not as exciting as it sounds. By standing in direct sunlight and using a magnifying glass, I could read the tiny, tiny writing on the leaflets inside the packs of the drugs prescribed to me by my cornucopia of doctors.

The possible side effects of legal drugs made recreational drugs look like a box of Smarties: nausea, vision impairment, breathing difficulties, suicidal thoughts, death ... My medicine cabinet was cluttered with perilous pharmaceuticals that could leave me more impaired than I already was.

There were, of course, more organic paths to menopausal health, a road paved with minerals and vitamins that ran through the supplements alphabet from A to Zinc. The celebrity snake oil sales reps of wellness were passionate advocates of the healing powers of nature: a spritz of lavender oil on your pillow, a handful of raspberry leaves and a sprinkle of bee pollen – all were touted as miracle cures for everything from insomnia to homicide.

But perhaps it would be wise to cover all the bases.

I dabbled in new substances such as black cohosh and turmeric; I carried round supplements like amulets against menopause symptoms I'd never even heard of: heavy legs, dropped arches, burning tongue syndrome. There was a tablet for everything except fun. My pill hill got higher, so to speak, and before long there wasn't room to stuff one more wild yam in the medicine cabinet. When I travelled, my luggage was so loaded with sprays and supplements I was overweight at check-in and, on one embarrassing occasion, borderline obese.

It was then that I realised I had gone too far, and anyhow there wasn't a shred of scientific evidence that any of Mother Nature's remedies did much besides give Gwyneth Paltrow a second career: her bespoke range of minerals contained more metal than a copper belt, hinting at a possible third career in mining.

I threw out everything except a bottle of liquid cod liver oil laced with orange juice I swigged at breakfast. That, I reckoned, took care of the secrets of Mediterranean longevity. Smelling like cod was the only unfortunate side effect.

*

I was intrigued to discover how many women I knew in my menopause self-help group rejected hormone replacements and courageously decided to enter the fray commando style.

A lucky few said their symptoms were too mild to bother about; others said they didn't want to risk the side effects of HRT – heart disease, stroke, breast cancer, *weight gain* – and would hold out as long as they could. One or two brave souls said they were simply going to bite down and take the rough with the smooth, even if they couldn't quite put their finger on the smooth. There were other coping mechanisms, they said, like drinking red wine from the Mediterranean diet.

One icy day in January I was having lunch with a colleague in a restaurant when she suddenly went the colour of boiled beetroot. 'I'm having a flush!' she said, rummaging in her bag. She produced a flamenco-dancer fan and a thermal-mist spritzer and commenced flapping and squirting water on her face through the rest of the meal.

We got looks from other tables, but my colleague didn't give a damn: she had chosen her weapons, and if the public at large found it all very amusing, they were *welcome*.

'You should see their faces when I do it on the Tube!'

Talk about owning your menopause – inspiring, really. I decided to give all my girlfriends fans and cans for Christmas. Gwyneth, meanwhile, had jumped on the legalisation of cannabis in the US, better known in my day as a crime punishable by a prison sentence with remission for good behaviour.

Would you believe it? Just when I decided to give up fun drugs on all but the most special occasions, cannabis was on the comeback trail (it had been legalised in South Africa, too, for personal use). Even in the UK, where over-the-counter procurement wasn't yet legal, an already stretched police force was unlikely to follow up on complaints about a funny smell coming from next door, unless it was a dead body sort of funny smell.

Boutique cannabis shops set out their shingles in suburban shopping malls. Doctors trumpeted the virtues of the weed, and a friend's mother-in-law – let's call her Mrs C – scored it at her local health shop. Around noon one morning I went to drop something off at Mrs C's house. She took ages to answer the door and eventually appeared in a bathrobe with her hair sticking up. 'Sorry,' she said woozily, 'I must have overdosed on the cannabis drops last night.'

It kind of takes the fun out of fun drugs when your mother-in-law is still stoned the next day.

Strange acronyms such as THC and CBD started cropping up in conversations: these were oily substances that came in little glass phials and could be popped in a handbag and dropped on your tongue whenever the need arose – to ease aches and pains, lull you to sleep, alleviate anxiety or simply put steel in your spine for Black Friday sales. One friend said CBD oil had even helped her get over Brexit. Some people I knew had taken the next step and were micro-dosing on magic mushrooms, more commonly known by their consumers as *edibles*. Edibles could be whizzed up in a super-food smoothie with leafy greens or sprinkled over a Thai stir-fry; you could even buy bars of chocolate with mushroom filling that would make Mr Cadbury spin in his grave.

Marijuana and hallucinogenic fungi suddenly seemed not only acceptable but *critical* to maintaining good health.

Plant-based 'medicines' contained none of the bad stuff: no preservatives, no colourants, no glucose, no sucrose, or any of the other no-nos we were all trying to avoid these days. Plant-based medicines were often 100 per cent *organic*, our absolutely favourite word after *authentic*.

Midlife, giggled my sister-in-law – the one with My Little Pony hair – certainly wasn't too short to stuff a mushroom. I noticed she giggled a lot these days.

All sorts of drugs that previously would have ended badly were going straight. Harder drugs such as MDMA and ketamine – *horse tranquilliser!* – were even being used by psychiatrists to help patients with post-traumatic stress disorder. I read somewhere that practically the whole of Silicon Valley was micro-dosing on LSD to 'stimulate creativity and productivity', which, I now understood, was how they were able to work twenty-four-hour days inventing idiotic apps that tell you when your toast's ready.

Oh dear, was I turning into a fun-drug prude? But surely half the point of taking them was not being allowed to?

I just had to wrap my head around the fact that drugs had gone respectable, and it was my generation's responsibility to teach our children how to use them responsibly. From now on teenagers wouldn't need to sneak around hiding things in their shoes. Instead, we'd gather round a crackling fire and play Pass the Brownie until we all fell down in a heap of high-functioning family.

There was always a dark side to drugs, even drugs that had been rebranded as nature's own cure for everything from psychosis to ingrown toenails. Basically, it was all about portion size: you couldn't scoff a whole bar of mushroom chocolate and hope to get away with it, even one composed of 70 per cent cocoa and Stevia. If you weren't careful, you might lose more than you'd bargained for – your mind, for example.

But as I was to discover, there were *loads* of people trying to lose their minds. On purpose! And they were paying good money to do so, too.

That's when I first heard about a drug – sorry, a plant-based medicine – called ayahuasca. Partaking of ayahuasca required a whole other level of commitment. In order to lose your mind in a meaningful way, you had to trek off into the Amazon jungle and hope you wouldn't dislocate a shoulder while wrestling your demons because there was no way out except the way you came in. And there was only a boat once a week. Ayahuasca was a risky business, a sort of bliss or bust deal with no refunds.

I knew all this because one of my friends had recently returned from the Amazon where she'd been on a three-week guided tour of the inside of her mind. Admittedly, she didn't seem any different than before she went, but I was sceptical about whether the benefits outweighed the risks. I couldn't wait to hear the gory details, though.

J had always been interested in the 'psycho-spiritual' benefits of ayahuasca – a combination of two plants, she informed me, found only in the Amazon and used by indigenous people in shamanic ceremonies.

By the time she turned fifty, J was showing all the classic symptoms of our age: she hated her job; she was burnt out, restless, at odds with the world and herself. She'd done her time on the therapist's couch and was ready to dig deeper, take a leap into the unknown. She wanted, she said, 'to have an internal adventure in an authentic setting'.

The authentic setting alone would have been enough to put me off. The Amazon jungle was already fraught with dangers without going looking for trouble. Imagine hallucinating that tarantulas were crawling all over you and waking up to discover you weren't hallucinating? What if the drugs blew your head off and you never found it again? I didn't think I was likely to go as far as she'd gone, or get as far gone: the best thing about the type of drugs I'd once enjoyed was that they never took me anywhere near myself.

When J finally arrived in the Peruvian village from where the boat would take her and the other initiates up the mighty Amazon river to the ayahuasca camp, she couldn't help noticing a fair number of bedraggled-looking foreigners wandering aimlessly about in tatty T-shirts. These turned out to be veterans of the ayahuasca experience *who'd never left*. I'd have taken this as a sign to leave right away, but J continued on her steamy Conradian way towards whatever lay at the end of the two-hour boat trip and another two hours traipsing through the jungle on foot.

When they woke up the next morning, the nervous initiates emerged from their thatched cabins and assembled for the introductory talk. The talk was given by facilitators – basically tour guides to the soul – who explained how everything would work. The facilitators reassured their charges that there would be a 'watcher' by their side at every step of the trip, or at every trip of the step, depending, because everyone reacted differently. At the end of the talk, it was announced that the group would now perform the *vomiting exercise* and everyone should put on their swimsuits because things were going to get messy.

For a month before the trip, the initiates had followed a strict diet to prepare their bodies for what was to come, cutting out red meat, alcohol and caffeine. The vomiting exercise would be a final purging of whatever toxins might still be lurking. The initiates lined up in their swimsuits at the edge of a freshly dug trench – never a good sign. Large pots of steaming citronella tea were passed around – not an unpleasant taste, apparently, but you had to keep drinking it until you vomited.

Let's just say, things got pretty messy. And this was all before breakfast.

Rehearsals over, the ayahuasca experience itself began that night with a yoga class in the *ceremonial space* – a vast conical structure with a wooden floor and net walls; proper walls, explained the facilitators, would have suffocated them in the heat and 100 per cent humidity.

This, I reminded myself, was costing my friend most of her life's savings.

After a while (time was already starting to warp) the indigenous healers arrived – *conveyers of the plant spirit*, they were called – carrying two-litre Coke bottles filled with the ayahuasca potion.

J remembered going up to the ayahuasca table to receive her dose in a shot glass. After that, she couldn't remember much.

'I had a sense of other people in the room – having a tough time, laughing, crying, whatever. I was aware of the healers working on me. They sang songs – well, they were more like sounds, *noises* – that were really incredible. I remember trying to stay upright in the meditation position but eventually I fell over – everyone did. We were all off our faces, including the healers. I do remember sobbing and sobbing with a grief I'd never expressed before. The whole thing lasted for about five hours, but I had no sense of time.'

The next morning, she felt *absolutely fucked*.

There were ayahuasca-free nights to allow the initiates time to recover. There were days when no one spoke. Everything rotted in the steaming heat and the initiates went to bed after supper at 6 p.m. because there was no electricity and nothing else to do: you couldn't read by the light of a cell phone because if you'd been daft enough to bring a cell phone, it was now a corroded lump of metal. Night walks into the jungle were not advised.

My friend kept this up for twenty-four days.

Was it worth it?

To be honest, she admitted, she hadn't come away with any answers to the meaning of life, as such, but she felt she'd done 'useful work on herself, in a non-specific way'. No, she said, it hadn't been fun, but that wasn't the point – ayahuasca wasn't a fun drug: it was a portal to the soul.

The following year, she did it again.

After her initiation into the school of ayahuasca, J kept up her studies, experimenting with what was known in the mushroom trade as 'hero' doses (read *a lot*). Unlike ayahuasca, hero doses could be tried at home, with a list of emergency numbers to hand.

It all sounded pretty scary, but then I had to remind myself that midlife was sometimes a scary odyssey through ourselves. Facing down our fears was part of the process. There was no right or wrong way to go about it.

For my birthday that year J gave me my first edible – a mushroom of priapic proportions, more of a large toadstool, really. I had no idea what to do with it.

In the end I stuffed it in an envelope and put it on a shelf out of reach of the grandchildren. A few months later while packing for a weekend away, I popped the envelope in my bag. We were staying on a farm with friends and there wouldn't be any accompanying children – in other words, we were in a safe place at a safe distance from endangering minors and making absolute fools of ourselves in front of anyone but ourselves. 'C'mon, said Husband on the second night, 'let's do it.'

After supper we all trooped into a field and passed round a plate of the chopped-up mushroom. I popped a thumb-size piece in my mouth and almost immediately spat it out. It was like chewing an old sponge that had been left to decompose under the kitchen sink. While the rest of the company was starting to experience exciting visual disturbances, I was crawling round the field on my hands and knees with a head torch, trying to find my semi-macerated mushroom before the dog did.

It was not a pleasant experience, and I thought that my first attempt at entering the portal of my soul would probably be my last.

It seemed that the midlife drugs of choice and I just couldn't get along. I couldn't eat edibles and cannabis drops just made me sleepy and antisocial. At the same time, I didn't want my life to gradually become a depressing series of *never again*s: never again would I wear skirts above the knee or stay up till dawn or flirt with strangers or know any new music. Never again would I have any fun, or *be* any fun.

Standing impatiently in line at the pharmacy's dispensary counter one morning, clutching my latest prescription, I wished the queue of mottled pensioners in front of me would shuffle up a bit faster. When it was their turn they hogged the pharmacist, slowly working through an inventory of aches and pains and predictions about the weather as if they had all the time in the world. Which in one way they did, and in another way, they really didn't. That'll be me in a few years, I thought sadly.

'Don't be silly,' said my mother. 'Look at me, I've never taken a recreational drug in my life and I'm having loads of fun!' Considering the most memorable edible she'd ever had was her first banana after the war, I felt she was coming off a low base.

After all was said, snorted, swallowed and spat out, I decided that *never say never* would be a more optimistic aphorism to live by than *never again*.

Rooting in my make-up bag one day I found an Ecstasy tablet. It was caked in the lipsticky gunk that lives at the bottom of a woman's make-up bag, but there was no mistaking it for one of my anti-inflammatories. With archaeological care I cleaned it with my eyebrow brush and revealed a tiny pink pill stamped with a skull and crossbones. It was like finding a fragment of gold from Tutankhamun's tomb.

Ah, Ecstasy, that 100 per cent illegal, synthetic, lab-manufactured fun drug of yore. I sealed it in an envelope and wrote on the front A B C D E and underlined the E twice: my clever code would act as a short-term memory aid and mystify anyone who might find it before I did. I hid the envelope somewhere so safe I only found it by accident two years later when I was cleaning out a drawer. Here was my *never say never*, my insurance against *never again*.

I hung on to the Ecstasy tablet, waiting for that special occasion, that rainy day, that final fling. It became a talisman, a promise to myself that I'd never be too old to have that kind of fun again. The longer I didn't take it, the more I savoured the *idea* of taking it. Who knew, perhaps I'd *never* take it and my children would find it among my possessions when I was dead. Or perhaps I'd save it up to take on my hundredth birthday. Then I wouldn't care about having a party hat jammed on my head by jolly carers who would blow out my candles and eat all the cake.

I wondered if Ecstasy had a sell-by date.

Lifestyle Choices

'The only way to keep your health is to eat what you don't want, drink what you don't like, and do what you'd rather not.'

— MARK TWAIN

When I was ten, my mother put me on a chocolate diet, all previous attempts to shrink me having failed. She'd already cancelled my subscription to the school canteen and packed my lonesome lunchbox with celery and lumps of cottage cheese, admittedly a negligible downgrade from spotted dick and custard. She and Auntie had even made Cousin and I join Weight Watchers, but really, what ten-year-old was going to be motivated by a bunch of fat grown-ups standing on a scale clapping each other? It was bad enough coming up with three good deeds a week for Brownies.

My mother intended the Chocolate Diet to be a form of radical aversion therapy, something she'd probably read about in the kind of parenting magazine that would be banned now. For three days I'd be allowed to eat only chocolate. There would be no fish fingers, Rice Krispies, spaghetti hoops or anything else considered normal, nutritious fare for growing children in the sixties.

Was I prepared to try it? she asked me in all seriousness. Because it would be harder than it sounded, and I'd have to commit …

I was out the door and in the sweet shop before she finished her sentence.

For three days I guzzled Bounty bars, Mars bars, Maltesers, Cadbury's Flakes, Curly Wurlys, Milky Ways, Walnut Whips and Smarties, which were permitted snacks in between meals. For three days this Willy Wonka wet dream materialised on my plate at breakfast, lunch and tea. Watching me eat drove my sisters, who weren't fat enough to be on the Chocolate Diet, *mad*.

On day four, my mother presented me with a bowl of cornflakes for breakfast and I howled, though not as loudly as my sisters did.

The Chocolate Diet was the best diet I'd ever been on, the only one I'd ever stuck to. Naturally, it screwed me up for life.

As middle age spread, my natural pear shape was transmogrifying into an apple shape; I began to look like a sort of *papple*. I refused to have a scale in the house in case I trod on it by mistake on my way to the bathroom in the night. I tried the Drinking Woman's Diet (misunderstanding – apparently, they meant water), the Your Jeans Will Tell You Diet (I bought a size up and cut the label out) and the Unhappy Diet (which only led to renewed bouts of comfort eating). The Eighteen-Hour Diet sounded promising until I realised that it meant fasting for eighteen hours a day, not getting thin in under twenty-four. My will-power was the only thing that seemed to be shrinking. The Smoking Diet probably saved me a few extra pounds, though.

Every sane person I knew had given up smoking, with the exception of my mother and Auntie, and their soundness of mind was questionable. They'd smoked on the labour ward, they smoked in the car, they smoked in the bath and they smoked in bed. I supposed they must smoke in their sleep too – I didn't see how else it would be possible to cram in the number of cigarettes they smoked between them. I could see the headline in *The Sun*: 'Sisters Spontaneously Combust!'

I'd smoked since I was sixteen, back in the days when hospitals provided ashtrays and smoking was a passport to being in with the Out Crowd at school. For a few weeks after taking up the habit I turned green and felt like throwing up, but eventually I got the hang of it. When my mother noticed I'd been pinching her cigarettes (it must have been that lovely damp tobacco reek in the loo) she begged me to wait, at least until I reached my majority, by which time I'd be off her hands and my lungs wouldn't be her problem. She even tried to motivate me by promising to buy me my own Zippo when I turned eighteen. Thanks to the Chocolate Diet, she knew that aversion tactics would have little effect on me and didn't bother trying to make me eat a pack of Player's.

Unbelievably, at the age of seventy-eight, my mother quit smoking. She who'd once flicked a butt out of the car window which had boomeranged through the back window and landed in my sister's ear; she who'd once called the manager over to her table in the fugged-up smokers' section of a restaurant and complained that, as she was paying the same price for her food as a non-smoker, she should be allowed to enjoy her fag in fresher air.

Her doctor had begged her not to stop on the grounds that it was too late and would probably kill her. She thanked him for his input and went cold turkey.

Like all addicts who lose a buddy, my admiration for her will-power was laced with envy and fear. I felt defensive, abandoned, betrayed; if she, a militant lifelong smoker and my DNA prototype, had quit, surely my days were numbered? How much longer could I carry on pretending smoking wasn't a disgusting habit and wouldn't kill me just because it hadn't killed her?

'Why did you do it, Mum?'

I had a sudden ping of terror that she'd had a cancer scare or could have emphysema and my sisters and I would be obliged to wheel her round Lidl with an oxygen pipe up her nose in one of those motorised scooters with a rain hood that made old people look like large, unappetising babies.

'I couldn't afford it any more.' She shrugged. She wasn't talking about her health, she hadn't made a lifestyle choice; it was pure economics.

For a year after stopping, she got every cold and flu virus going around and felt ghastly as her lungs resisted the brutal withdrawal of their fix. She ate cream cakes all day and piled on the weight. Slowly, her lungs came back to life.

Occasionally, she still asked if she could light my cigarette, which set me on the horns of a dilemma: on one hand it would be fun to share a puff with my mum again, like old times; on the other, it would be like giving a reformed alcoholic a glass of wine. I would be her enabler; I would go straight to hell. But then I decided she was a big girl and could take responsibility for her own decisions. She only ever took a single drag. 'Ooh, that was lovely,' she'd say; she never smoked properly again. Giving up smoking was one of the few *never again*s that was hard to argue against at any age, let alone at mine. 'If I can do it, you can do it,' Mum said.

Auntie had cut down from two packs a day to one-and-a-half. She had also cut down her intake of Mars bars from five a day to 'two or three' – or so she said. She had a lifelong addiction to Mars bars and kept them in a tin in the glove compartment in case she got peckish on her drive to the shops, fifty metres from her flat. Despite Auntie's largely sedentary existence and the Mars bars, she never failed a health check-up or put on weight – in fact, her doctor told her she should try to gain a few pounds. Meanwhile, could he use her as a case study for a paper he was writing in the *Lancet*? For her eightieth birthday, Sister Two gave Auntie eighty Mars bars.

Still, Auntie balanced out the Mars bars by getting in her other five a day at lunch.

'It's important to stay healthy, darling,' she told me, lighting up a cigarette. 'I cook a proper meal every day, fish with broccoli and carrots, and I've been very good about the Mars bars, though I do still love my eclairs with Belgian chocolate on top. Oh, and Aldi's double chocolate gateau.'

Could anyone blame me for thinking I wasn't genetically predisposed to death?

In a culture that has become more and more infatuated with youth, old age is the new taboo, the club nobody wants to belong to. The wellness narrative is merciless: you are expected to maintain goal weight and a youthful glow and exert ruthless control over your bladder, your brain and your intake of fatty acids. Anything less is your own fault and can be avoided if you just put in the hours, like Helen Mirren.

The head-spinning array of lifestyle choices for those of us fortunate enough to have choices can feel oppressive sometimes. The guilt and shame induced by failing to get with the self-care programme is like being a teenager approaching the confession box with impure thoughts. Wellness and agelessness are a perfect match, and being older is no excuse for not being younger.

Anti-ageing implies that time can fly backwards and death be put off long enough to get a birthday card from the Queen.

My grandmother had lived long enough to get two birthday cards from the Queen: the first was on her hundredth birthday. It was a large, handsome card on stiff cream paper with a blue tassel and a photo of a much younger HRH in a tiara. When a second card arrived from the Queen on her hundred-and-first birthday, Grandmother's mind was no longer what it had been, even a year earlier. Still, she rose to the surface long enough to notice that it was the same card as last year. She thought it was 'a bit shabby' of the Queen to send the same card twice, especially as there was no shortage of photographs of Herself to choose from. I felt a bit sorry for the Queen, who was no spring chicken herself and must have had writer's cramp at the rate the centenarian population was exploding. Thanks to the NHS, which was now having regrets, a hundred was the new seventy-nine.

Shortly before her hundred-and-second birthday, just in time to be spared another birthday card from the Queen, Grandmother died of – well, I'm afraid to say, old age. She'd held up her end as long as she could.

Grandmother was a Christian Scientist and had raised her children on the founding tenets of the faith, chief among which was the practice of mind over matter. Auntie said mind over matter took quite a lot of practice when you fell off your bike and got gravel in your knees and there wasn't so much as an aspirin in the house to prepare you for having it picked out with tweezers. Most things Grandmother diagnosed as non-fatal were treated with a stiff cup of tea and a lie down with Radio 4.

There was a war on, which meant there wasn't exactly a party going on in the pantry, let alone in the medicine cabinet. There was little sugar or fat, and butter was rationed to two ounces per person per week – about what I'd spread on a slice of toast. The war generation practically invented portion control: they called it *having enough*. Grandmother kept chickens in her suburban garden and grew vegetables. Even Hyde Park, said my mother, was turned into a giant vegetable patch.

Moderation wasn't a lifestyle choice in wartime, it was a necessity, and treats were held back for special occasions. In the neighbourhood air-raid shelter during the Blitz of London, Grandmother would keep the children calm by giving them each a Petit Beurre biscuit. My mother could make a Petit Beurre last for hours, nibbling one frill at a time; it took her mind off the ominous whine of the doodlebugs and dogfights shattering the night sky above their heads.

Sunday roasts at my grandparents' house began with a cup of what Grandmother called 'greens water' – the liquid from the cooked spinach or kale that in our house would have been poured down the sink. 'Drink up,' she'd say as we held our noses. 'It's full of goodness.'

In 1950s Britain there were no fizzy drinks, no MSG, no double-deep-fried takeaways. Petrol was strictly rationed and largely reserved for emergency vehicles, which meant that people had to walk everywhere. One Christmas my grandparents walked five miles with my mother and Auntie and baby brother to see a pantomime. Auntie and Baby went in the pram. My mother, who was four, walked, and when she couldn't walk any more, her father carried her. Five miles there, five miles back, at night, in the blackout.

My sisters and I couldn't get enough of these gruesome tales of unimaginable deprivation.

True, back then everyone over the age of twelve smoked – which must have upped the national happiness quotient when you were being bombed by the Luftwaffe – but no one was fat. Along with portion control, the war generation accidentally invented wellness.

When I asked my mother what lifestyle choices meant to her now, she was uncharacteristically lost for words.

'Well, I'd like to have a garden ...'

Once an enthusiastic gardener, she'd recently moved into a small, ground-floor flat with a miniscule square of concrete outside onto which she'd squeezed a few plant pots.

'No, Mum, gardening isn't a lifestyle choice – it's a hobby.'

'Alright, alright,' she snapped, 'I'm thinking.'

Lifestyle choices, I explained rather primly considering I hadn't made any yet, were about opting to do healthy things instead of unhealthy things – like being gluten free or taking up running or meditation; things that would improve your quality of life, your self-esteem, your life span. 'Like you giving up smoking, Mum!'

She shrugged and said, 'I told you, it was for financial reasons.'

She brightened. 'How about a neck lift? I'd like one of those.'

I sighed.

'I'm sorry I can't be more helpful, darling,' she said a little waspishly, 'but I really don't know what lifestyle choices are, maybe because we didn't have any in my day. We didn't think like that. If Auntie and I had a bit of red lippy and a straight pencil line up the back of our tights we were happy, and unless a man took me out for dinner I lived on porridge and saved my money for clothes.'

In Mum and Auntie's day no one had food intolerances, they just had food. Today, practically everyone I know is wheat intolerant or won't eat carbs or is allergic to dairy or has given up sugar. Only two of my friends have what I consider to be legitimate allergies: one of them went into anaphylactic shock after eating a peanut; the other one blew up like a medicine ball and had to be rolled to A&E after eating a curry laced with tamarind. As far as I'm concerned, the rest are attention seekers. Having them round for a meal is a nightmare – though, interestingly, nobody seems to be allergic to alcohol. I'm not intolerant of anything (except, it could be argued, of picky friends): I'd eat whatever was put in front of me with hearty abandon and worry about bloating afterwards.

It seemed the more lifestyle choices we had, the more pressure we were under to make them. It was all pretty stressful.

*

I wasn't completely tone-deaf to the tales of friends who, as we advanced into our fifties, had begun to listen to their bodies, but I couldn't see what it had to do with me. Denial loves company, and Mum and Auntie were excellent companions: by some dark magic, they seemed to have managed to make their bodies listen to them.

A typical food day for my mother began with nothing for breakfast, crackers and cheese for lunch, cornflakes with cream for supper and cake for pudding. Auntie believed in a good glug of malt vinegar to flush out her insides. They both drank a lot of tea. My mother's mugs got so stained with tannin she'd put liquid bleach in them once a week and leave them to soak on the kitchen windowsill. Auntie once took a swig, thinking it was water. Luckily, she managed to spit most of it out before she swallowed and seemed to suffer no ill effects.

When it came to exercise, Auntie – who wasn't a great believer in the benefits of fresh air – maintained muscle tone by climbing in and out of her car, while keeping her knees pressed together. The driver's door of my mother's car had been stuck for years, forcing her to clamber across the passenger seat and do the splits over the gearbox.

Apart from rattling off like AK-47s after their first ciga-rette of the day (a cough that disappeared when my mother quit smoking), they were fit as fiddles, poster girls for glowing health. As genetic role models went, my mother and Auntie had led me down a merry path.

Still, as time went by, I found that clapping my hands over my ears when little warning bells went off in my body didn't help – I could still hear them. I couldn't run up a flight of stairs without panting; I could just about squat at toddler eye level to play with the grandchildren, but I'd struggle to get up again and have to do little bounces on my haunches and spread my arms out like aeroplane wings to get lift-off. Perhaps it was time to get off my denialist high horse while I still could without causing myself or the horse an injury.

'Look, Mum,' I said the next time we spoke, 'I know you and Auntie will probably outlive carbon emissions, but what about our DNA ancestors? What did they die of? *Did* they die? Please don't say they're in the attic.'

It would be helpful to know these things before making any rash lifestyle decisions that might require me to take action that wasn't strictly necessary, plus every time I went to see a doctor these days they'd ask me what hereditary diseases ran in my family.

Somehow, I never got around to asking my father what hereditary diseases ran in his family. His parents had died long before I was born. I knew there had been a sister who died of polio when she was thirteen. It was whispered that my unknowable, grief-stricken grandmother had taken to her bed and died a few years later, when her youngest, my aunt, was just ten. There must, I thought, be many ways to die of a broken heart.

My matriarchal line would provide the only clues as to what I needed to know to make informed lifestyle choices to head off my heritage.

My mother commenced to rattle off a list of fatalities on her side of the family: breast cancer, brain tumours, heart attacks, strokes … The evidence that almost no one had died peacefully at home in bed took me somewhat by surprise considering Mum and Auntie's supernatural powers of survival. They weren't all very old either: Great-Aunt was forty-eight; Uncle was fifty-four. Grandfather was in his sixties when he had a fatal heart attack while pruning his roses. 'It was lucky, really,' mused my mother. 'Papa would have been absolutely *furious* if he'd had to lie in bed with my mother flapping about.'

All in all, it seemed that far from being immune to the consequences of poor lifestyle decisions, I could go at any moment. I went to see my trusty GP, Dr R – always my first line of defence – and embarked on a battery of health checks: blood pressure, cholesterol, kidneys, lungs, heart, bone density and my first ever mammogram. Having a mammogram felt like getting my breasts slammed in a fridge door, but it was nothing compared to the colonoscopy Dr R ordered next. The best thing about having a colonoscopy was the oral enema I had to drink the day before – I practically dropped a dress size. I don't like to think what the best thing was for the gastroenterologist.

I was in the clear, but Dr R wasn't letting matters rest there. Over the years, Dr R had never judged my lifestyle and in return I had never lied to him about it. For the first time, my blood pressure was higher than normal. He tentatively suggested that I'd perhaps been less than … fully attentive to my health. He rattled off a list of things I should swear off – pizza, pasta, pastry, wine, chocolate, Chinese takeaways, basically anything worth eating – for the rest of my life. Then, I should be fine.

There was an awkward pause before Dr R slapped his knee and said, 'Only joking!' Wiping a tear of mirth from his eye, he adopted a more sombre tone: 'Seriously, it's a good time to quit smoking while you're ahead, lose some weight' – he mentioned a frankly extortionate amount – 'and start exercising.'

There was a drum roll. I waited for the punchline. 'Are you still joking?'

Lifestyle choices were like Forrest Gump's box of chocolates, without the chocolates.

Dr R and I struck a bargain: giving up smoking, eating and lying on the couch all at once would only set me up to fail. So, we'd start with the exercise (there was that 'we' again) and hopefully this would kick-start the weight loss and give me an incentive to stop smoking before I stopped breathing. We shook on it.

What type of exercise to take up required deep thought. Someone told me it was important to pick something you actually enjoyed doing, otherwise you'd never keep it up. This massively narrowed down the field of possibilities.

Loads of people I knew went to the gym, including Husband and Son. They did something called spinning, which involved cycling for an hour on a stationary bike to house music while being yelled at by someone in a Lycra onesie with a six pack. Son also *pumped iron* which caused him to get *ripped*. The last time I got ripped I had to be put to bed with two ibuprofens and the only thing spinning was my head. But I took the plunge and joined a gym and promised Son I'd keep out of his way. I spent most of the time lurking in the sauna trying to sweat off a few pounds without having to introduce myself to the StairMaster. I found the change room among the biggest challenges of going to the gym. In the steamy gloom of the sauna no one could see anything, but in the change room naked women sat around towel-drying their fairies and checking their messages. I admired their lack of self-consciousness. I envied their confidence, especially the older women who didn't seem to mind exposing themselves to discreet scrutiny, unflattering comparisons and fluorescent lighting. They were not all slim and toned; some were flabby and droopy, yet they seemed comfortable enough in their imperfect skins, and I silently applauded them without having the gumption to follow their example. Instead I'd lock myself into one of the modesty cubicles used mostly by the Muslim women and only come out when I was buttoned to the throat.

The best part of going to the gym was the muffin I treated myself to from the gym's coffee shop after my workout in the sauna, because I felt I'd earned it, and calories don't count when you've been sweating for twenty minutes. Three months later I'd gained two kilos and tried to get a refund on the lifetime subscription I'd foolishly taken out.

It was back to the drawing board. What sort of exercise would I enjoy? More critically, what sort of exercise would I be able to sustain?

They say you never forget how to ride a bike, though I hadn't ridden one since I was twelve and banged my fairy so hard on the crossbar it was a wonder I could still have children. At school I'd been a fair-to-middling swimmer, but the chlorine turned my hair green, and considering how much I spent on highlights, any sports that involved getting my hair wet were out of the question. The width of my hair alone ruled out wearing a rubber cap – it was like trying to get a condom on a bear.

My younger sisters were all starting to show me up: Sister Two had taken up cycling – across-Mallorca-type cycling; Sister Four did a hundred squats a day and was carving out a booty like Beyoncé's. Sister Three lived on the fifth floor of a block of flats with no lift.

Cousin was a year older than me, the big sister I'd always wanted. At school she taught me that when a boy kicked a ball at your head it meant he fancied you. When we were teenagers she showed me how to steal testers and use tampons. In our forties we lamented the state of our bodies while knocking back vodka martinis. As we moaned our way through perimenopause, Cousin was the fattest she'd ever been – a direct result, she said, of having a baby at forty and a bakery over the road. We bought industrial-strength spandex undies which, we marvelled, must have been engineered by the same people who made BMWs.

When Cousin turned fifty-five she made her move. She stopped eating, joined a gym and dropped two stone. She worked out six days a week. She did *burpees* – a sort of hand–knee spring thing that made army push-ups look like meditation. In between she did boxing, yoga, running and something called an Insanity Class which she couldn't really describe but said was very intense. Her back went out and a doctor told her that her spine was degenerating because she was exercising too much. Cousin gave up the burpees, but carried on doing everything else. She said she'd rather have a flat stomach than a spine. She said you got used to drinking black coffee for supper once your stomach shrank. Ever thoughtful, she said I could take my pick of her fat clothes. I still looked like an airbag.

Cousin was obsessed, *possessed*, and although I'd followed in her footsteps, for better and for worse, since childhood, I knew I didn't have what it took to follow her down the path of perpetual will-power.

In the end, though, I hit on a solution I thought *would* work for me. I liked walking. Not up mountains on goat paths, just regular old walking through the 'burbs. A walker didn't need special equipment. A walker simply had to walk out of her own front door and turn left or right. A friend who belonged to a walking club convinced me to join. 'It'll teach you discipline,' she said. Ah yes, discipline, that would be a useful new skill.

Everyone at the walking club was very friendly and I quickly felt at home. The members seemed to be mostly women, many of them older women. Not being the sporty type, I didn't know what to wear the first time I went to the walking club. I didn't own any tracksuit pants, so I put on a khaki safari skirt and took a cardigan in case it got chilly. I revived a pair of vintage hiking boots from the back of the wardrobe. My children were in stitches.

The atmosphere at the walking club was pretty casual and most of the other walkers were wearing T-shirts and leggings or baggy ethnic-print pants. Many of the older women wore full-metal make-up and their lipstick looked freshly applied: I took this as a positive sign that it wasn't going to be a sweaty business.

The club manager was an elderly German who wore a net singlet and very short nylon shorts that did nothing for his varicose veins. But I was not there to judge.

Shorts was a perfectionist who ran things strictly by the book. Before I could be unleashed on a public road with the real walkers, he said I'd need to train under his supervision. We began with warm-up lunges and hamstring stretches – a modesty challenge in my skirt – but otherwise all went well. After the warm-up, Shorts told me to walk around the school playing field as fast as possible while he timed me with a clock he'd hung in a tree. 'Faster!' he'd yell. 'You have to walk faster! Pump your arms. *Breathe!*' Each time I puffed past the clock I had to take an elastic band from a box and put it on my wrist to help me remember how many laps I'd done. Afterwards, Shorts would count the elastic bands. Six weeks and four hundred elastic bands later, Shorts pronounced me ready to walk unaided. Handing me a high-vis safety jacket, he released me into the wild. Holding my high-vis jacket aloft, I felt as if I'd won an Oscar.

The training had taught me that walking wasn't as easy as it looked, but I felt confident in the brand-new trainers and vilely unflattering track pants I'd purchased for this moment: some of the walkers were older than me, and a few of them were *much* older than me. The club's living legend had just turned eighty. I was one of the spring chickens. This was going to be a walk in the park.

I shot out of the school gate at a fair lick and accelerated away from the pack.

A block later I was surprised when a knot of pensioners whizzed past me with a cheery wave. You're doing great, they shouted over their shoulders, keep going! A mile later I had to stop and bend over in the vomit position. From between my knees I saw the eighty-year-old living legend coming up hard on my left.

'Hot day, isn't it, dear?' he said, sidestepping me and speeding away up the road. The last three miles passed in a blur of disbelief. My lungs heaved; my legs shook – even my eyeballs were sweating. At last, I saw the school gate up ahead. I also saw Living Legend hobbling through it with blood streaming down his legs.

'Tripped on the corner of 4th and Main!' he warbled gamely. By the time I crawled over the finish line, everyone was too busy tending Living Legend's wounds to notice that I'd completed my maiden voyage.

These were not people to be trifled with.

I never did beat Living Legend, though I eventually drew level. 'Hot day, isn't it, dear?' he always said, come rain or shine or frostbite.

After a few months I could walk five miles without retching. I was fitter, if not much thinner thanks to the carb-loading I felt entitled to before a 'race'. But I enjoyed it, and I kept it up. I became obsessed with counting steps on my pedometer. I felt more … on top of things. I discovered something called endorphins, and my mood swings had definitely slowed to more of a gentle sway, though if someone pushed me hard enough, I could go flying up with a sickening lurch.

I started to think that my body needn't be my enemy; it could be my friend. In spite of the neglect I'd heaped on it, it worked. My legs carried me across the line, my lungs went in and out, my bone density improved.

'Excellent,' said Dr R at my next check-up. 'How's the smoking going?'

'Very well, thank you.'

There was no point lying to a doctor.

My attempts to give up smoking had been pretty half-hearted (I probably only had half a working heart by now). Some years later I would spend a few months of every year in France, and France was not a good place to try to give up smoking. Despite the fact that more and more French people were quitting the habit, smoking remained deeply embedded in French culture: the louche glamour of association with the nation's fabled intellectuals, artists and stars of the *nouvelle vague* cinema seemed not yet to have worn off. In summer French cafés couldn't keep up with the crush of smokers demanding pavement tables, forming human smoke rings around appalled American tourists. Smoking in France made me feel like Jane Birkin instead of Bet Lynch.

*

Sebastien, the owner of my local tobacconist, ground out his cigarette on the kerb and scuttled back behind the counter. 'What can I get you today?'

Even in France, which still *had* tobacconists, cigarettes now came in black boxes that looked like little coffins. The message emblazoned across them no longer said SMOKING CAN BE HARMFUL TO YOUR HEALTH, which at least was debatable, but declared unequivocally SMOKING KILLS.

The cigarette packs came with photos on them, lurid full-colour photos of people in various states of extreme suffering. It was like Hieronymus Bosch's vision of hell.

Sebastien handed me a pack with a photo of the inside of a mouth that appeared to be full of truffles. The caption read SMOKER'S TEETH.

Seeing my face, he said, 'Let's try another one.' He flipped out another pack from the rows on the shelf behind him. This one had a photograph of a grossly fat man with a large hole in his torso. The caption helpfully explained that the large hole in his torso was as a result of REPEATED LUNG SURGERY.

Sebastien started shuffling through the packs like a deck of tarot cards.

'This one's not too bad,' he said, showing me a photo of a young mother blowing smoke out of the side of her mouth to avoid a direct hit on the baby on her lap.

Didn't we all do that to keep our children from harm in the eighties?

'Wait,' he said, 'here's a good one – The Lovers!'

A man and a woman lay on the floor in a state of wild disarray; he was in the missionary position, her skirt was hitched up and she had one leg flung across his thigh. Her palms were pressing down on his chest. His face was the colour of chalk and his mouth was hanging open. The caption said SMOKING CAUSES HEART ATTACKS.

Sebastien shuffled the deck again.

'Aha!' he cried. 'The Thinker!'

A pasty, sad-looking young man sat with his chin on his knuckles, seemingly lost in thought. SMOKING CAUSES IMPOTENCE.

I took four packs of The Thinker, impotence not being one of my problems.

The next time I saw Sebastien he told me he'd stopped smoking.

It was getting cold out here.

*

Beyond making encouraging noises about how easy it was to not smoke once you stopped smoking, my mother never proselytised, and she always kept an ashtray handy for Auntie and me.

Since quitting, her own fitness levels had greatly improved. She took Dog on even longer walks and convinced Auntie to sign up with her for an introductory tai chi class.

How was she going to chop bricks in half with her arthritis?

Mum said she didn't think tai chi was that kind of martial art, but promised to report back.

'We *loved* it,' she said after the first class. 'We learned to *sweep the moon* and next week the instructor's going to teach us how to tap.'

It was worse than I'd imagined. I pictured Mum and Auntie hoofing across the scout hall in fishnet tights and top hats.

'*Tap?* That's even more dangerous at your age!'

'Now you're being silly,' she said. Tapping, she explained, was the latest thing from ancient China; apparently you simply tapped lightly with two fingers on certain meridian points of the body, which would reverse the wear and tear of decades and enable your body to miraculously *leap back to life*, like Lazarus. She didn't know exactly how it worked, but she'd let me know.

As promised, she called after the second class – this time with good and bad news.

The bad news was that Auntie had developed sciatica after the introductory class and had missed the tapping session. Auntie claimed that the excruciating pain in her left leg was the tai chi instructor's fault for making her take off her heels for the first time since 1985 to sweep the moon. She was never going back.

The good news was that my mother was tapping away and could stand on one leg in the prayer position and watch *Strictly Come Dancing* at the same time. The next time I saw her she demonstrated how to tap on my meridian points. Then she demonstrated how to breathe, which it seemed we'd been doing all wrong since birth. She was sleeping better, her arthritis had improved, she was considering taking a course in Mandarin.

'I think I've just made a lifestyle choice,' she said – a little smugly, I thought.

At eighty-three, my mother was on a path to living to a hundred-and-eighty-three and doing her bit to contribute to the collapse of the NHS. Auntie was back on the Mars bars.

It was never too late to make lifestyle choices.

Big Swinging Chicks

'A man came up to me and said, "Don't you think you're too old to be running around the stage like that, singing rock 'n' roll?" I said, "I don't know, why don't you ask Mick Jagger?"'

— CHER

'What do you do?' is such a dull conversation starter.

To be fair, the person starting it is usually the stranger seated to your left at one of those interminable awards ceremonies where no one knows anyone and everyone has to suffer through four hours of sponsors' speeches, sobbing winners, a terrible comedian and one bottle of wine per table.

Once upon a time it was, at least, an easy question to answer: I was a journalist. I knew exactly who I was and what I was for. Most people say they don't like journalists. We're like dentists – no one wants us until they need us. But we do come in handy every now and then, often when someone who considers themselves a *personage* is on the lookout for a human voice-recorder to write a book about their riveting life, which they'd write about themselves if only they weren't so terribly busy being riveting. The personage – not infrequently the stranger seated to your left at the interminable awards ceremony – behaves as if they're offering you the chance of a lifetime, a glittering prize: why wouldn't a lowly scribbler wish to spend two years listening to them drone on about their incalculable contribution to society then jot it all down precisely as they'd told it?

At least at that point I still had professional standing: someone paid me to pitch up at work in the morning.

But there would come a time when I'd dread the 'what do you do' question, because I didn't do it any more. 'What do you do?' really meant 'Are you worth bothering with?' By now I was no longer really sure who I was. Lapsed journalist currently living off Husband while waiting for something less humiliating to come along? Middle-aged has-been starting to think I might have thrown the baby out with the bathwater when I quit a perfectly good job to go off and *find myself* in a foreign country where I didn't speak the language and, well, actually it's a really interesting story ... But already I'd be talking to the stranger's back, because they'd have turned to the person on *their* left, hoping for better luck.

Loss of confidence, loss of influence, loss of interest: these were words I heard over and over in conversations with my girlfriends.

Some said they were bored with their long-standing careers that seemed to have got stuck on Repeat; others felt they still had a lot to offer but were getting too old to be considered for the juicy parts. Still others felt as if they'd gone into a sort of career coma – they could hear everything going on around them, but they couldn't move.

Leaving the security of a dependable job to take a leap into the unknown, well, it was a huge risk that could mean never getting employment again.

As my lapsed lawyer friend put it, 'There's a fundamental loss when you come to the end of a shit-hot career. You can be an excellent salad maker, a keen theatregoer, a devoted mother, but there's no real substitute for it.'

Then again, few women I knew of my age were ready to get out their rocking chairs. Rather, they wanted to reinvent themselves, ignite new purpose and passion, find new ways to use their skills and experience or do something completely different, while we still had options, before the email informing you of the non-negotiable early retirement package landed from the HR department.

The catch was, once you'd worked out what you didn't want to do, you still had to work out what you did want to do.

And that, said Lapsed Lawyer with characteristic wisdom, was why we needed a gap year.

*

Work had been a fundamental part of my identity. It was where my vanity lay.

From the very first day at the community paper I'd found by going through the telephone directory, I'd loved my job. I covered church fêtes and cake-icing contests and school sports days. It was drummed into me that the most important part of any assignment was to cram as many people as possible into the photograph, so that everyone in it and all their relatives would buy the paper.

I was nineteen and had no tertiary education to speak of – I lasted one year at journalism college and one year at university: the only useful skills I came out with were touch-typing and how to drink tequila without falling off a bar stool.

This may have had something to do with why I suffered from imposter syndrome for much of my career (I have heard a few far-better-qualified women than I confess that they've had it too, though I have never heard of a man with this condition). It might also explain why, early on in my career, I'd get picked to take minutes when the editor's PA was off sick. I felt like Melanie Griffith in *Working Girl*. I never quite got over the novelty, the spectacular luck of finding myself, a school leaver with no contacts and zero certificates, employed in the best job in the world – *and I'd got my big break out of a telephone directory!*

I loved office life: the gossip around the water cooler, the camaraderie at crunch time, working as a team when a big story broke, getting dressed for success in the mornings. I even enjoyed the post-2008-crash Christmas parties when sushi and champagne stations were replaced by sausage rolls and warm white wine in paper cups: there was always the thrilling possibility that someone would behave inappropriately and provide weeks of post-party entertainment.

But around the time I turned fifty I started to feel that I'd gone about as far as I could – or wanted – to go in my career. At the media house where I worked I'd accrued all the status symbols befitting my seniority, under-cover parking and my own office, pathetically coveted perks in an open-plan workspace where employees were squished together like battery hens squeezing out eggs.

I was running low on inspiration and losing the boundless curiosity I'd once had for peering into the human kaleidoscope and observing the colourful fusions and confusions produced by society in all its rich diversity and ever-changing temper.

Covering conferences where speaker after speaker kicked off by telling you what they were going to tell you, proceeded to tell you, then concluded (eventually) by telling you what they'd just told you, made me want to slide down a wall. Strictly monitored thirty-minute interviews with bored celebrities in blank hotel rooms, going through the motions of talking up their latest project with an interchangeable rote of reporters, lost their star appeal. No wonder they looked half-asleep by the end of another round of 'intimate' chats – answering the same questions, refusing to talk about the really juicy stuff, desperate for the hawk-like publicist to hustle you out so they could call their children/watch the test cricket/try out new expressions in the mirror, or whatever celebrities did when they were left to their own devices. I stopped thinking that I would be the one to extract confidences that no one else had, some thrilling new titbit about their personal life, an unguarded comment that they would live to regret and would give me a great headline. It was all so transactional.

Things that once I'd so keenly wanted to communicate, I could barely be bothered to think any more. Healthy scepticism was turning into cynicism; my competitive streak seemed to have run its course. Quite simply, I no longer got a kick out of my dream career.

A colleague approaching a similar career crossroads

said it felt as if she had a slow puncture, as if the air was going out of her tyres.

My own slow puncture was combined with another feeling, a suspicion that I was no longer essential to operations, that I was an expensive nice-to-have, that ambitious younger colleagues were eyeing my office over the top of their workstations, watching for the signal to rush my flimsy plywood door.

Media was a young industry. By the time I was fifty, I was almost always the oldest person in meetings – meetings that couldn't start without me only because I was punctual. The boss was ten years younger than me. The reporters were thirty years younger than me and listened to music through headphones, posted tweets, updated their Instagram, watched news feeds and wrote copy all at the same time. They were the future, the very near future. It was their turn to rise and shine.

'I want to be like you one day,' sighed one of the interns, whose star was rightfully rising, as we clinked paper cups of noxious office coffee to celebrate the end of a long-running assignment.

'Really?' I said incredulously.

'Uh-huh,' she said, 'old and fabulous.'

It took me a moment before deciding, *I'll take it*.

Yes, perhaps it would be wise to get out while I was on top, before I turned into one of those lemon-lipped lifers in droopy cardigans who sellotaped their name to their tea mug.

As the twenty-first century entered its teens and my fifties got underway in earnest, I realised something else: unless you worked in IT (no people skills required) or were already top dog (people skills no longer required), the powers of charm and seduction were vital to any successful career. Seduction was about getting noticed, persuading others to take your ideas seriously, whether you were wooing a client, giving a presentation or trying to get a class of fidgety kids to put down their phones and pay attention. A glowing CV counted, but so did first impressions. A friend working at a high level in a corporate where money and status were measured by how much new business she brought in admitted that she was feeling the heat of younger, fresher colleagues at her back, the stars of tomorrow.

'My job begins with seduction,' she said, 'so how do I keep doing that when the first impression I make on a potential client is *who's the old lady?*'

Colleagues had begun to ask her when she was going to retire.

Over and above being good at what we did, our youth had conferred certain advantages – a foot in the door – and youthful looks, especially youthful good looks, never did any harm, whatever we might tell ourselves to the contrary.

An old friend had started out in the film industry as a runner. As the lowliest dogsbody on the set, one of her jobs had been to run to the airport and pick up more illustrious members of the cast and crew flying in from all over the world. She'd stand in Arrivals holding up her white board with the director or actor or producer's name on it, and escort them to their swank hotel. When the Very Important Person was a man – especially a young man who wasn't so bad looking himself – the flirt factor helped the atmosphere on set. My friend's bouncy youth implied that the job was going to come with perks, that the director/

actor/producer wouldn't need to spend the evenings skulking in his hotel room with CNN: nothing debauched or disgusting had to happen (this is not a Harvey Weinstein story) but the prospect of hanging out with cool young people who knew all the best bars and clubs could lift the jet-lagged director's spirits.

Now, more than thirty years on, Old Friend had moved up in the movie pecking order. One day, she offered to do a VIP airport run as a favour to a filmmaker friend whose new runner was still being broken in on the coffee run (skinny, decaf, extra shot, hold-the-sprinkles ... getting the coffee order right was arguably the hardest job of all on a film set).

Old Friend stood in the Arrivals hall holding up her board with the VIP crew's names in big black letters. Three likely-looking candidates wearing sleeve tattoos and pork-pie hats emerged through the automatic doors. Old Friend waggled her board and smiled as they walked towards her. Seconds before they almost walked *over* her, the trio split up and swerved around her as if she was a traffic interchange.

'They literally looked right through me, even though I was planted in front of them waggling my board with their names on it.' Old Friend sighed. 'It was obvious they were looking for the usual young, sexy runner ... It was definitely a moment when I felt like an old, frumpy person.'

Only once was I aware of having been hired partly for my fresh young looks. I knew this because my new boss at the red-top tabloid told me so: it was the eighties, the age of paparazzi supremacy and everyday sexism, which didn't bother disguising itself because it didn't know it existed.

'You'll get your foot in the door,' winked New Boss.

Unfortunately, his crafty plan (to which I don't recall taking offence – it was the eighties et cetera) didn't exactly work out as planned, and most days I'd come hobbling back to the office with an empty notebook and a slammed foot. My charms soon palled on the management. After a freezing night outside the house of a C-list celebrity whose door remained locked against my pleas that I was young and considered to be good looking and was about to lose my foot-in-the-door to frostbite, I quit. Still, my brief encounter with the mucky end of Fleet Street went onto my CV and my career did not suffer as a result.

It was hard being honest enough with ourselves to admit that we might have exploited our youth and looks to get what we wanted at work.

Straight after graduating from college, a friend had landed a juicy plum of a job on a grungy culture magazine in Los Angeles. In a competitive market, LA Friend wondered what had made her stand out from the crowd of candidates with degrees *and* work experience. But deep down, she knew the answer, or at least part of it.

'The editor wanted to get into my pants.' She shrugged. 'I was never intentionally *oh, hello, here's my boobs*, but I'm pretty sure I got the job partly because I was cute, he had the hots for me and I didn't mind playing the dumb blonde in order to advance my career.

'If anyone had said to me at the time, "That's why you got the job," I'd have said, "Bullshit." But in hindsight, I'd have to admit that it's pretty much what happened.'

In her forties, Not-So-Dumb Blonde encountered a different type of discrimination at work – this time as an older woman. Now she was a boss, and among the men who reported to her, there were some who didn't take kindly to instructions from a woman.

She had to take charge of the game another way. She got tough; she made few friends. She no longer cared. 'I don't need them to like me, I just need them to do their job.'

*

In Auntie's day, most women were still attached to the end of a hoover. Auntie would never be a boss or even dream of being a boss, but she had a career, and that was unusual enough in the late 1950s. It began in the typing pool and moved through the ranks until she was an executive assistant to the CEO. I pictured her perched on the edge of his desk taking dictation in a cone bra like Joan in *Mad Men*. PA level was about as high as a woman could rise in the world of work in the 1950s, bar the occasional spinsterish odd-ball with ideas above her glass ceiling and a hide like a rhinoceros. Auntie didn't set out to have a career: she had only taken a course in typing and shorthand to tide her over until the man of her dreams came along and turned her into a housewife.

Unfortunately, the man of her dreams turned out to be a nightmare – meeting and marrying Uncle, her true prince and survivor of the frying-pan incident, was still in the future – and Auntie sued for divorce. In an era of put up, shut up and get the kids fed before he comes home, this was no easy matter. Auntie had to go to the Old Bailey and ask a judge for *permission* to get a divorce: as a woman, her request would be granted or denied at his discretion (all judges were men). After hearing the evidence, the divorce was granted. When she was asked how much maintenance she wanted for her daughter, Auntie said, 'I want nothing, my Lord.'

And so, in her early twenties, she became a sole bread-winner and a single parent – terms barely heard of, let alone accepted. Even to get a flat she had to submit to an interrogation by the property manager, who said he'd never heard of anyone renting to a woman. She was told to get her father's permission, in writing.

'Women didn't have their own cheque books. Women didn't drive. The husbands had the money. I got my driver's licence, I got a cheque book, I got an apartment.'

Long before anyone burned their bra, Auntie was independent of any man. I thought Auntie was an extraor-dinarily brave, on-the-ground, realpolitik feminist. 'No, darling,' she demurred, 'I'm just a woman.'

While Auntie was occupied with single parenting and sole breadwinning in London, my mother was attached to the end of her hoover in suburban Bromley. She loved being a housewife. She had coffee mornings with her girlfriends, redolent with gossip and cigarette smoke, and fetched us from school in the Mini Cooper my father bought her one birthday – an icon of swinging sixties Brit cool along with miniskirts and the Beatles. Dad brought home the bacon; she cooked it. She had an allowance, pin money for her pins. He went skiing with his mates; she didn't mind. She told me it was one of the happiest times of her life: she felt fulfilled in her role as homemaker, mother and wife. She didn't want a career; her ambition was to have three chil-dren and a fur coat by the time she turned thirty. Which she did.

But when my parents divorced a decade later in South Africa, my mother, at forty, abruptly found herself having to provide for four daughters with no back-up plan. The house was sold. The car went. The telephone went. The washing machine went. After moving back to the UK and settling in Devon, where the rest of her family had slowly migrated, my mother took whatever work she could get – cleaner, carer, shop assistant and finally, best of all, barmaid (she never thought of herself as a 'bartender': this conjured up images of Tom Cruise juggling with cocktail shakers and there was certainly nothing like that in *her* job description). In the market town where she and my sisters ended up living, she was an ice-n-slice gal in the tradition of British pubs with bizarre names involving farmyard animals. The work was exhausting, atrociously paid and demanded heroic levels of tolerance and diplomacy.

She loved it.

The happy-hour hum; keeping her mahogany counter polished to a gleam; memorising her regulars' preferences and peculiarities; getting 'tarted up' and putting on high heels, though as she got older she had to take anti-inflammatories and painkillers to get through a shift.

Over the years my mother worked in several pubs around the town: sometimes the owners moved on, or she'd get poached, or, occasionally, the boss would be a total *dick* who could stick his miserly ways and dirty kitchen. It was one such case that led to her final appearance behind a bar counter, at the age of seventy-nine. She was working shifts at the Conservative Club but quit when the new owner turned out to be a *complete wanker* and, really, she was far too old to be treated like a skivvy and still have to curtsey for five pounds an hour. But she missed it – the pub quizzes and banter, old Maggie tottering in for her nightly pint; even the punter who'd get legless and throw darts at the portrait of Winston Churchill, the scuffle and drama of having to call the boys to march him out. Nobody messed with Winston.

Even after she retired, you couldn't walk down the street without her being hailed by an old colleague or customer. I felt proud to be her daughter.

Mum and Auntie didn't have much truck with words like *identity* and *self-worth*. Neither of them set out to have careers, but their work ethic was stitched into the fabric of who they were: they took their work seriously and put food on the table for their families during some very lean times.

For a while after Mum stopped working, I know she missed it; but if her days lacked structure, seemed a little emptier, I never heard her complain, though I did overhear her telling a former colleague who was moaning about being overworked that she'd be glad to help out on Quiz Night, as long as the wanker wasn't around.

*

Yes, I would need to give careful thought before giving up my job, relinquishing a career that had felt vocational, that had been good to me. Work gave shape and purpose to my days. Work paid the rent. On balance, I'd probably spent more waking hours with my colleagues than with my family.

Work was a brilliant excuse for procrastinating, putting off boring chores like visiting the licensing department and cleaning the kitchen cupboards. I could say I was in a meeting even if I was in a nail bar (usually with a few other women who, I could hear from the way they answered their mobile phones, were also in 'meetings'). Work had status; other people took my time seriously. I could wave the work wand and duck out of dreaded arrangements ('Groan, I'm stuck at work!'). It was even better than having to get home for the babysitter. Work was also a pretty good way of avoiding too much self-examination: I didn't have time to peer into the Petri dish of whatever writhed in my inner world, take a temperature reading of my relationships and risk being forced to confront uncomfortable truths about what and who I might be sorely neglecting. Keep busy, keep moving, don't think too much, don't look too hard. Work was a highly effective displacement activity.

Of course, there was also the money. Money had never stuck to me or driven me, but earning it not only paid the bills but was deeply affirming. Lapsed Lawyer agreed: in a capitalist society, getting paid at the end of the month, someone saying 'I value you to the tune of ...' was inexorably tied up with our sense of self-worth.

I'd always earned my own money, through two marriages with a single-parenting stint in between: for a while Daughter and I had lived on frozen hake and spaghetti. Having your own money gave you leverage in a relationship, evened out the balance of power; paying your way meant never having to stuff shopping bags at the back of the wardrobe and say 'Oh, this old thing?'

But how would I ever know what I wanted to do until I stopped doing what I didn't want to do? Something would have to give, starting with the money. That was the trade-off – less money, more freedom. I quit my job.

The boss made a farewell speech; there was warm white wine in Styrofoam cups and plates of sausage rolls. It was very moving.

I watched with interest as one by one my girlfriends began to shift gear too. Some were slowing down, going part-time, adjusting to being smaller, happier fish in the pond: they felt they owed it to themselves, that after decades of being run off their feet and beholden to deadlines and alarm clocks, they'd earned the right to bow out, breathe out and work out whatever it was they might want to do next in a quieter, more contemplative environment. Others were cranking up the handle, taking bold risks and reinventing themselves: turning hobbies into businesses, running their too-big empty-nest homes as guest houses, retraining as life coaches and hypnotherapists. One friend was investigating opening her dream green funeral parlour. My Little Pony sister-in-law had started selling organic rainbow-coloured henna online – she was killing it.

All I'd done since quitting my day job was blow a hole in my company pension payout and lie on the couch eating Pringles while contemplating my navel, which was a lot easier to see when I was lying down than it used to be. I felt like a gap-year failure.

'Take your time,' said Lapsed Lawyer, who was well into her third gap year. 'Give yourself a moment to declutter your mind and let stray thoughts come into it.'

Lapsed Lawyer had quit smoking and taken up breathing, mindfulness and yoga. She had also dabbled with several full-time positions outside her professional comfort zone, but so far nothing worth giving up her new-found freedoms for. She decided that the thing she missed most about having a corporate career was *the chase*: being wooed and pursued, even fought over by prospective employers – the glow that came with getting plucked from the chorus line for a second-round interview because you were hot stuff, up there among the damn-near perfect tens. But lately, Lapsed Lawyer confessed, after the initial rush of getting the callback and curating her interview outfit, she'd get as far as the tube station before realising she didn't really want the job, just the confidence boost and a new pair of boots. It wasn't unlike dating – you didn't have to fancy the boy in order to get off on him fancying you.

'Enjoy the lull in proceedings,' she said. 'It's like everything else that's happening to us, and we should think of this time in our lives as a ceremonial pause, like handing over Hong Kong.' I didn't like to remind her what had happened to Hong Kong.

I took on various freelance work, which paid a few of the bills; Husband generously offered to take care of the rest while I concentrated on my ceremonial pause and waited to see whether my flag would go up or come down. It was a privileged position to be in and I was grateful to Husband, though it was a bit awkward when his birthday came around and he had to buy his own present.

A major online news site invited me to contribute a weekly blog. 'Obviously, we don't pay,' said the section editor. 'It's a blog.' It was funny how language worked in the digital world: surely content was content, whether it was in the form of a blog or an old-fangled newspaper article? The only difference as far as I could tell was that anything you wrote online, regardless of the time and effort you put into it, was for free. I blamed

Bill Gates: back in the nineties when we all thought the internet was the greatest innovation since cave-dwellers learned to rub two sticks together to produce the world's first cooking show, Bill was going around saying that the internet wanted to be free while making his first billion. Well, that was the situation back in the early twenty-first century – practically antiquity in tech time. Putting aside clearly redundant thoughts that my self-worth was partly invested in getting paid to do a job, I jumped at the chance: if I was serious about seizing my moment and opening my mind to a world of possibilities, blogging might lead to Other Things.

As ever, Lapsed Lawyer cheered me on. It was the perfect time to have faith in our experience and abilities, she said, and, oh, the *relief* of not being at someone else's beck and call, a big upside of not getting paid. New opportunities would come our way if we put ourselves in *their* way and worked our corners. To Lapsed Lawyer's credit, she admitted that some ideas were never likely to leave the tube station. But this, she said, was all part of the process: failure to gallop off to the next horizon was going to be as critical to our success as success!

Between my blog and the freelance work, I still had time on my hands. Quite a lot of time. Sometimes it seemed as if time was all I had. On one particularly slow day, I ironed the carpets and watched a chicken defrost.

But this was what I'd wanted, wasn't it? Room to declutter, get fresh perspective on the future, reignite purpose and pay closer attention to the health and welfare of my relationships, starting with myself.

Such questions swung in the air above my empty desk.

*

An old school friend got in touch. She'd been the head girl; her blazer clanked with badges for everything from academic achievement to javelin throwing. Despite the special powers bestowed by her authority, she didn't throw her weight around and was popular with staff and students alike. While Head Girl was collecting silverware, I was awarded a season ticket to detention and had been banished from French class for disruptive behaviour (result!). Yet somehow, Head Girl and I became friends. Looking back, I probably wanted to be more like her than like me: like a lot of kids identified as troublemakers at school, we were mostly just troubled – problems at home we had no control over made us angry and unhappy. It was around the time my family was imploding in the lead-up to my parents' divorce.

After school, Head Girl and I had gone our separate ways and hadn't stayed in touch. When she found me, we hadn't seen or spoken to each other for more than thirty years. By then I'd quit my career and was living semi-permanently in France, in a village close to Toulouse in the south-west. Incredibly, it turned out she lived in France too, in Paris with her husband and children. Head Girl spoke fluent French: she had, of course, been the top French student at school. I, having recently landed in France, was now wishing I'd put more effort into conjugating *avoir* than into upsetting the French teacher.

A few months after renewing our contact by phone, Head Girl and I met up in Paris. Thankfully, she didn't look like one of my mother's friends – even without the badges she was instantly recognisable as herself. We rapidly dispensed with thirty years' worth of polite catch-up – marriages and children, the health of our mothers, the passing of our fathers, and speculation about whether the biology teacher and the PE instructor who'd been caught in flagrante in the stationery cupboard had lived happily ever after. Fast forwarding to the present, we compared our midlife crises – a chance for me to bend a fresh ear about how I'd recently given up a solid career to seek out the Next Big Thing, which now seemed to be shrinking to a series of Next Small Things.

I was not surprised to learn that Head Girl had already made her big midlife career move and now ran her own business online. She also sat on several boards, including that of a fledgling radio station that was looking for contributors and said she'd put a word in with the station director – no previous broadcast experience was required, they were that desperate for content. It was the first and thus far only English-language radio station in France, explained Head Girl, a shoestring operation, meaning no one got paid, but I was getting used to not being paid. And who knew? The station might climb the rankings, attract advertising, win awards and *then* pay for content! Meanwhile, I'd be learning new skills and getting a chance to practise them on real-live listeners, although Head Girl said I shouldn't get my hopes up on that score as to date there were only about four of them. I'd always loved radio, even more now that practically any station in the world could be streamed directly into my ears while I did the housework. Anyway, it was early days and the name of the station alone was enough to set my blood racing: World Radio Paris. WRP for short. I rolled the words around my tongue and could practically taste the glamour.

World Radio Paris!

World *Radio* Paris!

World Radio *Paris*!

It sounded impossibly sexy and I imagined the thrill of telling the next person who asked me what I did for a living that I worked for WORLD RADIO PARIS. It wouldn't be strictly true, but it wouldn't be strictly untrue, either.

Head Girl took me to the studio and introduced me to the station director. I told him my idea – a dispatch from where I lived in the remote French countryside, aimed at enlightening Parisians who believed civilisation ended at the *périphérique* that there was life out there.

He said I had the 'job' and that he hadn't really needed to meet me in person because most of the contributors recorded their shows from home, and anyway it was radio, so appearances didn't count. The WRP 'studio' was basically a padded cupboard in the corner of an office at the American University. Every now and then someone in the office would rap on the window and make slashing gestures across their throat. This, Director explained, meant they were going into a meeting and we had to stop speaking until they rapped on the window again to signal that the meeting was over and broadcasting could resume. It was quite hard not to speak when you were recording a radio show, but, shrugged Director, beggars couldn't be choosers. I knew the feeling.

When the office staff went on lunch, we did a trial run. Director gave me an enormous pair of headphones and put me in front of the mic. I felt almost like a real presenter. I read aloud a piece I'd prepared and learned my first lesson in broadcasting: writing for radio is not like writing for reading, so unless you're Judi Dench, sentences longer than twelve words will cause you to run out of breath halfway. Breathing in the wrong places on radio is the equivalent of having spinach in your teeth on TV.

Take Two.

Director says he can hear my bangles.

Take Three.

Director says, 'Try not to swallow the mic – you sound as if you're in a wind sock.'

Take Four.

Director says he *thinks* he has something he can use and sends me on my way with a bulbous foam-covered mic with a WRP sticker on it. I'd arrived!

Back home I made my own padded studio with pillows and a duvet. I loved the mic and did one-woman karaoke shows after hours. My self-worth soared.

WRP paddled along gathering listeners, and I paddled along with them for a year or two, though I never managed to master the art of reading without sounding as if I was reading, and I certainly never managed to shoot the breeze without a script. But my brief flirtation with broadcasting had given me an appetite for writing again.

Writing for radio had been a humbling experience. In career terms I'd gone from top to bottom: no one knew me, no one expected anything of me; there was no pressure to succeed. As I adjusted my sights to the muddy bottom of the pond, I began to see that the muddy bottom could be a promising place to start. Stripped of the vanities of being good at what I did, I learned, as Lapsed Lawyer said, that failure was part of the process: nobody started out at the top.

All journalists were supposed to have a book in their bottom drawer, including some who should have left it there. But once I'd acknowledged that I was mostly just scared of doing anything I might not be good at, I realised there'd be nothing to lose by trying because I'd already lost it. Once I'd worked that out I felt liberated.

Bit by bit, an idea for a book took hold. It percolated then went off the boil; it hovered at the edge of my vision then vanished; by turns it gained and lost my attention. One day it seemed silly; the next it seemed there could be something there, something of value that might surface if I screwed my butt to a chair and *tried*. 'The muse will come,' said a friend who'd just finished writing his second book, 'but you have to be present.'

*

A common theme that emerged from the many conversations I had with friends – mostly women friends – was a (frequently misplaced) nostalgia for certain things we felt we'd lost or left behind: being in the thick of things, at the heart of the action, even, on occasion, indispensable to it. But such rewards had come at a price: constantly being up against the clock, stuck in meetings that ran way over time that you couldn't leave, even though you'd promised the kids a date night, because it would only reinforce the stereotype that women didn't take their work as seriously as men did. Once, when I knew I was getting sick, I went on a business trip to Atlanta, US, because I didn't want to appear weak. By the time I got back I had double pneumonia.

When you were in the high-pressure thick of things, the contest between the professional and the personal was one that the personal seldom won. And there were times when I had put my work before my children – the dressy events and openings and after-hours networking that had once seemed so vital had not always served them well. More than one of my friends admitted to having forgotten to fetch their kids from school.

Had our Big Swinging Careers always been worth the candle?

'Nope,' said Lapsed Lawyer, 'I have no sense of glamour about what it was like working full-time.'

'Nope,' said a friend who'd worked in war zones. 'I can't say it was great when there were grenades going off and I was cowering under a table.'

At least dodging a grenade would make it a memorable day at the office. It was easy to forget that sometimes work was deadly dull, a featureless slog to the end of the day, hanging around the tea urn, recycling stale gossip while waiting for the next blip of excitement: on slow days the highlight might be the appearance of a birthday cake, compliments of someone in IT you'd never heard of, which we'd rush to get at, like starved bears.

*

Midlife career changes were becoming almost routine in my circles, but nothing could have prepared me for the news of an actress friend's new career.

Actress Friend was about to turn sixty and she wasn't going to take it lying down, though, actually, she did take it lying down, not metaphorically speaking. The idea came to her after she'd been rejected for three jobs, all well within her competency and experience.

'I felt as though I'd been tick-boxed just by getting the interviews: sixty-year-old female. Tick.' She was positive her age had played a part.

After giving the matter some thought, she came up with an ingenious way to repurpose her God-given talents and smoky nightclub voice to earn money and be her own boss. And that was how she came to join a phone sex agency. She wrote a script and created a character called Candy. Candy was twenty-four and had long blonde hair and breasts like Barbie: she was an instant hit. Actress Friend rolled her eyes. 'You wouldn't believe how popular the Candies are, however corny.' Being Candy meant Actress Friend could work flexible hours from home, so she took the 'breakfast show' from 6 a.m. Getting up at dawn was one of the little jokes of ageing: the days of being shocked into wakefulness by the Marimba ringtone and stumbling round the house in the dark looking for a stray school shoe were over, but once past fifty no one slept later than 5 a.m. without heavy medication.

Getting ready for work had never been easier: Actress Friend would get up, put on her dressing-gown, make a cup of coffee and clear her throat. Once she got the hang of things, she found she could even do a little light dusting during phone calls.

She was back in charge. 'It was a very powerful feeling. I loved having a different persona. No one knew how old I really was and it creased me up thinking if only they could see me in my fluffy dressing-gown, doing the dusting!' Multitasking was one of the perks of the job: unfortunately, she had to wait until she knocked off work to do the vacuuming – too noisy – but if she groaned loudly enough in the right places, she could whizz round the bathroom with the Ajax. Actress Friend acquired regulars and the money was pretty good. But best of all, she said, was 'being a sixty-year-old woman getting away with being twenty-four'.

Actress Friend's appetite for the phone sex business palled after a while – being an OCD cleaner, she was more turned on by the hoovering. At the time of our conversation she was thinking about how to reinvent herself once more. Perhaps she'd start a painting and decorating business or be a dog walker or monetise her formidable cleaning skills.

'I might even do the odd blow job,' she mused.

I think she was joking, but with Actress Friend you never could tell.

I was learning new tricks too, attempting to write something longer than nine hundred words for a 4 p.m. deadline on Friday that someone other than my mother would read. Surprisingly little of what I'd done before had prepared me for this challenge: I had a few tools in my box, but for a long time I struggled to find any that would unlock the next door. More and more I was convinced that, even if I didn't succeed, in some significant way I'd be in a different place when I'd finished. Trying something new that was out of my comfort zone was like starting piano lessons and wondering if I'd ever get better than 'Chopsticks'. I practised my scales and set myself daily goals; I treated myself to an ergonomic office chair that was easier to stay screwed to for protracted periods than the kitchen chair. On bad days the house sparkled and shone with displacement activities: Actress Friend would have been proud of me.

My time spent in liminal space, the space in between, in transit from one place to another, had been essential: it was like being in an airport – a nowhere place that went everywhere if you just hung on in there and waited for the Boarding sign to come up.

Little by little, I began to believe that even if the world was no longer my oyster, it was definitely a clam with potential.

Fashion Forward

'What does "age appropriate" mean? Does it really apply to me or anyone else in this world? They need to throw out that term, period.'

— BADDIE WINKLE

Even as I began to see the advantages of giving up my career and sensed that there would be new opportunities ahead, my clothes begged to differ. As my wardrobe flashed before my eyes, I could see that most of its contents were no longer a fit.

I didn't want to turn into a frumpy old bag, but I worried that if I didn't change certain things about the way I dressed, I might wind up looking like Grayson Perry. I too had a weakness for six-year-old-girl drag – baby doll dresses with puffed sleeves, Peter Pan collars and pinafores. Being a famous artist and trans icon, Grayson got double-page fashion spreads in the *Observer* while I just started to look not quite right in the head, like one of those poor things on an outing from the Home. I tried to steer away from dresses that looked adorable if you were three years old and experimented with pleated skirts, black tights and sturdy lace-ups – part Doc Marten, part prison warder. I went through a Victorian-blouse phase and a smock-top phase to disguise the onset of middle-aged spread that made me look like thousands of other woman trying to disguise their middle-aged spread. As I got older and rose in seniority at work, I bought a crisp white shirt, which I hated, but as I was on my way to being the oldest person in the room, the best I could hope for was authority.

Sometimes I envied people who had to wear uniforms to work – nurses, police officers, nuns: nuns don't get up in the morning wailing 'Oh God, I've got nothing to wear', even though they probably have more of His ear than most of us. I imagine a nun rising from her virginal bed with a song in her heart and a clear vision of what she's going to wear – a voluminous black robe with bell-ringer sleeves that will hide a multitude of sins and is machine washable. No dithering about which shoes match, only one piece of statement jewellery to choose from and the baddest of bad hair days banished beneath her veil.

But old habits die hard, and by our fifties, most of us have settled into our fashion faults and defaults: we've travelled so far down the road of our signature style it's not easy to change direction. One of the ironies of the wild ride through middle age is that not unlike nuns we're on a maiden voyage through virgin territory.

*

For thirty years I'd worn the same style of shoes – black Mary Janes. Every pair looked different to me and served a different purpose: there were the high-heeled black Mary Janes, the flat black Mary Janes, the buckled black Mary Janes, the button-over black Mary Janes ... office-y ones, casual ones, evening ones, schoolmarm ones. And still I would be surprised when a friend held up a pair of black Mary Janes in a shoe shop and said 'These are so *you*'. All I knew was I needed them, just like I'd needed the other twelve pairs hanging bat-like in the dim recesses of my closet.

In three decades, probably my most significant style breakthrough was turning my boring old skinny jeans into ripped skinny jeans, though, like all great discoveries, it was by accident. I loved ripped jeans. I felt they gave me an edge without going over the top, and I made sure they were never ripped higher than the knee: even I knew that thigh-gape was strictly for firm-fleshed adolescent girls. Still, a rip was a rip, and I wondered how I would know when it was time to turn in my jeans to the nearest fashion police. I was having my doubts about leggings too. Leggings were best friends with my smock tops and I had a drawer full of them: leggings never judged you, they simply accommodated you; they didn't fit at a stretch, they stretched with you; leggings were effortless, like nuns' habits. The late Karl Lagerfeld, high priest of the House of Chanel, once said that women who wore leggings had *given up*. Which was pretty rich coming from a man who'd worn the same outfit for forty years. Still, perhaps I should make a bit more effort.

It was time to clean out my closet, get a new look, step out in different shoes. It felt a bit like being a teenager again – a second chance to work out how to express myself while overcoming paralysing bouts of insecurity. Who was

I now? Who might I become? What would my clothes say about me? I'd pin things from Pinterest, make a mood board, mash-up style icons, tear pictures out of *Vogue* and *Good Housekeeping*, just to be on the safe side. I was determined to make dress sense, even as I struggled to make sense of everything else. This, I thought in an optimistic moment, could be FUN.

First, I needed makeover inspiration, and where better to start than with a masterclass in the classics – Paris.

Parisian women weren't fashion risk-takers. Sometimes it was hard to distinguish between mothers and daughters and grandmothers because they frequently wore the same clothes – unfussy, timeless, immaculate. I loved watching the *soignée* madams tripping lightly along the Right Bank in their seasonally appropriate ballerina pumps (spring and autumn) and tightly belted trench coats, the wind-screen-size Jackie Os they never seemed to take off, and the scarves they learned to tie six different ways before they were allowed to graduate from nursery school. True, some of the older women seemed to have had rather too many fillers and appeared to have difficulty smiling – but Parisians didn't set much store by smiling; it would have ruined the expressions they wore that managed simultaneously to convey chilly confidence and intimidate fat tourists in fleeces.

But I suspect you have to have been born and raised inside the *périphérique* to achieve the kind of *je ne sais quoi* Parisian women made look a birthright, and I'd probably left it too late to pull off their haute-hauteur.

Turning my gaze to provincial climes closer to home in the sunny south of France, the street-fashion contrast was striking. There seemed to be a frilly thing going on: frilly skirts, frilly tops and even frilly leggings. Older frilly women, at least those of doll-like proportions, wore their frilly things very short with very high heels. 'That's southern style,' shrugged my unfrilly French friend who only shopped at the *friperies*, the French version of charity shops, more commonly known as *la frip*. I'd once been obliged to buy a frilly sun dress in a *frip* when a strained button popped off as I was trying it on. 'Take appetite suppressants and eat only apples for three days,' advised the assistant, handing me the button and the dress from which it had separated. 'By the fourth day it'll fit you.' The *frip* assistant drove a pretty hard bargain for a dress that cost five euros.

One thing all French women had in common, from Paris to the provinces, was their ruthless pursuit of thinness. In a country where you couldn't buy a Disprin at a supermarket but had to go to a separate pharmacy selling drugs and medical supplies (which in turn was a different pharmacy from the one that sells cosmetics), appetite suppressants were available *everywhere*. In the toiletries section of my local supermarket they took up half an aisle.

Frilly clothes definitely weren't going to work for me, plus French clothes in general seemed to be cut on the small side: in the interest of blending in I spent fruitless hours trying to squeeze into them. Which, I saw now, was never going to happen.

Instead I turned to the street markets which, along with French staples like cheese and wine, sold vintage farmer's clothing. At one of these I purchased a roomy farmer's nightshirt that looked as though it had been in service since the Revolution. There was some demand for these, being authentic relics of a bygone age when burly pig farmers wore embroidered nighties to bed.

Black was a gift from God and Coco Chanel. But unless you really were a nun, it didn't play in the south of France. The sun boiled and beat and made a cotton cardigan feel like wearing a fur coat. Jeans, even ones with holes in them, were too hot. A belt was too hot. A bra was too hot. Semi-naked was the preferred southern dress code, and in August everyone stripped off and came out of their houses barely covered, regardless of their age, shape or gender. Women I knew who were well into their seventies tended to the flower beds outside the church in gardening gloves and bikinis. Local men stripped down to Speedos – practically a national costume in France and the only apparel men were allowed to wear at public swimming baths. But men always ripped off their tops when they got hot, and even the old ones seemed impervious to the effects their straggly grey chest hair had on the general population. But older women? I knew I should take their exposed flesh in my stride, be humbled by it, be on their side and celebrate my sisters for being comfortable in their skin *and so little else*. But secretly, I was shocked.

The first time I saw older women going topless on a beach in Spain I tried not to gawp. A trio of granny types in bottoms only sat on their towels, chatting away, *just as if they had clothes on*! Everything wobbled and flopped as they passed round the baguettes. I sat, practically invisible under a heap of sarongs, trying to decide whether to be appalled or envious. The last time I'd worn a bikini was before the birth of my children, before eating their leftovers in between meals deprived me of the will to live on rice cakes and water. Since then I'd run the gamut of swimsuit options in search of the right one for me: there was the yummy-mummy-gone-bad tankini, the industrial-strength floral one-piece with a built-in underwire bra; there was the racer-back no-nonsense one-piece with boy legs, which Husband said made me look like a Baltic weightlifter. For weeks after I dumped this one he called me Belarus. Why couldn't I be like these European women who didn't care who saw them in their natural state? By day three at the beach the local customs were beginning to rub off on me: I'd loosened my sarongs and the trio of topless grannies looked so ordinary, I stopped looking.

*

Peering out from my comfort zone in search of adventurous, age-appropriate fashion inspiration had thus far been a failure. I was going to have to widen the search area.

By now, even going clothes shopping fully clothed was a risky business: the perp walk from the change room to the communal mirror, the mounting humiliation of trying to find that special dress and being steered by a twelve-year-old to a rack of laundry bags with pockets. Young girls shopped in packs: on Saturday afternoons they went on hunting expeditions to Zara and H&M, crowding into cubicles, giggling and oohing over that *cute* playsuit. Those were the days. Now, like many of my friends, I preferred shopping alone; taking my time, guarding my privacy; burying my mistakes in the Oxfam pile with the tags still on.

As once I'd turned to the gurus of menopause for guidance on how to overcome irrational behaviours and murderous impulses, I now turned to the style guides on YouTube offering tips to the over-fifties about what, and what not, to wear.

Remember Trinny and Susannah on the TV makeover show *What Not to Wear*? When I was in my forties, Trinny and Susannah were required viewing. It could be grisly watching their makeover models standing in the change room in their tired underwear getting their boobs jiggled by Trinny and Susannah at the start of each show, but stripping down to your M&S knicks and letting them poke your back fat was the price you had to pay if you wanted the fairy wardrobe mistresses to wave their wand over your closet. Trinny and Susannah drew gasps for some of the amazing magic tricks they performed, but every now and then, they seemed to run out of ideas and just bundle everyone into a V-neck wraparound dress. The wrap dress was their one-style-fits-all solution to a range of unruly body parts – big boobs, flat chests, short necks, wide hips, narrow shoulders: no one could afford to be without at least one wrap dress in her new improved life. I confess I was never convinced by the healing benefits of the wrap.

Daughter – who was too young to remember *What Not to Wear* – mentioned that she was a big fan of Trinny's fashion tips on Instagram; she said Trinny had good advice for all ages and I should take a look. Twenty years had passed since *What Not to Wear* and Trinny was now in her fifties. Daughter was right: she did have inspiring fashion ideas for older women – clothes that were wearable, affordable and put together in ways that simply hadn't occurred to you yet. Teacherista Trinny did not require her students to undergo a personality change or grow three inches taller, only to keep an open mind, apply a dash of derring-do and invest in a pair of white trainers. I took notes.

Trinny was a class act in a booming market in home-spun midlife makeovers on every internet corner. Upbeat matrons took up their posts in suburban living rooms scattered with many cushions, in front of flattering floral arrangements that matched their lipstick. They favoured necklaces of giant brightly coloured beads that covered their necks and tunics that covered their bottoms. They draped themselves in animal prints and posed against swag curtains, or sometimes, it appeared, the other way around.

My friends and I passed these videos around like the comedy gems they were, and if any of us were in any doubt about what *never* to wear, all we had to do was watch one. We were obsessed with a woman who described herself as an inverted triangle. Inverted Triangle showed us how to turn ripped jeans into *funky, mature* jeans by sewing animal-print patches over the holes. She demonstrated how open-toed shoes could *elongate the foot* and teamed them with knee-length pink tuxedos with shiny lapels. Sometimes, Inverted Triangle wore the entire animal kingdom all at once. Every now and then a large, shaggy German shepherd would wander into frame: we couldn't wait to see how Inverted Triangle was going to wear it.

The welter of conflicting fashion advice for the over-fifties could be paralysing: black was timeless and black was ageing; 'artists' smocks' that could comfortably accommodate *Guernica* flattered the fuller figure but could also make you look fuller figured; hats could create a style stir but needed to be handled with care; scarves were a neck's best friend, but only if you *had* a neck.

Would I end up creating a style stir by following their advice or end up getting mistaken for a pile of coats at a party and sat on?

Certain guidelines were just common sense. For instance, there was no need to debate whether to give up plunging necklines because my neckline had plunged all by itself. But there was murkier territory that required more thought. Trinny said take risks. Maybe I *could* rock red tights, not only at Christmas. Perhaps 'contour'-hugging knitwear *could* be managed with the right scaffolding underneath. Having accepted that these days my body could be more aptly described as a figure, it would probably be a wise move to get a professionally fitted bra. A good bra, I discovered, cost more than a mini-break in Barcelona. I booked a return flight to Barcelona.

Resisting the cheap, cheerful temptations of the 50 per cent off sale rail in fast-fashion stores and investing in fewer better-quality *pieces* was one of the Ten Commandments of the older woman's style bible. A pair of sharply tailored trousers, a silk shirt and a cashmere sweater – these were classics that wouldn't bobble or split or catch fire on impact. Still, it was all very well saying that one Ted Baker was worth ten Primarks, but when you got the Primark home and realised you must have been temporarily blinded by the price, you didn't have to feel guilty about turning it into a duster.

I turned to Daughter for help. Daughter was born stylish and could be trusted to tell me the truth without hurting my feelings.

'I only want what's best for you,' she'd say, prising anything with an elasticated waistband out of my grip. Daughter taught me that the whole point of secret socks was that they remain secret; she said my favourite puffer jacket made me look like a hand grenade and should be thrown a safe distance away; she said three-quarter-length cargo pants were the devil's work.

When I got it right, I was rewarded. 'Now *that*,' she'd say, 'looks fabulous.' Having Daughter to guide me through the style thickets was like having Trinny on tap.

*

We are constantly fed the message that being older means we can stop caring about what other people think of us. This notion is sold to us – mostly by ourselves – as one of the advantages of ageing. To me this is just another way of saying that as we become less visible in the world at large, more blurred around the edges, other people aren't going to think much about us at all, so there's really no point worrying.

But of course, we cared: there was no going back, but we weren't giving up on ourselves. And in a fashion age where there are no such things as plus-age departments and grannies and teenagers tote the same shopping bags, the stakes are rising all the time. I thought of my grandmother and how bewildered she'd be at the thought of taking her granddaughters shopping in Zara and finding something nice for herself too. It's true that Auntie still wore thongs to prevent visible panty line, but Auntie was a special case and was possibly having a delayed reaction to the Heath Robinson-like underthings her mother wore.

Grandmother laid the foundations for the structure of her clothing with so many ramrod undergarments she couldn't bend from the neck down.

When my sisters and I were young, we'd beg her to let us watch her get dressed, which she did in the airing cupboard for warmth. Once she had on her first modest layer, we'd be allowed to sit in a semicircle in front of the cupboard. The door would open and there she'd be, unbuttoning her quilted dressing-gown. A cotton vest went over the cross-your-heart bra, followed by a 'step-in' which required expert twisting to manoeuvre into position. Then came the rolling of stockings, the snapping of garters and, finally, the rustle of a flesh-pink nylon slip.

It was like watching a striptease backwards.

Only now was Grandmother ready to put on actual clothes – a Margaret Thatcher pussy-bow blouse, a tweed skirt, a brooch. She had special driving shoes to prevent her good courts getting scuffed on the pedals. Grandmother wasn't exactly stylish, but she was immaculately groomed. I never saw her in trousers or without lipstick. Her hair was always set and waved. She would have been in her mid-fifties back when I sat giggling with my sisters outside the airing cupboard: looking at photos now, I see that even then she looked like a granny.

Catching the sixties wave, my mother's generation was somewhat more casual and less constricted below stairs. The invention of pantyhose and a brief craze for disposable knickers must have seemed to them as liberating as the pill. But when she got on a plane, my mother dressed *to the nines* – she even had a smart little suit made for air travel. In those days flying was still rare and impossibly glamorous, like being invited to a party thrown by Elizabeth Taylor and Richard Burton: there were glamorous hostesses, the bunny girls of air travel, and drinks in real glasses, after-dinner cigars and chit-chat with the captain on the flight deck. Everyone wore hats.

In the seventies my mother went through a cheesecloth phase before settling on what would become her signature style for the next thirty years – fishnet tights, slit skirts and skyscraper heels. It was a look I vividly remember from parent–teacher evenings when I'd try to pass her off as someone else's mother; to be fair, she probably wished I was someone else's daughter when the report cards were handed out. When she fetched me and my sisters from school, we'd make her park half a mile from the gate and forbid her to get out of the car. My friends thought she was the coolest mum ever.

Recently, Mum and I had a good laugh about this. When I asked her to define her style back then, she replied without blinking, 'Slutty.' Her clothes, she said, had expressed an important part of her identity *at the time*. Not wishing to probe the possible reasons for this, I moved the conversation briskly back to the present. How would she describe her signature style now? 'Comfortable,' she said: flatties, skinny jeans, sweaters in autumn-y shades. Her red hair, which she'd allowed to fade just enough to stop looking as if it was about to burst into flames, served as her pop of colour. Occasionally Mum went a bit off-piste and finished off an outfit with a cracked leather pirate's belt with a giant brass buckle that she'd had since 1965. This was her vintage look, she said. When she snuggled down to watch *Strictly* or *Housewives*, she'd wind herself into a leopard-print blanket and tuck it in under her arms: this, she said, was her tribal chief look.

Next door, Auntie continued to make her own signature style statements. Apart from her thongs, which were pale and lacy, Auntie wore black: black trousers and turtlenecks that complimented her choppy platinum blonde hair. She refused to wear flat shoes, but when she was at home alone, Auntie cranked up the central heating, put on her favourite satin spaghetti-strap nightdress (also circa 1960-something) and went barefoot. 'I've always liked to slip into something more comfortable, darling,' she winked.

These were their happy clothes.

At the outermost reaches of the happy-clothes galaxy lived Baddie Winkle. Baddie was a drinking, smoking, scrappy Kentucky gal somewhere between ninety and immortality. She'd become an overnight Instagram sensation when her great-granddaughter started posting pictures of her in boob tubes, cut-off denims and rapper jewellery. Soon, Baddie hit the red carpet, trading fashion tips with Miley Cyrus and making guest appearances on TV in cheerleader skirts and rhinestone bootees. Baddie was having the time of her life, living proof that sensational style could triumph at any age. She told interviewers that she'd decided to embrace who she was. Baddie really didn't care what other people thought of her. She was living her dream in dayglo lipstick and fun-fur bikinis. Drag queens prostrated themselves before her thigh-high velvet boots. Once you'd got over the shock of seeing a ninety-year-old in a biker jacket and aspirational T-shirt emblazoned with the message 'Be a Slut', you realised that she was the very definition of style – confident, original and unabashedly true to herself. Whether anyone was watching or not. Baddie was so bad she was good.

Baddie's philosophy was simply 'live and let live'. She would wear whatever made her feel *fabulous* and others were welcome to do the same. She scoffed at the term 'age appropriate': she had no idea what it meant and, anyway, she couldn't think how it applied to her or anyone else. In Baddie's opinion, only God was entitled to pronounce judgement, and she was pretty sure He didn't have a problem with the way she dressed. Either that or He was speechless.

By covering up very little, Baddie just about covered everything: be yourself and the world will smile with you – or at you, *whatever* – and the gods and possibly even Anna Wintour would turn a blind eye.

Taking a leaf out of Baddie's book, at last I saw the light. I didn't need to make any drastic changes: my style was my style! It was me, whoever me was *at the time*. I didn't need to turn in my wardrobe to the authorities, just tweak it here and there, as I saw fit. Oh, the sweet relief of letting myself off the midlife makeover hook. I eventually outgrew the Mary Janes and donated my dirndl skirt to the von Trapp family museum. I tugged a hemline here, a sleeve there. I introduced a few bold new staples to my wardrobe: a cropped leather jacket that made me feel like Madonna, a cashmere sweater that made me feel all grown-up in a good way, and a pair of white trainers with very secret socks. I consigned my ripped jeans to the dustbin of history.

It was like therapy: in the end, you answered your own questions.

When I'd asked Sister Two to describe her happy clothes, she'd replied, 'Anything that doesn't attract attention.' As our Invisible Years drew nigh, I knew we'd be less likely to attract *any* kind of attention, least of all admiring attention. Sister Two mulled this over. 'In that case,' she said, zipping up her hoodie, 'even better.'

I wasn't sure I was quite ready to disappear in *that* way.

The Silence of the Wolves

'Personally, I find the wolf whistle one of life's more cheering sounds. It has a … jauntiness that rings out rather innocently in an age where misogyny has gone underground into the dripping caves of the internet.'

— ALLISON PEARSON, *DAILY TELEGRAPH*

Did I miss it, the wolf whistle, those phwoar noises men in hard hats had once made as I scurried past building sites?

In the #MeToo era I wasn't sure it was permissible to even think such thoughts, let alone speak them. But truthfully, every now and then I'd ask myself: *did I?*

If a Hard Hat called out 'hey, beautiful!' I felt beautiful. I liked to be looked at – not leered at, not accosted, not stalked, but when being seen in a certain way made me feel good, well, then it *was* good. Let's face it, there were far more toxic insults than a wolf whistle: the colleague who addressed your breasts as if you weren't there, the date who accused you of being frigid when you weren't suitably grateful for the free dinner.

I was a reporter in my early twenties when a celebrated civil rights lawyer who was in town for the duration of a long-running trial that I was covering invited me to a 'small gathering' at his hotel. I was incredibly flattered to be included. Arriving at the hotel, I was directed up to his suite, which seemed a bit odd, especially when I saw a single bottle of wine in an ice bucket on the table in front of a sofa and no other guests. It turned out be a very small gathering indeed. After a few minutes of cursory chit-chat he pounced. In between maulings I'd break away and make for the door, but he'd overpower me and pin me to a wall or try to drag me over to the bed. After what seemed like a very long time being chased around his fancy hotel room in this manner, I managed to get out. He pursued me along the corridor to the lifts, but now it was to beg me not to tell. And I didn't. A few years later he was appointed to the bench and had a long, illustrious career as a judge. I heard a fawning interview with him on the radio to mark the occasion of his retirement. He was mouthing off about how important it was to keep up the good fight against racism and sexism, blah blah, and how very shocked he was that in this day and age, men were often still considered to be the superior species.

Why didn't I tell? Because he was a powerful public figure, fêted for his commitment to equality and social justice. I almost didn't believe what had happened myself. Would I have told if he'd succeeded in raping me, which, without a doubt was what he intended to do? My older, bolder self would like to think so, but I suspect my younger, more timid self might not have. There would always be predators and woman haters, the Weinsteins as well as the whistlers. But I don't think these categories should be confused.

The dangerous wolves were the ones who dressed up as your grandmother and asked you to come closer. But when the whistlers went quiet it meant something else. The game was over, our race was run. It was one of the ways we knew.

'Do you miss it?' I asked Lapsed Lawyer.

She thought for a long moment before replying. 'No, I don't think so,' she said, 'but now that men in hard hats don't skip a pneumatic beat when I walk past, I think, rather, do I miss the thirty-year-old who could make them drop their lunch?'

Yes, that was it. What we missed – were missing – was that magnetic part of ourselves we'd taken for granted when we were too young to know we wouldn't always have it.

There was another kind of attention I seldom attracted these days, an altogether subtler, more welcome kind. This was the Look: the attractive man who glanced up as you entered a train carriage and held your eye for a beat longer than necessary; that second glance on the street, that passing flicker which said *I like what I see* and moved on just as quickly. The Look had never happened to me often enough to be taken for granted, but you didn't have to be a traffic stopper when you were young. Such moments – over in a blink – made me feel alive, desirable and 100 per cent visible. Was I a pathetically willing object? Perhaps. I only knew that I'd enjoyed being seen in *that way* by anyone not old enough to be my father and not young enough to be my son. Especially now that I wasn't being seen in that way.

Then there was flirting. In my experience flirting was never heavy-handed, but the lightest of touches without the touching, sexy without the sex. Flirting was about the possibility of something happening that probably never would. Flirting took two to tango; it required mutual consent. If flirting wasn't reciprocal, it either fizzled out or moved into the realm of harassment. Lately, it seemed to have fizzled out altogether.

Our trumpets were getting rustier and there was no point, said Lapsed Lawyer, in trying to play the same tune on an inferior instrument.

Ageing was incremental, like frogs being heated up in water so slowly they barely noticed until they were good and boiled. We didn't disappear to the naked eye overnight – it was a gradual erasure – but we couldn't say we weren't warned. Lapsed Lawyer closed her eyes and sighed. 'All those taps on the shoulder in the ten or fifteen years before the door closes and someone in charge hustles us towards the exit. *But we've been telling you, we're closing!*'

*

My mother said she'd made peace with the fact that she'd never get – never *seek* – that kind of attention again a long time ago, though she confessed it had taken her a while to get out of the brass section. Mum had been a man magnet: after the divorce, she was seldom without one, if not two at the same time; she specialised in doomed affairs. There was another complicating factor: as she got older, she decided she was only attracted to younger men – *much* younger men.

Her last doomed affair was with a man twenty-seven years her junior. He ticked all her boxes: he was young, he was a Marine ('*uniform*, darling!') and he was married (no strings attached).

I'd met him once: he and my mother were sitting at her kitchen table with mugs of tea, playing Scrabble. He didn't look like a pervert. In fact, of all the men my mother had brought home, he seemed the most normal, the least trouble, the nicest and by far the best looking.

The day my mother turned sixty, she decided she had to let him go. It couldn't go on – her vanity wouldn't allow it. Her trumpet was rusting; it was time to get out while he still wanted her, while she still had her dignity.

It was, she said, the worst birthday of her life.

'Suddenly I was confronted with the harsh facts of growing old. I could no longer keep my stomach sucked in, my wrinkles hidden; I had this wonderful lover and I knew I had to give him up. I didn't want to be one of those over-made-up old ladies clinging to a young man's arm, looking ridiculous.'

In coming to this conclusion, her *decision*, my mother was influenced by two of her favourite novels, the French writer Colette's *Chéri* and *The Last of Chéri*. Léa, the ageing beauty, forces herself to give up her young married lover, Chéri, before he starts to find her old and disgusting. In *The Last of Chéri*, he returns from a six-year absence to find Léa old and disgusting. Unable to get over either his shock or his obsession, Chéri kills himself.

My mother found in these books a salutary lesson – not that she thought anyone was going to kill themselves over her, but that she had no choice but to get out while she was on top, so to speak.

'If you're going to be a cougar you have to face the music: you know it's got to end, and probably not very well. It broke my heart, but I knew I had to get rid of him before he got rid of me.'

It took another two years after she turned sixty for my mother to extricate herself from the relationship. She pushed him away, he came back, her resolve would crumble. Of course, she never told him the real reason why she'd begun to blow cold: he would never know, she made sure of that.

I felt as if I'd just heard the saddest story in the world.

'Don't be sad for me,' she said. 'It was terrible when it ended, but that's when I decided to embrace getting older. After that, I just went with it. I knew I'd never have another lover because, as you know, darling, I don't like old men.'

My sisters and I had once tried to hook her up with a retired judge with pots of money who'd made it clear to my mother that he was looking for a wife and she would do nicely. By all accounts he was a kind man and quite sprightly for eighty-five. We encouraged the match: Mum had barely a penny to her name – this way she'd be taken care of for the rest of her life and we wouldn't have to worry about her being old and cold and alone. We plotted and schemed, like Mrs Bennet trying to marry off her daughters in *Pride and Prejudice*, until Mum put her foot down and said he was a nice enough old bloke, but imagine *waking up next to him*. This was not something my sisters and I had imagined or ever wished to imagine. 'Well then,' she said, 'what makes you girls think *I'd* like it any better?'

No, my mother was never going to pick on someone her own age, and we would never speak of it again.

The trouble with a lot of old men, said Mum, was that they didn't know when to stop. Old men didn't seem to *get* that their expiry date had come and gone: they still thought they were in with a chance.

And that, she said, was the difference between us and them. 'We know when it's time to change our tune – they just keep banging away like kettledrums. Speaking of kettles, shall we have a cup of tea?'

'Changing my tune didn't mean I had to stop *flirting*,' she called from the kitchen. 'No one ever has to stop flirting. You just have to learn to be a bit more selective. Flirting isn't always sexual, you know – it's really just another word for *charm*.'

Womance

'Whether you're throwing up or breaking up, you want your girlfriend right there. I don't trust women who don't go to their girlfriends.'

— DREW BARRYMORE

Where would I be without my girlfriends? They're my happy triggers, the human equivalent of serotonin. Champions and comforters, trusted confidantes and intrepid companions, each and every one of them delighted and inspired me in her own way. My girlfriends helped me view the world and myself in new lights, from different angles, because what I saw when I looked in the mirror was not necessarily what they saw – for better and, on occasion, for worse. Girlfriends rejoiced in your successes, spun your failures and agreed that your boss was behaving like a dick, based solely on the fact you said so. Girlfriends were always on your side, even your worst side; they made you laugh, they kept your secrets, they had your back.

But as we crunched across the shells of one another's midlife fragility, there were bound to be a few breakages. Take *touchy* plus *tense* and multiply by two, and the odds of nothing ever changing, of all staying friends forever, weren't in anyone's favour. It was indeed crunch time: skins got thinner, quirks got quirkier; we were all starting to wobble like jellies, setting in our little ways. How come she only dropped *my* books in the bath? Was she going to bang on about her ex all night? Tolerance and patience were called for at precisely the moment in our lives when they were in shortest supply, when we were our least stable selves. We forgot we'd already told each other stuff and told each other again. I'd had gossip gleefully reported back to me that I'd told them in the first place. My pain threshold had definitely sunk a few notches, but when the going got tough, I'd grit my teeth and remind myself, *she's your people*. Thanks to all this gritting, I had to wear a gum guard to bed: my dentist said I'd been clenching and grinding. Once, I might have taken this as a compliment.

Yes, certain relationships would begin to weigh us down as we trudged through the existential badlands together. Some friendships would simply run their course, drift apart in a puff of unspoken agreement, dwindle to a friendly wave on Facebook with no hard feelings. Others came around and went around on a bobbing carousel – now you see them, now you don't. These were the easy ones – no commitments, no timetables, just good fun *whenever* friends. Then there were the ones that were never going to go quietly, that spoiled for a fight, that demanded a duel to the death. As with bad old married couples, these waters ran deep. These were the break-ups that would kill you or cure you, the ones where someone was bound to get hurt.

Unless she was sleeping with your husband, these break-ups seldom happened overnight. Slights and grievances mounted over time, in between kissing and making up, turning over new leaves and promising to be a better tempered, more considerate, less annoying friend in future. Breaking up with a girlfriend was like a divorce without the fight over money and the kids. And its ending could be just as miserable.

*

She smacked her hands on the table and reared back. 'Are you *breaking up* with me?'

In the bar where we'd met for sundowners, our frozen margaritas shivered. Heads turned.

We'd been friends for twenty years of holidays, children, marriages and divorce, careers, confidences and an awful lot of shopping.

For twenty years, we'd been there for each other: through thick and thin, in sickness and in health, in H&M change rooms where tact was tested to its limits. But now, as I looked at her across the table, sitting on my hands to stop them trembling, I struggled to think of anything to say that I wouldn't bitterly regret later.

Things had been bumpy between us for a while. It was obvious – to me anyway – that we were growing apart. Or maybe it was just me. We just didn't seem to have much to talk about any more, less in common than we once had. What had changed? How had it changed? I didn't know the answer, but the relationship grew more and more strained and meeting up began to feel more like a chore than a pleasure, a habit rather than a treat. Frankly, she was starting to take up more emotional bandwidth than I had to give her. I knew this wasn't what a healthy friendship was supposed to feel like, and deep down I knew it couldn't all be her fault.

On that last date, we'd barely made a dent in the free peanuts when she said something – I don't even remember what – that pulled the pin on my grenade. I tried to stay calm and count to ten. I tried to resist succumbing to the temper I'd worked so hard to leave behind. It was no good: angry, hurtful things spewed out of my mouth like verbal tics I could no sooner stop than stuff back.

More heads turned.

One of her false eyelashes was coming unstuck, but I wasn't about to tell her that. No, sister, the days of tucking in each other's labels, discreetly miming *spinach teeth* and alerting each other to price stickers left on the soles of shoes were *over*.

There was a shocked silence.

'It's not you, it's me,' I finished lamely. It was the oldest break-up lie in the book.

Without another word, she got up, took out her purse, threw too many bills on the table and left. *This is terrible*, I thought, watching her through the window of the bar as she vanished into the night and I felt my body sag with relief.

I did not skip away unscathed from the end of this friendship. For a long time afterwards I felt ashamed when I thought about some of the things I'd said – I wanted out, but I hadn't wanted to hurt her, or had I? We had mutual friends; I prayed I wouldn't run in to her. Sometimes, I missed her.

Culling a friend was a gory act of self-preservation, and it came as a nasty shock the day I got the bullet – obviously it had never crossed my mind that *I* could be excess baggage, a surplus member of someone's herd.

A friend working in another city was back in town on a visit. I only knew this because I happened to bump into someone who'd been at the *fabulous dinner* she'd thrown the night before for her friends. Well, everyone except me. The air went out of me. It had to be a misunderstanding. Perhaps she thought *I* was out of town, which I often was. We'd laugh about it over lunch. I called her. 'I didn't know you were back in town! I hear you had the gang round for a *fabulous dinner* last night!'

There was an awkward pause: it was all very spur of the moment, she didn't know I was around, blah blah.

There was another awkward pause during which I wondered if she'd ever heard of WhatsApp, SMS, MMS, email, Messenger, Skype or two tin cans and a piece of string.

'Did I do something wrong?'

'No, no, no,' she said, but well ... it was kind of obvious we'd been drifting apart for a while, wasn't it?

This was news to me. *I* hadn't drifted apart.

'It's not you,' she sighed, 'it's me.'

It was all deeply uncomfortable. I sent her an email the next day seeking written confirmation of my retrenchment from her affections because I still could not quite believe it. What had changed? How had it changed? I got a swift reply back from her that left me none the wiser. She thanked me for the good times we'd shared and wished me all the happiness in the world. She never had been one to pull the plaster off gently: it was one of the qualities I'd admired about her – the ability to confront facts, take remedial action, get the unpleasantries over with and move on. Which was all very well as long as she was doing it to someone else.

There seemed no point in prolonging the agony. I had to face the fact: she just wasn't that into me any more.

*

I loved being a woman; I loved other women. I'd grown up in a household of noisy, larger-than-life females. None of us was exactly shy and there were precious few subjects we felt the need to tiptoe around, and a good laugh, even at someone else's expense, was almost always worth the risk that it might backfire. All was fair in love.

Born and raised long before a time when a rich and complex alphabet of gender options became available, I identified as a girl, an unapologetically girly girl. Whether I'd been brainwashed from birth or biologically made this way I couldn't say, only that I was comfortable in my pinafores and patent shoes and pink sparkly things. When I got a new pair of shoes, I'd put them at the end of my bed, nestled in their box, so they'd be the first thing I saw in the morning, like a Christmas stocking. I loved watching my mother put on make-up; I didn't like getting dirty. I kept my precious things in a shiny plastic handbag with a butterfly clasp that closed with a ladylike snap. If I'd ever wanted to transition, it would most likely have been to a drag queen.

Sister Two could not have been more different: she identified as a tomboy and got Scalextric and cowboy hats on birthdays. One Christmas, my parents bought her a doll, which I had to take into care because she neglected it so badly. Sister Two was allowed to stay up late to watch *Bonanza* and refused to cry when she fell out of trees. She wore boys' clothes and had once auditioned for a boy's part in a movie; she didn't get the part, but no one mistook her for a girl. The day she came home and threw a fit because she'd been picked to play Sleeping Beauty in the school play and had to wear a stupid princess dress, I wanted to throw up.

One of my earliest memories was of being kept home from school when I was sick and being allowed to lie on the sofa during my mother's coffee mornings, those sixties seedbeds of desperate housewives on the brink of throwing in the tea towel for Mrs Robinson-esque deflowerings of young men in the church choir. They didn't burn their bras, they simply whipped them off and put them back on again afterwards. Thankfully, most of their conversations went over my head, but I inhaled enough of the fragrant allure of femaleness to know that this was what I wanted to be when I grew up: the lowered voices punctuated by sudden bursts of laughter, the musky wafts of perfume as they leaned down to kiss me in their wet-look boots and short shift dresses.

I was desperate to be a woman.

From the day my very first best friend and I skipped off hand in hand to big school, I always had a bestie. Someone I knew would pick me first for the netball team; someone whose house felt as safe and familiar to me as my own; someone whose birthday parties I never had to worry about not being invited to.

In my teens my best friend was a year older than me. I was infatuated with her and the way she effortlessly fitted into the social life at school without ever quite conforming to it. She smoked a pipe and had a Françoise Hardy album *in French*! I immediately copied as much of her as I could, including her hair, a super-cool Bay City Rollers mullet. She was the pal who held your hair out of your face over the toilet bowl after four tequilas. On Saturday nights we'd spend hours talking on the phone while I lay on my bed twisting the cord around my finger and smoking my mother's menthols. Looking back, it was a lot more fun than lying on the back seat of a Cortina with a spotty sixteen-year-old trying to get his hand down your hotpants. She was always the one who decided what we were going to do and who we were going to do it with. If she'd told me to stick my head in a gas oven I'd have seriously considered it. I was her number-one fangirl, her second-fiddle, her straight man, though it took me a long time to notice or mind this. After school we went our separate ways – something to do with a boy – and I moved on to the next new best friend.

Next New Best Friend and I met on the first day of our first proper job as interns on a daily newspaper. Together we made our debut into the grown-up world of work. With our first salaries we rented a flat together. We slept on mattresses and sat on cushions on a thread-bare rug we found in a skip. We didn't have chairs or a table, but we had scarves we threw over lamps and piles of clothes that reeked of incense, which we never hung up and happily shared: it made sense to have a bestie who was roughly the same size as you. We seldom washed dishes or cleaned the bath. At last, real life had begun. It was brilliant.

These were formative friendships, friendships stitched into the DNA of my childhood and youth, regardless of whether they lasted or ended life in the archives of nostalgia. These were friendships that shaped me.

When my own children came along, friendships took another turn: I became a paid-up member of the school mums' club. We huddled together over plastic cups of vile coffee on the frozen sidelines of soccer matches; we watched our daughters wobble through ballet classes to the strains of Mrs Plink-Plonk's piano. We toiled side by side on the tombola stall and held the line when the PE teacher tried to make us sign up for the mums' race on sports day. We saved each other seats at prize-giving – despite having sent our kids to the school because the brochure said their ethos was that taking part was more important than winning, regular ceremonies were held to crown the winners.

It was fun making new friends through our children – if your kid liked their kid, there was a good chance you'd get on with the kid's parents, at least for the duration of the soccer season, united against a common enemy, the coach. Meeting other parents was kind of like being back at school yourself: there were the overachievers, the teacher's pets, the rebels and the scary ones who ran the snack shop like the Marshall Plan. Anyone who could bake a cake that looked like a fire engine or sew an angel costume that looked like an angel, not a sheet with a head sticking out, was unlikely to be my type, nor I theirs. Much as I had in my own school days, I wanted to hang with the Out Crowd, the mums who came screeching up to the school gate five minutes after the bell rang looking as if they'd been shot, the mums most likely to open a mercy bottle of sauvignon blanc when a five-year-old's birthday party ran amok.

These back-to-school friendships with the parents tended to fade away with the dying notes of the school anthem on graduation day. Mostly they'd been circum-stantial, but they had been critical to surviving the school years. You swore to keep in touch. You meant it – you really liked each other. You'd definitely do lunch. A few years later a name would pop up in your contacts and you'd think, gosh, I wonder what happened to her?

There was one mum I kept up with in a haphazard sort of way after our accidental reunion twenty years later at the Botox doctor's office. If our foreheads had been able to move we would have looked as surprised as we felt. She hadn't changed a bit. She said I hadn't changed a bit. We gave due credit to the doctor. And so we found ourselves together in the trenches once more, only this time the common enemy was our necks. Our daughters were still friends, mostly on Facebook, the young mums' equivalent of Happy Hour. We swopped photos of our grandchildren. We promised to do lunch. It never happened, but that was one of the nice things about getting older, the ability to appreciate friendships for what they were as much as for what they weren't.

Other friendships drifted during my school-mum days, notably friendships with my child-free friends. Child-free friends suggested doing outlandish things like meeting up for cocktails after work, because their Happy Hour hadn't been replaced by Suicide Hour. Child-free friends had to do most of the running if they wanted to maintain mean-ingful contact. It was easier for a child-free friend to visit me than it was for me to get a babysitter, and it was easier for both of us than me bringing the kids along to her place and spending two hours catching family heirlooms and flying fruit juice. Child-free friends had to put up with a lot – incomplete sentences, only getting half your ear while the other half attended to the screaming in the background, having to reupholster white sofas bought with scant regard for who might sit on them.

Recently, I asked a child-free friend what it had been like for her. Our friendship was one of those that had drifted during the food-throwing years, but thankfully we had made a comeback. Daughter invited Child-Free Friend to her wedding without any prompting from me, and Child-Free Friend bequeathed her Peter Rabbit plates to my grandchildren.

'Hmm,' she said thoughtfully, 'put it this way, I knew that if I wanted to continue seeing my friends with children and keep our friendship alive in a meaningful way, my plans had to revolve around yours. I think I more or less accepted that the adjustments would mostly need to come from my side.'

The intimacy and intensity of even the most solid friendships could waver according to the constraints and opportunities of work and love and just generally where you were *at* in the world at different times in different places, and sometimes simply in different *spaces*. Child-Free Friend and I were a case in point: we had drifted apart and come back together again more than once, not only during my breeding years.

When Daughter and Son reached the age of infinitely preferring to be left to their own devices, I found myself with more free time to spend with my friends. But Child-Free Friend had just entered the honeymoon phase of a passionate new relationship that seemed to leave *her* little time for much, or anyone, else. She and New Man travelled a lot, and when they were at home they seemed to be otherwise engaged, probably on a bearskin rug in front of a log fire. Now it was my turn to make the adjustments. I awarded Child-Free Friend the Friendship Sabbatical. The Friendship Sabbatical was an offer I extended to anyone who was involved in a new relationship, had recently given birth, was getting divorced or had just moved house. The Friendship Sabbatical entitled the recipient to a calendar year off from being a good friend back: they were allowed to forget my birthday and never had to explain their absence. For one whole year I would not take their sketchy communications and cancelled arrangements personally, because it *wasn't all about me.*

Unless they forgot my birthday again the next year.

Once Child-Free Friend's relationship settled down and the log fire phase had been replaced by fights about whose turn it was to take out the trash, we picked up again, pretty much where we'd left off. We'd been friends since our twenties; we knew each other's tastes and triggers and back stories inside out. But soon our lives would hurtle off in different directions again.

We were older and busier; at work we were either peaking or seeking new horizons; ailing parents had begun to enter the picture; family life was somehow more consuming, even though everyone could wipe their own nose. The ground was shifting beneath our feet once more: energy see-sawed, capacity shrank and elaborate, long-running dental appointments took precedence in our crowded diaries. Time seemed to speed up just as it should have been slowing down. Increasingly it felt as if there was a finite number of people and things I could give my best self to.

Everyone I knew was feeling like a stress ball being squeezed by an invisible hand.

Cocooning, putting up soft borders, craving time alone – time to think, time to lie on the sofa with a takeaway and a TV series ... we all needed more Big Nites In with ourselves. I added menopause to the list of criteria for the Friendship Sabbatical.

In fact, the friends who were becoming more protective of their own time and space were the ones I gravitated towards, felt closest to: if we saw one another less, well, we made up for it when we did see each other. We mostly remembered birthdays. No one laid guilt trips. But when a girlfriend was in crisis, we dropped everything, including the next root-canal appointment. For much of the rest of the time we rapped out messages on pipes in a show of solidarity. Everyone understood.

But, even un-needy friendships required tending to, and I made sure to water the ones that mattered. Gone were the days when we'd spend hours painting each other's toenails and share beds in hotel rooms, but true womance never died: from now on we'd share sleeping pills and reading glasses and learn to withhold judgement of each other's driving.

Lapsed Lawyer said we were too old anyway to have *besties*, that BFs and NBFs and BFFs were adolescent constructs we'd surely outgrown. This came as a bit of a shock because I thought she was my bestie.

'However,' she continued (thank God, there was a 'but'), 'we are the best of friends.' This, she said, was a description more befitting of our maturity and one that wouldn't make our other besties feel left out.

*

My friends and I played a game that was arguably more suited to oncoming second childhood than to maturity. The game was to pretend that our children were sick of us and our husbands were dead or fled – not really such fanciful notions – and we had packed up and migrated to proper old age in a remote spot on the planet where we had set up our own community. Wouldn't it be fun to all live together, just like in our flat-share days, only this time with dishwashers?

It would take the pressure off growing old gracefully. No longer would we have to twist ourselves into knots trying to fit in with a patriarchal, celebrity-obsessed, youth-worshipping world of rappers and vloggers and billion-dollar tech babies dating robots and chairing board meetings barefoot. We'd be liberated, accountable only to ourselves; it'd be like one big pyjama party and we'd never even have to take off our pyjamas!

When I found out that there were women who'd actually done this, I investigated further. The migration movement began in the seventies in the US when doughty bands of women, galvanised by the emerging women's lib movement, trekked off into the wilds to establish brave new worlds in environments where they felt safe and powerful. They chopped down their own damn trees and built their own damn houses. Biodiversity, bee-keeping, sawdust toilets – pioneering off-grid stuff.

Few of these women-only communes survived into the twenty-first century but had become more like quaint ideological throwbacks to another era: the original settlers confessed they were struggling to attract new, younger members, and the founding mothers, now in their sixties and seventies, were starting to feel their age – wonky knees, hip replacements, pacemakers – which made climbing a telegraph pole with a mouth full of nails more hazardous.

I wasn't sure after all whether I was cut out to roam the plains in hiking boots and share a sawdust toilet with my neighbours. Still, with the addition of a few modern conveniences, I thought the idea still had merit. In *my* fantasy village groceries would be delivered by drone, there'd be a solar-powered hair salon, no one would be judged for eating bacon and ice-cream sandwiches and everyone would have their own bathroom. But what if it all went wrong? What if it turned out to be more like living in a TV prison drama? What would happen when everyone started sleeping with everyone else's girlfriend and the shampoo ran out? What if you refused to hand over your Elizabeth Arden Eight Hour Cream to the leader and got your hair set alight in the exercise yard?

Yes, embracing the sisterhood could go horribly wrong, especially if they were, actually, your sisters. I knew how fast solidarity could turn into a punch-up in the backyard, how gang wars could be started by a missing styling wand, blood feuds triggered by an empty

Easter egg wrapper: it was called my childhood. I felt bad that I had not always appreciated my sisters' good qualities – it was just that when we were children they didn't appear to have any.

But in adulthood, even though I lived so far away from them, my sisters became my NBFs. How was it possible I hadn't noticed how wonderful they were, how smart and funny, how loving and loyal? The bonds forged by our common experiences in childhood, for better and for worse, were unbreakable, and they belonged exclusively to us. When my sisters and I were together we didn't need anyone else: we made our own fun and drama, we had our private jokes and secrets. Once we were able to see one another as real people instead of competing interests, it turned out that we actually liked each other. In fact, we couldn't get enough of each other. We were like *Little Women*! We were BFFs!

If it wasn't for the fact we still gossiped behind each other's backs and had the occasional brawl for old time's sake, we'd have been insufferable.

*

Mum and Auntie had travelled a long road together as sisters and friends. Auntie was just seventeen when she and my mother, then twenty-one, moved into a flat together. It was the olden days, when fathers ruled by *not under my roof*, so if you wanted to paint your nails 'whore red' and meet boys, you had to leave home first. My grandfather put my mother in charge of Auntie's safety, chastity and intake of leafy greens. Inviting strange men home was strictly forbidden. Smoking was strictly forbidden. He would be conducting spot checks.

After moving in to their flat, Mum and Auntie got a black cat on a gold leash and took it for walks, waggling provocatively around the park in cigarette pants. They invited strange men home and smoked like gangsters.

Grandfather never knew the half of it.

When my parents moved to South Africa in the 1970s, Mum and Auntie kept up a witty and revealing correspondence on crackly blue aerogrammes. (I know they were revealing because I found them tucked among my mother's files and read them. They were far superior in their racy detail to the Mills & Boon pulp I was briefly enamoured with.)

Over the years Mum and Auntie had their ups and downs, their spats and silences, but that was one of the advantages of having sisters as friends – they could never divorce you. Their lives came together and strayed apart, until, in their seventies, to everyone's delight and surprise, Mum and Auntie moved in next door to each other.

They still smoked like gangsters and kept their figures, though they no longer invited strange men home, only the ones they knew. They had their own dishwashers and bathrooms. Auntie painted her living room 'whore red'.

As their circle of friends began to shrink – cancers and strokes, the drawn-out diseases of muscle and brain, the dreaded dementia – the sisters drew still closer. The coffee-morning gals, once so glossy and vital in their flirty skirts and wet-look boots, were vanishing, one by one. My mother tried to be philosophical about these losses: 'It's terribly sad when your friends start dying,' she said, 'but at my age, darling, what can you expect?' Still, she was inconsolable for a long time after the death of one particularly close friend.

I knew how she felt. Sometimes, I even talked to my dead friend, the one who'd lived for seven years after being diagnosed with cancer. *Listen, they're playing your song on the radio!*

I didn't expect to make new friends in my fifties. I felt lucky to have the ones I had, the ones who brought joy to my table, made me laugh and held my hand in times of trouble, if not my head over the toilet bowl after four tequilas. I kept up rich epistolary relationships with cherished far-away friends, who I knew I might never see again.

But, as I was about to find out, friends weren't like cars – you didn't have to trade one in to get a new one. And one fine day, a shiny new friend came roaring out of the showroom.

Part outlaw, part earth mother, part snob, I'd never met anyone like her. New Best Friend had holes in her tights and sunbathed topless; she was partial to the occasional party drug, but refused to take HRT because it wasn't *natural*. She was a stickler for good manners at the table, though she had been known, on occasion, to dance on it.

I wanted to know everything about her; I wanted her to know everything about me. We had sleepovers at each other's houses, and when she forgot to bring her toothbrush, I lent her mine without thinking twice. We loved the same books and music; we laughed at the same things; we even shared clothes until she dropped two dress sizes after her divorce. She gave me an Armani suit that now swam on her that she'd found in a charity shop.

If I thought I'd outgrown this sort of adolescent girl-crush stuff, I was wrong. I'd always loved a good womance, and I guess I always would.

Old Married Couples

'We've been married for 50 years and I've been gone for about 47 of those. But the truth is, we've always been very compatible [...] and we've always had a good time together. He loves staying home and I love staying gone, so it's worked out really well.'

— DOLLY PARTON, VANITY FAIR INTERVIEW
WITH BENJAMIN LINDSAY, AUGUST 2016

Husband and I had been married for twenty years and been together for even longer; my mother said our marriage was the envy of the family. For a woman who thought safe sex was a sprung mattress, she held romantic views on marriage, or at least on mine.

Husband and I had house-trained several dogs and raised two beautiful children; we knew each other's cell-phone numbers without having to look them up. We laughed a lot, developed the same taste in soft furnishings and, through it all, our bed had stayed warm. To the best of my knowledge, we'd been faithful; if there'd been a one-night scuffle here or there, I didn't know about it and I didn't need to.

Digging into each other's private doings and thoughts was something we never did. Once, I'd had a boyfriend who would interrupt my quiet daydreamy moments and suddenly say, 'What are you thinking?' And if I said, 'Oh, nothing much,' he'd say, 'No, really, what are you thinking?' What I was thinking was usually along the lines of whether we had soy sauce for that Nigel Slater recipe I wanted to make, or whose turn it was to have Christmas this year. But Boyfriend seemed to want to climb inside my head, pry open my private thoughts like an oyster; possess every part of me, including my imagination. He was always trying to catch me off guard, because if I wasn't thinking of him, I must be thinking of someone else: *So, who's this Nigel Slater?*

Little by little, my thoughts strayed to thinking of almost anyone else. Needless to say, the relationship didn't last.

Suspicion has no place in a healthy relationship, and I think Husband and I both appreciated that a little bit of mystery could go a long way. We did not look at each other's messages or share a bank account or send out joint emails with our names coupled together in the address line. Anyhow, we didn't have the same surname – he kept his and I kept mine. Over the years we'd pursued very different hobbies and interests and, sometimes, different friendships. There were confidences I'd share with girl-friends that I'd never dream of sharing with him: in certain particulars, even the most stable and democratic of marriages was no substitute for the friendship of women.

Of course, we were friends too and shared confidences I wouldn't dream of sharing with my girlfriends, but we never lost sight of the fact that we were individuals and I was convinced that this had played a part in our success as a couple: according equal rights and respect to our needs, desires and limits as individuals while agreeing on the really important things such as the welfare of our children and what colour to paint the front door.

Lately, however, I'd begun to think that some of the values that had kept us together for all these years were the same values that might be our undoing. In the restless turbulence of midlife, it was becoming increasingly clear that, in certain fundamentals, Husband and I just didn't want the same things any more.

I began to have thoughts, private thoughts, seditious thoughts: people and their needs changed over time. Life was dynamic, constantly shifting in shape and temper. Stasis was impossible. Stasis was death. What were the chances that any two independent-minded people, however much they liked and respected each other – *loved* each other – would stick together till death did them part?

I only had to talk to my old married girlfriends to know that there were many ways to skin a marriage.

*

I was astounded to learn that several of my girlfriends were having affairs or had had affairs or were contemplating having affairs or would be open to having affairs: was this a sign of late-blooming gender parity – our turn to have our cake and eat it? – or a last toot on the trumpet in an attempt to stop it rusting up?

Either way, they weren't getting sufficient assurances at home that they were still vital to proceedings in ways that made them feel strong and sexy. But very few of them wanted a divorce. On the contrary.

One friend revealed that her marriage had never been better since taking a lover – *and her husband agreed*. Admittedly, she went on while I tried to absorb this news, it hadn't been easy at first – the creeping around, the discovery and the confession. But in the end, they'd all come to an amicable arrangement. It was very convenient, she said, when the family went on holiday and he looked after their cat.

Other friends were having crushes and flings the old-fashioned way: behind their partners' backs. In strictest confidence, a colleague told me she'd met a man at a conference. Her husband would never know, she said with the reckless conviction of anyone who'd ever found themselves in a similar position. She'd hate to hurt him or put their marriage at risk. But wouldn't he notice her radiant glow, the skip in her step, the extra workload that kept her late at the office? No, she said, he wouldn't. That was the point.

Most of the women who shared these secrets and sighs with me had no intention of venturing beyond their own backyard; they were simply going to rearrange the yard.

As I poked around, stoking confidences, I would learn many interesting things about what was going on behind closed doors – boredom in the bedroom, the humdrum of habit and routine, him falling asleep in front of the TV with his mouth open.

Then again, show me the couple who after twenty years together spend their weekends in rumpled sheets reading poetry out loud and feeding each other ice cream. No matter how close you are, if you've been together longer than a piece of string, the moony phase is over.

'Don't get me wrong,' said a girlfriend whose marriage appeared to be rock solid, 'I love him to bits, but these days I'd rather go to bed with a good book.' I didn't like to ask how he stacked up against a bad book.

Another described her husband as her best friend, even though they slept in separate bedrooms because *that* side of their marriage had been over for a long time, plus he snored like a horse with a hangover. She looked thoughtful as I topped up our glasses, then said she was going to tell me something she'd never told anyone before: around the time she turned fifty, she'd had a fling – well, it was a bit more than a fling: it went on for two years. As her husband frequently travelled for work, she and the fling sometimes got to spend the whole weekend together in rumpled sheets, feeding each other ice cream. She was pretty sure her husband never knew about it, but if he suspected that something was going on, he hadn't said anything. Perhaps he was relieved, she pondered, perhaps it took the pressure off. Perhaps he was seeing someone too ... All she knew was that the affirmation she got from the affair had made turning fifty a hell of a lot easier.

God no, she didn't want a divorce. She and her husband had a good life together, a sister–brother-type arrangement. Selling the holiday home, splitting up the furniture, upsetting the children, custody battles over the grandchildren – at this stage of their lives, the unravelling of such things was really *quite* unnecessary. They knew each other's little ways, they'd earned their wrinkles together, they had a lovely circle of friends and she certainly didn't want to divide *them* up. As long as you got on, she said, it was a pretty good way to live. Why go looking for trouble?

Snoring frequently came up in conversations with my girlfriends as one of the chief reasons they slept in different rooms. Snoring appeared to be the new headache – code for 'not tonight, dear'. It might also, I thought, be a way of glossing over a waning of interest in that department without making a big deal of it. Perhaps the ones who kept separate bed chambers maintained conjugal relations by appointment, like the Queen and Prince Philip in *The Crown*.

Husband and I both snored, but over the years we'd worked out how not to let it come between us. When Husband snored, I gave him a hard poke in the back and told him to turn over, and he extended the same courtesy to me: in the matter of snoring we set aside our differences and worked as a team. We had our anti-snoring routine down pat and could practically do it in our sleep.

As with most things in a marriage, staying on active service in the bedroom required a degree of commitment, like not skipping more than two Pilates classes in a row. Surprisingly, it was harder to find friends who were prepared to admit they were still having sex with their husbands than it was to find friends who were prepared to admit they weren't. I mean, you couldn't just go up to someone and ask them if they were having sex. 'Just say "Are you active?"' suggested one friend who was, very. I tried this approach but when the first woman I asked replied that she was thinking of taking up marathon running, I lost my nerve.

Active Friend, who'd been married for eighteen years, said having regular sex with her husband was vital to the ongoing health of their relationship – even when she didn't feel like it and there was a bestseller vying for her attention on the bedside table. She shared her secret – a technique she called the *ten-minute investment.*

'It's not always the best sex,' she admitted, 'but it only takes ten minutes and it has an enormous impact on how I think about myself; it makes me feel attractive to the world, and afterwards everyone's happy.'

As far as keeping her marriage alive *and* kicking went, it was, she said, the best ten-minute investment she'd ever made. Our chandelier swinging days might be over, but if you're going to invest in the future, you have to put your money where your mouth is.

*

I fancied Husband from the moment I first saw him: we sat at desks next to each other in the office, separated only by a half-dead pot plant. He had a poster above his desk that said Capitalism Kills, but lust at first sight didn't need candlelight.

We came from vastly different backgrounds and had very different cultural outlooks. He wore harem pants and bangles and belonged to a Marxist reading group. I'd long ago jettisoned incense-infused cheesecloth and believed in retail therapy. He'd grown up playing sport; I'd grown up baiting my sisters. He lived in a commune where they grew their own vegetables and nobody shaved, notably the women. His idea of romance was to throw a scarf his ex-girlfriend left behind over a lampshade.

And, oh, I almost forgot, I was married.

At the time, Husband One and I were living in a nice sub-urban house with our new baby. Husband One was twenty years older than me. We'd met when I was nineteen, shortly before my mother decided to leave South Africa and decamp back to the UK with my younger sisters; I seldom saw my father, who had moved to the other side of the country with New Wife. I'd had to grow up pretty fast after the family split up, and consequently I thought I was much older than I was and perfectly capable of making my own far-reaching decisions. Looking back, I see that Husband One was a little bit sugar and a lot daddy, but we were happy for a while, and I have no regrets because together we produced Baby. Baby was eight months old and I was twenty-five when Future Husband came jangling along in his bangles and the Turkish harem pants you could fit your shopping in.

Baby's father and I parted ways. It was as amicable a divorce as divorces almost never go – we didn't even have lawyers. I made sure he saw Baby as much as he liked. After an interval of dancing around one other like boxers, Ex-Husband and Future Husband downed gloves and shook hands. Baby was the glue that held us together.

For a few years Future Husband, Baby and I lived together in relative peace and harmony, and I began to wonder when he was going to get around to proposing. I wanted to be married; I wanted security for Baby and me, which was a bit weird considering my only experience of marriage – my parents' and my own – was that it didn't last. Future Husband loved me, I loved him, he loved Baby: I couldn't see the problem. Future Husband muttered about not believing in marriage, but he liked children, so maybe we could get another one of those instead.

A little brother or sister for Daughter would be the cherry on top – but only after he put a ring on my finger. I pointed out that it was almost the 1990s: nobody took free love seriously any more, and in case he hadn't noticed, rebellion had been replaced by irony. Madonna was doing shows in white wedding dresses. Couldn't we at least have an *ironic* wedding?

I threatened to leave if he wouldn't marry me. I threatened to stop shaving. Nothing seemed to help.

Little by little, I realised that there was another obstacle to my wedding plans that I hadn't planned for: this obstacle was called Future Parents-in-Law. Future Parents-in-Law were Orthodox Jews, and I was from the wrong tribe: to them I was the *shiksa*, the wild oats nice Jewish boys sowed before settling down with nice Jewish girls, preferably doctors or lawyers. Any children from my union with their one and only son would not be considered Jewish because I wasn't Jewish, and Jewishness was passed down through the maternal line. It didn't matter who the father was as long as everyone knew who the mother was and that she was Jewish: in the Orthodox religion, being half-Jewish is like being a little bit pregnant. This rule went some way to securing the purity and growth of a race that knew what it felt like to be hounded to near-extinction, so I tried not to take it as a racial slight. Equally, there was nothing I could do to make up for not being a doctor or a lawyer.

I hadn't exactly made a dazzling first impression on Future Parents-in-Law when I'd been taken home to meet them. It was during Passover, hardly the most joyous festival on the Jewish calendar to begin with. Passover commemorates the exodus of the Israelite slaves from Egypt after God put pressure on the Pharaoh to let them go by inflicting ten plagues on the Egyptians. Water turned into blood, carpets of frogs covered the land and everyone got lice. And that was just the warm-up. Passover food includes bitter herbs and, for some reason, boiled eggs, the one food in the world I can barely be in the same room as, let alone eat: the egg shivered on my plate like a peeled eyeball. Boundlessly ignorant of Jewish customs, I had presented Future Parents-in-Law with a basket of Lindt bunnies: as Easter and Passover coincided that year, I thought it would be a fun way to launch our multicultural relationship. I didn't know they didn't eat chocolate at Passover; Future Husband had explained none of this to me.

While Future Husband didn't care about tribal taboos, he did care about how his parents would react if he was to announce that we were getting married. Non-confrontational by nature, Future Husband went out of his way to avoid conflict: he knew with absolute certainty his parents would be unhappy about our union because there was precedent. He'd witnessed first-hand the gnashing and wailing that had gone on when his sisters got married. Both of them had married out of the faith – three times apiece. Six times in total! Not a single Jewish husband between them! His sisters' stunning record of multiple marriages to a succession of non-Jewish men had devastated their parents, in particular their father, the uncontested head of the house, in whose mind family values and Jewish values were synonymous. As his daughters embarked on their marriage relays, my future father-in-law did not cry, 'Where did we go wrong?' He bellowed, 'Where did they go wrong?' All his roaring had made no difference, but it was enough to put the wind up Future Husband. But all this I found out only years later.

Despite this rocky start to our relationship, Future Parents-in-Law were always friendly and hospitable to Daughter and me, possibly hoping I was a phase their son was going through. Future Husband assured me it wasn't personal.

Future Parents-in-Law were a textbook old married couple: they weren't the touchy-feely types, and Father-in-Law certainly wore the pants, but you could tell it was a till-death-us-do-part partnership, and whatever relationship challenges that must surely have cropped up over the decades were kept firmly behind closed doors. In some ways I envied their family set-up: compared to my own, it was staid, but also solid and dependable. Future Husband's sporting trophies were still displayed on the shelves in his boyhood bedroom and a few of his clothes still hung in the wardrobe.

All I could do was cross my fingers and hope Future Husband would cross the line. Finally, after four years during which I became increasingly vocal about him popping the question (in the end I got him down on both knees), my persistence paid off and a date for the wedding was set. We wouldn't be allowed to get married in a synagogue or a church, but by that point I'd have done it in a car park. I hurried to the registry office to book it myself in case my intended changed his mind. The first opening they had happened to be *on the same date* as my first wedding: ready as I was by this point to seize practically any day, it could not be that day. Decorum overcame desperation and I wrangled a cancellation slot two days later.

As the Big Day drew nigh, I couldn't help noticing that Future Husband still hadn't informed his parents of this major development. When he eventually worked up the courage to break it to them, I could see what had held him back. On hearing the happy news, they said ... nothing. Future Mother-in-Law was the first to recover. Murmuring her congratulations, she took out her diary and checked to see if they'd be available.

For a long while the only sound in the room was the rustling of pages.

'Aren't you happy for us?' I asked Future Father-in-Law, who still hadn't said a word.

'For what?' He shrugged. 'It's not my wedding.'

At least I was marrying into a family with a sense of humour.

Years after marrying into a Jewish family I still found Jewish weddings thrilling. At the end of the service the groom would smash a glass underfoot to symbolise something that was never quite clear to me. Then the dancing would begin: the bride and groom would be hoisted on chairs above the shoulders of the crowd and energetically jiggled up and down to the catchy strains of 'Hava Nagila' while the guests clapped in time. It was impossible not to get caught up in the excitement. A respectable Jewish wedding would not have been complete without being wildly over-catered for. At a family wedding many years after Husband and I had been married, I was standing in line with Father-in-Law as we inched towards the groaning post-nuptial buffet tables. After a couple of whiskies, Father-in-Law was in a jolly mood; surely after all this time he no longer minded that his son had married me? Moved by the festive spirit of the occasion and half a bottle of Chardonnay, I asked him, 'Aren't you happy now that your son and I got married?'

'Not really,' he chuckled. I waited in vain for him to explain the joke. He was still a funny guy.

My mother, by contrast, couldn't have been happier about our match.

She'd always loved an *oppressed minority* – well, not all oppressed minorities it has to be said, but anyone black, gay or Jewish was in her good books. She was over the moon that her firstborn was about to mingle blood with a member of a proud, persecuted people. The Jews, she said, had given so much to the world despite their suffering, including *Fiddler on the Roof.*

I bought my own wedding ring, a plain gold band I'd spied in an antique shop on a work trip. To be fair, Husband paid me back.

We were married in court on a cool spring morning. Having had the big white church wedding little girls like me dreamed of the first time around, I wore a short black suit that made the proceedings feel rather more business-like. Daughter, then five, was our bridesmaid. Putting aside their disappointment my new Parents-in-Law threw us a lavish reception full of people I'd never met.

I didn't know it then, but I was three weeks pregnant with Son. Life was perfect.

*

But now, here we were, Husband and I, twenty years later, up a tree-house without a paddle, being quizzed by a couples counsellor about what had gone wrong and whether it could be fixed. Having been diagnosed as 'Selfish A-Types' and sent on our way with a warning not to topple down the stairs of his work-from-home-tree-house on the way out, all that remained to be seen was who would win.

The differences that had once been part of our charm as a team might this time prove irreconcilable. I wanted change; he wanted everything to stay the same. I was ready to strike out for new horizons, take risks, make big decisions about how and where to live that I was convinced would be better for both of us. He said he liked our life just the way it was and had no plans to go anywhere. These days when Husband and I looked out of the same window, we saw different views. The glue that had held us together all these years was still strong: children, friends, Netflix series, the ten-minute investment; above all, a steady flame of love that could be explosive, but as far as I was concerned, that was what helped to keep things exciting.

Everyone wanted to find true love, didn't they? Well, I'd found it. Family and friends told me how lucky I was to have a man who loved me for who I was and never tried to turn me into someone else. Ever my number-one champion, Mum said, 'Not as lucky as *he* is to have *you*, darling,' though when pressed for details she went a bit vague. She settled on my *je ne sais quoi*.

But my *je ne sais quoi* no longer seemed to be having the desired effect. Restlessness propelled me on.

Husband refused to budge; I refused to budge. Now when we fought, I simply waited for his lips to stop moving so that I could carry on arguing, always the same argument, over and over. The louder I shouted, the less he seemed able to hear me. Our fights were like *Groundhog Day*: they never went anywhere, and in the morning the movie would start all over again.

One night, after another shattering row, we lay clinging to our separate sides of the bed pretending to be asleep; the same lumpy old king-size mattress where once we'd lazed on Sunday mornings with tea and toast, the children burrowed between us smearing crumbs on the sheets with buttery fingers.

Into the electric silence, Husband said something so softly I didn't catch it at first.

'What did you say?'

'I said, I don't want to live like this any more.'

And all the balled-up rage in my body gave way to a fathomless sadness that was far, far worse.

How could two people who loved each other make each other so miserable? At the back of my mind was another unsettling thought: perhaps the person I was falling out of love with was myself. But as much as I loved Husband, I couldn't live his life, I could only live mine.

For weeks and months and sleepless nights, the counsellor's question went around in my head. Did we want this marriage? In the end the answer was always the same: not at any price, not any more.

New Romantics

'Love never gives up.'

— CORINTHIANS 13:7

While our marriage froze in the headlights of an oncoming decision, I looked to my girlfriends to see how they were rising to the challenges of changes in their own relationships, relationships that started with how they related to themselves. If I'd been surprised to learn how many women I knew were having extramarital flings or parking their husbands in the spare room, it was inspiring to count up how many more were gunning for happily-ever-after in a variety of imaginative ways.

In the space of a year I went to three weddings where everyone involved was over fifty, including the bridesmaids. I witnessed a close shave with a dodgy engagement, a liberating divorce, a coming out and multiple dips into online dating.

The last time I'd seen B she had short, spiky red hair and wore the sort of clothes that were ... hard to say. The woman who pulled up her trolley next to mine in the supermarket and said hello had long, wavy silver hair and was wearing a gauzy white dress with turquoise jewellery. I almost didn't recognise her. B and I didn't know each other well, but through mutual friends we'd been acquaintances for a long time. But it wasn't only the hair, the dress, the jewellery; there was something else different about her – the smile? The skin? Something had happened, and I didn't think all the credit could go to Botox, even though, she happily admitted, she'd had some. Plus a few other things.

'Wow, you look amazing.'

'Thanks,' she said. 'It's because I'm having the best sex of my life.'

She had just turned sixty-one.

Considering she'd cut straight to the money shot, I felt no compunction about abandoning my trolley in frozen foods and hustling her off to the coffee shop next door to tell me more.

B had been single for many years since her divorce when her children were still young. An artist and a self-described introvert, she spent much time alone, chiselling away through the night in her studio, creating her monumental, otherworldly sculptures. B's work was both her mistress and her muse. And, for a very long time, it had been fulfilment enough.

Then, two years before turning sixty, she hit a low point.

'I had beautiful children, a house, friends and a successful career. But I felt that if I carried on living the way I had been for the previous thirty years, I'd become more and more reclusive and probably end up living in a tent on my own in the desert.'

She needed, she said, to push her boundaries, start a new adventure – perhaps even one with a man in it. She made a mental list of the things she'd never had, or even known she'd wanted.

'I realised I'd never had a good sexual relationship – even, maybe, that I was incapable of having one. I wanted to see what the kind of intimacy I'd always run away from would be like.'

Like other women I spoke to in their forties and fifties who were taking off in search of new aspirations and hidden corners of themselves, B did not exactly have a stable, loving relationship with her body. So that was where she decided to start her journey – in the boldest way imaginable that had nothing to do with joining a gym. She booked herself into a retreat that would have had me running a mile in the opposite direction: for a start, everyone was naked. Not German-tourist naked with sandals and a sock tan, but more ... *sensual* naked. She described the retreat as being 'all about celebrating the body and physical pleasure'. At first she was 'overcome' by shyness and the intimidating fact that most of the other participants were in their twenties. But little by little she shed her inhibitions and various items of clothing, until by the end of the programme she was walking around starkers. In the space of three weeks, B said, she had learned what Brazilian women had known all along: loving your body, flaws and all, made you sexy.

My coffee had gone stone cold.

When the all-new unselfconscious B came home, she spread the word that she was in the dating game and joined an online matchmaking site. But taking off her clothes in front of a bunch of twenty-year-olds turned out to be less of a challenge than getting a date.

It was a high-end service and she got her own personal matchmaker who said he couldn't guarantee he'd be able to fix her up with someone her own age – one of her must-tick boxes. Men her age, he said, wanted someone *much younger.* The matchmaker said she might have better luck rolling her dice in the direction of men in their seventies, in whose eyes women in their fifties were still frisky. 'And while you're about it,' he said, 'you might consider dyeing your greys.' The grey hair? B stood her ground: she told the matchmaker that if a potential date wasn't prepared to meet anyone with grey hair, she didn't want to meet them either. There followed six months of near silence before the matchmaker managed to strike a match: and that, she said, was how she got hooked up with the man she called 'the best sex of her life'. He looked even better than his photograph, she said, and he was *her age*! On their first date they met for lunch and talked till midnight.

After our fortuitous meeting in frozen foods at the super-market, another year went by before I bumped into her again – this time in a restaurant. I couldn't wait to ask her how it was all going with her man. She waved her hand and blew a raspberry. 'Oh, that's over,' she said, 'thank God.'

Their relationship had lasted six months before B started to feel *crowded*: he was around all the time, asking when she was going to finish work, what time they were going to eat supper.

'He took up all the space in my head – there was no room left to think.'

Ending it had been a relief, she said, which wasn't to say she wasn't grateful for the experience. Quite the opposite. She was extremely grateful: at the age of sixty, she finally knew what the best sex of her life felt like, and that gave her a massive confidence boost.

'It opened a door, and I found a part of me that I'd kind of forgotten about – spent so long running away from – and it was in pretty good working order too. It made me realise that I'd been rather repressed. I'm more sexual now than I've ever been in my life, and I want to explore that further. At last, I'm comfortable in my crepey skin, and it feels good.'

Having shot out of the starting blocks after a few false starts, B was finally running her race. The last time I saw her she was still dating, this time having a 'casual on–off affair' with someone who slotted in more comfortably with her lifestyle and work, someone less … *domesticated*. She hadn't given up on finding true love: 'I'm still a romantic at heart,' she said, with a shake of her wavy grey hair, 'but first I had to learn to romance myself.'

*

Of all my friends, R had arguably the most conventional marriage of any of us: she cooked and took care of the children; he fixed squeaky doors and brought home the bacon. It came as a surprise to everyone – not least to her husband – when she packed her bags and left: her children were grown and flown, and her nest felt as empty as her heart. R didn't regret her decision to leave, but she missed having what she described as the 'protection of a husband'. During her marriage she had inhabited a world very different from my own, living in a small, conservative town where the men busied themselves doing manly things and the women did everything else. R and her husband had been part of a clique of kindred couples who wandered in and out of each other's homes and kept an eye on one other's kids. The husbands played cricket; the wives made sandwiches. On Sundays they took turns to host barbecues. Everyone knew everyone's business. Of course, the women and the men in the clique could be pals, have a laugh, swop views on the latest global fiasco, but if your husband came home and found Kevin leaning up against the sink while you got the supper on, it would imply something very different from coming home and finding Kevin's wife in the kitchen peeling potatoes. By the unspoken codes of the clique, friendships between the women and the men could happen only through their respective marital intermediaries.

By leaving her husband, R had effectively separated herself from the herd, and a darker side of the clique, one she'd never imagined possible, rose to the surface. Suddenly, she was the odd one out and one or two of the women began to treat her – surely she was imagining it? – almost as if she was a threat to the stability of the nucleus. Most upsettingly of all, she noticed that one or two of the men in the group were starting to look at her differently: she might catch one staring at her across the table; another would sneak an arm, almost proprietorially, around her waist. One of them was even more explicit and made it clear he fancied having something with her *on the side*. She wasn't imagining it: men who'd consulted her about the perfect anniversary gift for their wives (her closest friends!) and gone on fishing trips with her husband were *coming on* to her. R burned with humiliation and fury, mostly directed at herself.

'I was ashamed – because I still felt obliged to let them down lightly, to be careful not to hurt *their* feelings, to pretend that nothing out of the ordinary had happened!' At the age of fifty-five she felt like a bewildered tweenie not knowing how to fend off the fumbling advances of a kid at a foam party.

In the end R fled town and struck out for new horizons, but before long she fell into the 'protective' arms of another man. Within a year they were engaged. Six months later she gave him back the ring.

'The engagement changed everything. When he came into my life he seemed so kind and considerate; he listened when I spoke and, really, all I'd ever wanted was to be cherished. He pushed the marriage thing, but almost as soon as I agreed, he became controlling, possessive, needy. He kept saying, "Soon you'll be Mrs So-and-So," even though I'd told him I didn't want to change my name.'

Financial security, the 'already taken' status conferred by marriage, a shield from a world she'd never had to navigate on her own – these were the things she'd always sought. But suddenly none of it seemed like a fair trade-off for falling into the same old traps. That was the turning point, realising that she'd merely replaced her suffocating marriage with a suffocating facsimile of it.

R stopped running away and settled down with herself. She moved to the city, made new friends and started a business from home. She seldom cooked any more – she'd always hated it. Financially she scraped by; emotionally she blossomed.

Still, R was hardwired for romance, and a few years later she was in a new relationship, only this time it was different: having 'learned the happiness of being myself', her *yes, dear* days were done.

'He's lovely – I really enjoy spending time with him. I don't know if I'm in love. I don't think I want to marry again, or even live with anyone again. But we're having a great time – on terms that suit me. I realise I like being autonomous and I would never have said that about myself before. It changed me, it changed everything.'

*

In one respect my friend M wasn't so different from R: neither of them was built to be alone. M craved mushy love – hearts on Valentine's Day, rose petals on the pillow. When M fell for a man (which was quite often) she fell hard. I'd seen her grazed knees. M's third husband was fifteen years her junior. A fortnight after their twentieth wedding anniversary, on the eve of her sixtieth birthday, M found out he was having an affair. She hadn't seen it coming – who ever did? He said it wasn't what she thought, that it didn't mean anything, that he loved her. The old story.

M got sick, she couldn't sleep, she couldn't eat, she raged; but she didn't take him back. The age difference between them was a decisive factor.

'I thought, in ten years I'll be seventy, and if we're going to separate it must be now. The feeling was so strong, despite the tears, the betrayal, the anger, and everything else.'

In some ways, she said, having a younger husband had kept her on her toes, made her feel young; in other ways it made her feel terribly old.

'I was often with people much younger than me because his friends were often younger than him. Trying to look fresh, keep up appearances in a room full of thirty-five-year-olds, didn't always feel so great. And then there were all those things I'd already done that he still wanted – you know, everything had to be fucking organic, everything was political. We still shared a lot of the same values, but I was no longer fuelled by the outrage and drive it took to spend my weekends on a protest march waving a placard. There were days when I just wanted to come home from work and crash out on the couch and eat chocolate.

'I guess,' said M, 'that's where the age difference came in.'

She had been comfortable with the prospect of their growing old together – not necessarily madly in love, but with an unshakable bond – after all, they had a young son (she was forty-eight when he was born).

'But he wasn't ready for that,' she said. 'I was happy with one thing, and he was unhappy with that thing – and I can't risk being hurt again at my age. I don't feel old, but the clock says otherwise, and now I need to accept getting old without having to see myself reflected in someone else's mirror in a constant state of anxiety. I don't want somebody jumping around reminding me of my age every five minutes. For now, I just feel I'm happy to be by myself: I am warm and comfortable in my house; I've got books and films and friends and the love of my amazing kids and grandkids.'

The end of their relationship was messy. The friends got divided up. As much as I liked her husband – in fact I had met him first – it just wasn't possible to be loyal to both parties at war, to have a foot in both camps. Friends had to choose.

A year later M showed signs of coming back to life. The odd door still got banged, angry messages were exchanged, scenes made. But little by little, M felt the mist lift on a brighter future.

'If I had to choose between rebuilding my marriage, knowing I'd have a husband, maybe for the rest of my life, or take the risk of reconstructing myself for me, I would 100 per cent take the risk of being by myself until the end of my days. I don't have time to mess around; I'm in a hurry to go on. I have nothing to prove any more, no one I have to impress. Who would I impress anyway? An attractive thirty-year-old man isn't going to be interested in romancing me. This is the reality: I have to lower my sights, drop my standards, ha! I certainly don't want to become bitter or closed-up, but there are fewer choices, so you resign yourself. It's my growing-old-gracefully revelation: change your expectations; see the world differently. That kind of seduction will no longer preoccupy me. No, I've spent too many years crying over men.'

It was good to see M bouncing back. But I knew she didn't mean the half of it, certainly not the half about being ready to give up on the possibility of new romance. She just didn't know it yet. Tempted as I was to say, 'Don't be silly, of course you'll find romance again, you're hard-wired for it,' I resisted, fearing that it would be like telling someone whose dog just died to get a new puppy. M was a wise woman, but she never let wisdom become an insurmountable obstacle to trying new things she might regret later. She and I had had a few misadventures together that we refused to regret later.

One night not long after her 'I'm through with men' keynote speech, we were at a party. M spent the entire night in the kitchen flirting with an attractive man in his thirties. They sat with their knees touching and their heads together in the kind of animated conversation that didn't invite participation. She and the attractive man in his thirties met up again the next day, and the next night and the next day, and so it went on all summer. M mooned about like a crush-struck fourteen-year-old: she experimented with smoky eyeshadow; she took her phone with her when she went to the bathroom in case she missed a WhatsApp from him. She had it bad.

Of course it was flattering to get that kind of attention from a younger man, and it was exactly the kind of boost she needed. Wise M knew it wasn't love, that it wouldn't go anywhere in the long run; Moony M went round sighing and texting and washing her hair. It wasn't easy being a relapsed fourteen-year-old's BF when you were fifty-nine, but that's what friends were for, wasn't it? And so I'd smile weakly when the twenty-ninth text message was relayed to me for analysis and feedback. Still, I was happy for her – back in the saddle instead of over a barrel, riding high on confidence.

By the autumn, relations with the attractive man in his thirties had cooled. They still enjoyed each other's company, even on occasion still slept together, but the heat had gone out of it, the fever had passed, and they settled down to being Just Good Friends. The gift that kept on giving was knowing that she wasn't all washed up at sixty. She was radiant and beautiful and, well, romance really suited her. She had not changed the way she dressed or tried to powder over her cracks. She had not pleased him at the expense of her own pleasure. The summer of her cross-eyed infatuation aside, she had stayed 100 per cent true to herself. In fact, she was more herself than she'd been in years.

Like R, she'd learned to cherish her own company, to nurture her independence, to be unafraid of a future without a man in it, even when there was a man in it. It was, they'd surely have agreed if they'd met, a most delightful paradox.

*

Two of my girlfriends were getting married – to each other. J and her intended, Ms Right, had been together for fifteen years. Ms Right knew she was gay from her first pubescent stirrings, but in our youth J had been a man magnet: her specialty was men who were married or emotionally dysfunctional, but she seemed to relish dancing with the drama that attended such liaisons.

She and my mother got on like a house on fire.

J was in her forties when she had her first sexual experience with a woman.

I knew the story off by heart – I'd even met the woman – but I still loved to hear it and she always obliged. J's debut lady tumble was typically colourful. We settled back on the couch, refreshed our drinks and steadied ourselves for an action replay.

'Well, as you already know, I repeatedly got involved with men who were either losers or married. Then one day, a very large, loud lesbian film-maker walked into my office. She had 44DD breasts, hairy legs and a hearing aid. I remember the first time I saw her Rubenesque plumpness in all its glory and I just thought, *Wow!* It came as quite a surprise.'

If J was surprised, I was *gobsmacked* to discover that she and Rubens were doing more on the cutting-room floor than editing footage.

As far as her sexual reorientation went, J never looked back, though she objected to being called a lesbian. Sleeping with women didn't mean she identified as a lesbian, she said, and if an attractive man came along, she could just as easily have *had a scene* with him. There was always going to be a scene. In the gender-fluid LGBTQ+ era, J slotted into the alphabet quite unremarkably. But back in the dark ages of the late twentieth century, there were only two respectable options – gay or straight. J was way ahead of her time, let alone mine.

Leaving a trail of Mr Wrongs in her wake, my old friend was launched on a path that led her from Rubens to Ms Right. 'I'd simply walked through a door into a world with more choices,' she said, 'and in this world lived the person I wanted to spend the rest of my life with, who just so happened to be a woman.' Some wag in our circle began calling J a 'late-onset lesbian', which was simply too good not to stick.

After fifteen years of happily unmarried bliss, it was, surprisingly, J who proposed, though wisely she didn't go down on one knee in case she couldn't get up again. An awkward flurry followed when Ms Right wondered if she'd heard correctly, being a little harder of hearing these days, but once the confusion was cleared up, Ms Right said yes. Like other couples of my acquaintance who'd been together in everything but the matching wedding bands for long enough to have arrived at an age where they could start comparing wrinkles, I was curious to find out what had propelled my old friends to the altar when they could simply have carried on the way they were. After all, they were hardly spring chickens – what would a formal marriage bring to their relationship, what novelty or benefit other than to give their friends a good knees-up, obviously metaphorically speaking?

They said they'd thought a lot about this and in the end had decided that marriage would provide them with greater emotional security, confirmation that they'd be there to look after each other as they grew older. As they grew old.

These struck me as sound reasons, but not especially *romantic* ones. Until J said, 'I don't think there's anyone in the world who knows me or cares about me as much as she does, and it's the same the other way around, even when we irritate each other.'

Now that was romantic.

I wasn't the only one of their middle-aged girlfriends jostling for a spot in the bridal retinue. The youngest of us was fifty-six, which had to be factored in when it came to choosing our bridesmaids' dresses: nothing puffy, flouncy, backless, frontless or in apricot; no hats, mermaid tails, spaghetti straps or satin-covered stilettos. We weren't remotely interested in what the brides were going to wear.

Depleted hormones clashed, anxiety leaked; squabbles among us bridesmaids broke out over the venue, the food, the table settings and whether anyone's teeth would survive sugared almonds. Who would walk who down the aisle? Would there be a Best Woman? No one wanted to be the Matron of Honour. The brides piped up to say they had no idea how they were going to do it or what they were going to wear but were open to suggestions, as long as it wasn't white. White, they said, would make them look enormous and clash with their rosacea, which tended to flare at the first sign of stress or excitement. Rosacea did not produce the same effect as a bridal blush and veils were briefly considered. J and Ms Right both hated shopping and said as long as their bridal garb didn't make them look fat, old, butch or red in the face, they didn't really mind. Ms Right proposed carrying J over the threshold, a motion unanimously quashed for health-and-safety reasons.

Plans came, plans went, plans changed, plans were dropped or forgotten in the mists of short-term memory loss.

When J remembered that she hadn't yet broken the news of the impending marriage to her mother, panic ensued: how could they invite her to the wedding? How could they not? J's mother was ninety-seven and had more marbles than her daughter – surely, she must have worked it out by now? J's mother and Ms Right had known each other for *fifteen years*.

'Who does your mother think Ms Right *is*?' I asked J.

'My *lady companion*,' she said.

'Well, there you have it! Gertrude Stein and Alice B. Toklas by any other name!'

But J couldn't bring herself to do it: at her mother's age, she said, she might not withstand the shock. At J's age, it seemed she might not either.

After endless brainstorming sessions during which the CBD oil got passed round like pretzels, the brides rebelled and said, 'To hell with it, things have got out of hand, we're eloping.' We pleaded and promised to stop making mood boards. Seemingly mollified, a few days later they announced that they would marry under the peach tree in their garden on Thursday at noon, which, at such short notice, was the only time the LGBTQ+ marriage officer was available. It was a crafty move on the brides' part, it being way too little notice for the bridesmaids to regroup.

The brides wore floaty Indian cotton tunics they'd bought that morning at a local market. A dozen of us gathered together to witness them exchange vows. A sunny day, a jar of roses, a fan of champagne bottles in a silver ice bucket. We bridesmaids wore our own clothes, hastily rustled from our wardrobes and given a quick iron. There wasn't a puffed apricot sleeve in sight.

Everyone cried when they said 'I do', though not as loudly as the bridesmaid who minutes before the ceremony cut her finger to the bone with a kitchen knife and was now dripping blood all over the naked wedding cake.

Like all the best wedding speeches, the bride's toast to her bride began with a joke. 'Well, here we are, my darling. Married at last, for the rest of our lives, till death us do part – which shouldn't be long!'

Old married couples had their little jokes, but new married couples who were old had better ones.

Leaving aside the bridesmaid who was carted off to hospital to get her finger sewn back on, it was a perfectly lovely day.

*

D's wedding – her third, when she was fifty-three – couldn't have been more different. She was determined that *this* one would be the wedding of her dreams. No expense would be spared, no ritual left to chance, no guest unturned. This time she was going to have all the bells and lace trimmings; this time she would wear *white*.

Her first wedding, when she was a twenty-one-year-old student, had been hastily put together – not for *that* reason, but because her Catholic parents were horrified that she was living in sin with her boyfriend. D's father had a heart condition – he could have another angina attack at any moment. Guilt got the better of everyone and the dazed young lovers got hitched a few weeks later in a registry office and afterwards repaired to the pub next door for lunch. It was the seventies. D was a Feminist with a capital F and more devoted to Engels than snagging a husband. She didn't want a ring, she didn't want a fuss and she certainly wasn't going to wear white. Her mother, a seamstress, ran up a wedding dress of watered silk in hues of blue and green: it looked, said D, like Monet's *Water Lilies*.

Though D stayed true to Engels, her marriage ended nine years and two children later.

Her next wedding took place in a registry office too: it was a hasty affair – not for *that* reason, but this time because her lover was a hunted political figure who had to leave the country in a hurry, and if she was going to follow him into exile, it made sense to commit to a status, if not a state, somewhat less ... precarious. She borrowed a jacket from one of their witnesses, and afterwards they repaired to the pub next door for lunch. It was a happy marriage, but the wedding, she said, was more bureaucratic than romantic.

D was forty-one when her husband died and fifty when she joined my book club, where she met her third husband. They were very under-cover when they started seeing each other, and it took the rest of us members ages to realise that they hadn't simply formed a breakaway group and made off with all the best books. Book Club Husband, said D, was very romantic, which made a pleasant change. They celebrated the anniversary of their first date with fireside picnics and champagne. They made romantic playlists. Love tokens were exchanged. But after three years of this malarkey, D wondered where the relationship was going.

As they'd settle down to another fireside picnic, she would think, 'He's going to ask me to marry him!'

From my own exhausting experience of trying to get Husband to bend the knee, I could sympathise: like me, D was the marrying kind.

'Part of me was thinking, look, we're having a good time, this is really fun, so if it ain't broke don't fix it. I'd been married twice – why would I push it? I decided that if it was going to happen it would be because *he* wanted it to happen, and that was OK.'

Then on a holiday in Paris, the thing that wasn't broken got fixed.

'We spent New Year's Eve in a tiny hotel room. We covered the tiny table with a white towel and ate the lobster we'd bought at a market. Suddenly he got down on his knee and proposed!'

They picked out a ring together, they wrote their own vows, and D got her big fat white wedding. Being older had made a difference, she said. Embracing life's rituals, marking rites of passage, living in the now: such things became more important with the passing of time because nothing was eternal. And there would be no more deferments.

*

It had been almost two years since M's separation from Younger Husband. She said she felt almost … *grateful* to her ex, that he'd done her a favour by having an affair, that one day she might even thank him.

'Steady on,' I said, 'aren't you going a bit overboard?'

But M was in a forgiving mood.

'In some ways he gave me a golden opportunity to grow old gracefully. It was the best exit possible – I had to take it. I feel optimistic really. I have faith in life. I'm not alone in the universe, and so I breathe deeply and think *you'll be alright.*'

As I listened to my girlfriends' stories, what I heard was that there were as many ways to love as there were to un-love. I'd been lucky in love, but looking myself in the eye, I saw reflected back at me an angry, resentful woman living on the borderline of bitterness. And if I no longer loved myself, who then would love me back? The person in the mirror was not the one I wanted to spend the rest of my life with.

The storm in my marriage was abating: there was nothing left to say between us that hadn't been said a thousand times. Husband and I reached an accommodation: we would stay together by living apart. From the moment we agreed to do this, we stopped sticking pins in each other and started sticking pins in maps. The result was that I would end up moving to France, half a world away. For us, living in the *now* hadn't worked out too well. But perhaps we could live happily ever after in the *now and then*?

Husband was the only man I'd ever truly loved; splitting up to stay together, to keep the romance alive, would be taking a huge risk, but we'd have to go the distance to find out.

Friends whispered about a divorce in disguise.

Why shouldn't it be possible to live two lives with one heart? On different continents? Six thousand miles apart? A friend who'd 'left home' and moved to another city for a great job opportunity confided that her marriage had never been better. She said that when she and her husband saw each other now, it felt like a first date. They had new adventures together and the time they spent in each other's company felt special, a hunger for something more than pizza in front of the telly satisfied. She said that they were never around each other long enough to wish they weren't.

As Selfish-A-Type-thinking went, Husband's and my plan seemed reasonable enough: if things didn't work out, one of us could always call a cab.

In the Family Way

'You don't have to give birth to someone to have
a family.'

— SANDRA BULLOCK

I'd just swallowed a sleeping pill when Son-in-Law called
from the maternity clinic.

'You have a grandson,' he said. 'Come!'

I knew Husband and I had about twenty minutes to
get there before I slumped drooling over the dashboard
and missed the magical moment. It wouldn't be the first
time I'd been the architect of my own downfall in family
matters.

But when I saw Grandson, pressed to Daughter's breast,
his mass of dark hair still slick with birth goo, my adrena-
line kicked in and cancelled out the Ambien. Grandson
was a wonder to behold, a transcendental creature still
cloaked in the mysteries of the unknowable world he'd just
come from. But it was Daughter who I couldn't take my
eyes off. Part Venus, part Madonna, her long fair hair, still
damp from the birth pool, fanned out on the pillow. I had
never seen her look so luminous, so … complete. I would
come to love that little boy more than I could begin to say,

but that night my heart flew to Daughter, *my* baby, and I could not have loved her more.

At the age of fifty-five I was a grandmother. Not 'at last', not 'finally' and certainly not 'too soon'. I did not feel too young to be a grandmother, though I didn't mind if anyone said I didn't look old enough to be one. These days, who *did* look old enough?

Being a granny was going to be great, but being called Granny was where I drew the line. Grannies got a bad rap: granny furniture, granny flats, granny clothes, granny cars … shorthand for fusty, spinsterish things.

Inconsequential. Amusing. Defining.

Admittedly, all that was changing as more and more grannies rejected old-fashioned notions of what it meant to grow old gracefully. Instead of melting into the background they were dying their hair pink and getting boob jobs and boyfriends. Still, no one I knew wanted to be *called* Granny.

Daughter said if I didn't want to be called Granny I'd need to come up with something better. Almost anything would be better than Granny, and I got cracking. For the first and last time in my life I'd get to choose my own name! I must not blow it: my granny name would need to be picked with care and attention to meaning – something that would describe the fun-loving, easy-going type of granny I was going to be, but one who still had presence and style, at least, the presence and style I planned to cultivate. As a spirited older woman with plenty left in the bag, why would I want to be a Nan or a Gran when I could be a Gigi or a Peach? If I was going to be labelled, it would be a label of my own design. It was not a decision to be taken lightly.

I googled famous grannies: Goldie Hawn was GoGo, Susan Sarandon was Honey and former *60 Minutes* presenter Lesley Stahl was Lolly. I quite liked Lolly until I read in Stahl's book about her own experience of becoming a grandmother that her husband's chosen grandpa name was Pop. And this was a woman who'd covered the White House.

One of the pitfalls of made-up granny names was overthinking them: there was a fine line between too-cool-for-care and she's-gone-gaga. Gaga, by the way, was another popular name in the modern granny-name canon. Gaga. Chichi. Boo Boo. They sounded like rescue chimps.

By contrast, I noticed that new parents these days were choosing names for their children that made them sound terribly grown up, even vaguely presidential: Kennedy, Jackson and Lincoln had all been on Daughter and Son-in-Law's top-ten list of boys' names. If Grandson was being moulded from birth to become a world leader, I needed to be equally careful to avoid choosing a chimpanzee name that would embarrass him on the campaign trail.

No, 'cute', infantile names were *out*, and elegant, aspirational names were *in*. In the end, I settled on Coco. Coco as in Chanel – perfume and navel-length pearls; not the kind of granny who'd get down on all fours and play horsey, but the kind who'd smell nice and dress her grandchildren in black.

One of the most rewarding things about being a grandparent is the chance to atone for one's sins as a parent. Helicopter Parenting hadn't been invented when I was a young mum; in any case, I'd say I'd been more of a sort of

Balloon Parent – colourful, but liable to go *pop*. Or even, every now and then, simply float away ...

When Daughter was three years old I left her with Future Husband for three months and went to Paris on a cultural exchange programme. *Three months!* Paris was six thousand miles from home in Johannesburg; it was years before the internet and cell phones. I posted Daughter care packages containing books and sweets and trinkets I found in markets and kept a framed photograph of her on the bedside table of my grimy digs in the 11th arrondissement, which had not yet become fashionable. When I came home, Daughter attached herself to my legs and didn't let go until she was a teenager. I developed a guilt complex and strong calf muscles.

When Son was born I remember looking down at him guzzling at my breast – so small, so vulnerable – and thinking, *How could I have left Daughter? What was I thinking?* I appalled myself. I would never dream of leaving Son, or either of them again.

A week after Son's birth by C-section, it felt as if a mule was trying to kick out my insides. The smallest movement was agony, and I was readmitted to hospital with a pulmonary embolism. I spent two weeks on my back watching the nurses tip my breast milk, contaminated by the blood-thinning medication, down the plughole. By the time I came home Husband had transferred Son out of his cot into the middle of our bed, which was where he stayed practically until he went to high school. At least Husband seemed to have everything under control on the domestic front, because I felt exhausted, at sea and, at times, utterly superfluous. Son and I both cried a lot, but

Husband was endlessly patient and never panicked. At night Husband put Son in the car and drove round the block until he (Son) fell asleep. Unfortunately, this trick didn't work for me.

I went to see a doctor who said I was probably just tired, like all new mums, and gave me a vitamin B shot in my buttock that stung like a hive of bees but had no other discernible effect. When Son was really upset he would become so hysterical that he'd turn blue and we'd have to blow in his mouth to get him to breathe. One particularly bad night, when Husband was thousands of miles away on a work trip to Stockholm, I paced up and down for hours with Son writhing in my arms. It must have been around 3 a.m. when I called Husband at his hotel. 'You have to do something!' I sobbed uselessly.

I wanted my mother, but she too was thousands of miles away.

Between Son and I, we made a lot of noise that first year. What was wrong with him? What was wrong with me? I ought to have been feeling blessed and Madonna-like, but mostly I just felt helpless. It was only later that Husband and I saw what had been under our noses all along: Son's lifelong aversion to milk – he wouldn't even touch a *carton* of milk – indicated that he'd probably been allergic to the cow's milk we were forcing down him rather than to me. No wonder he'd screamed. It was only years later I realised I'd had all the classic symptoms of postnatal depression.

I loved my children unconditionally. I'd have died for them, *killed* for them, and I still would, but I was never what you'd call a natural. Leaving Daughter when she was too young to understand that I'd ever come back, struggling to connect with and comfort Son in the first months of his life: these were the abiding regrets of my life.

If Son had been a challenging baby, he was an easy teenager. He got his quota of tattoos and went through an iron-pumping phase that made me suspect he was on steroids. But he enjoyed school and was good at sports and art; he didn't crash cars, get anyone knocked up or ask for unreasonable sums of money.

Unexpectedly, it was Daughter and I who clashed when she was a teenager – the strops, the sulks, the door slamming – and that was just me. The first year of Daughter's life had been difficult in different ways to Son's: her father and I split up, we moved out of the house, and I had to put her in a creche; the part-time job I'd taken at the start-up paper where I met Husband bled into the afternoons – start-ups did not observe hours – and Daughter spent much of that first year on a playmat next to my desk chewing newsprint. But I'd always thought of Daughter and me as a team. She was a contained, orderly child and independent beyond her years: at two she announced she was perfectly capable of bathing by herself and would call me when she needed a towel. She liked playing quiet games that involved stationery, she could be trusted with scissors, she colour-coded her wardrobe and organised her books by author. Her adolescence caught me completely off guard – she even became *untidy*.

To this day, there hangs a prickly question mark over whether I forced her to go to boarding school or she went willingly: had I cruelly cast her out of the nest, or had she said that everything sucked, especially me, and she couldn't wait to go? Didn't everyone's mother suck when they were sixteen? Didn't all mothers and daughters turn into frenemies when their hormones collided in a storm of pimples and withering oestrogen? Whoever was to blame for the decision, in the end Daughter went, emerging two years later with a clean record and perfect skin, poised to enter adult life as capable and meticulously organised as the early promise she'd shown when she was two. We were friends again.

Daughter got a job and moved to another city. A few years later Son got a job and moved to another city. I was proud of them; they were not afraid of flying.

Some parents were happy when their children left home – finding their wings and soaring up to their own altitude was what we'd brought them up to do, right? But there were others who threw themselves down on the fainting couch and went into a decline. It was called Empty Nest Syndrome. It seemed unfair, said the afflicted, that just as you were hitting your midlife stride – slowing down a bit at work, finding time to source twenty-four ingredients you'd never heard of for an Ottolenghi recipe – your children were being *snatched away* by dark forces beyond your jurisdiction. One abandoned mum I knew had ENS so badly she wrote to her eighteen-year-old son at his university, setting out her complaints. Why didn't he come home every weekend? Why had he left her? Was it something she'd said?

'The gist of his reply was that he was enjoying spreading his wings and wanted to spend more time with his girlfriend. *Incredible!*'

Two years later, Abandoned Mum's younger son flew the coop too. At least, she said, this one called home when he needed money, which meant they kept in regular contact. Abandoned Mum was pathetically grateful for these hustler calls, though she understood that they were largely transactional: he got money and in return she got to ask him whether he was eating properly. She took what scraps she could get.

ENS came with side effects. What, wondered Abandoned Mum, would she and her husband talk about in their empty nest now that their lives no longer revolved around the children? She couldn't recall when last they'd spoken to each other in full sentences. It was a whole new relationship dynamic. What would they *do*? She didn't want to sail around the world (her husband's suggestion) or take up watercolour classes or wild swimming. She pined for the days when she'd fall in the door from work and have to get the dinner on and shoo the kids from underfoot and get their names mixed up with the dog's – *Have you done your homework, Chewy?*

In the end, she and her husband got a new puppy to talk to: the puppy appreciated the trouble she went to over Ottolenghi's chicken with za'atar and sumac and didn't appear to mind when she got its name mixed up with the children's.

'We have such a short window with them,' she wailed.

And yet, she conceded, so long: the drudge of having to feed them every day for years, the Olympian logistics of juggling playdates and the extracurricular activities without which they'd have few options in life but to hang out in tunnels tagging train carriages. And she certainly wouldn't miss the humiliation of skidding into parent–teacher meetings just as everyone was packing up the chairs.

When Daughter and Son left home, Husband and I sold the house, practically from under their feet, and downsized to an apartment, which was advertised as the perfect lock-up-and-go lifestyle opportunity for empty nesters and first-time buyers. In other words, the entire flat was about the size of our old dining room. Still, it had a second bedroom that could be turned into a snug work-from-home office, plus there was no garden to maintain, no shin-banging bikes in the hallway, no dogs, no dog shit. Voila!

The children acted most put out when we sold the sprawling suburban home they'd grown up in instead of preserving it as a shrine to a million Lego pieces and Son's collection of fossilised Easter eggs.

But it was time to clean out the closets, edit down, let go of stuff that had outlived its usefulness and move on. Emptying the nest after the little birds had flown was a cathartic rite of passage and a sentimental journey through the museum of their childhood. Coin collections, sports trophies, ballet shoes, Ninja Turtle suits and a coat hanger marked First Fairy gently swaying in an empty wardrobe. Every object told a story, lit up a memory, tugged a heart-string or a smile. It took ages to decide what went in the trash, what went in the charity pile and what would be sold to defray expenses if they didn't come and get it. Out went punctured paddling pools, recorders, board games with pieces missing and the creepy doll with eyes that followed you round the room.

I kept a few nursery-school scribbles, a small selection of turd-like pottery and a couple of wildly ambitious letters to Father Christmas. I kept their favourite story-books, the ones I knew off by heart I'd read them so often. Unfortunately, a few things fell through the curatorial cracks, such as Daughter's milk teeth and Son's first edition of *Harry Potter and the Philosopher's Stone*. The book had been a gift from his godmother before anyone realised it would one day be worth more than the contents of Tutankhamun's tomb and that Husband and I could have retired to the Bahamas on the proceeds. It must have got mixed up in the charity pile, and I could only hope that it had found a good home, most likely at Sotheby's. Son never gave up believing that one day it would fall out of an old recipe book, but, as I said to him at the time, 'Son, we have to be philosophical about it, because when all's said and done, it's just *stuff*.'

Losing Son's inheritance is the other biggest regret of my life.

Still, it was a wonderful purge. I loved our decluttered new nest, and if I felt just a little bit guilty about not having ENS, I hid it well. Anyhow, I wasn't the only woman I knew who'd skipped this step – lots of my friends didn't even have children.

I wondered if any of them regretted not having children, now that it was too late, but I didn't have the nerve to ask: how would I feel if someone asked me whether I regretted having them?

There were studies arguing that, in evolutionary terms, women lived beyond menopause primarily for the purpose of being grandmothers, to nurture the youngest members of the tribe and leave the mums free to go to work in the forest foraging for bugs and berries. But all this was prehistory, and I was surprised to read that Miriam Stoppard – the sensible celebrity doctor whose books on childcare had been my go-to guides during my own pregnancies and early motherhood – seemed to buy into this idea. Interviewed about a book she had written on grandparenting, she said she believed that women were programmed to live beyond the menopause to help their children with their children and that the presence of a grandmother enhanced the community's fitness and ability to reproduce.

'It works for whales, African lions and olive baboons,' she said, 'so why not for us?'

I liked to think that a mutual obsession with grooming aside, there were bigger differences between me and an olive baboon. The idea that as members of the older female species the defining purpose driving us forward rested in our reproductive legacy did not sit well with me.

I was reminded of the words of Dr Z, the French doctor who had advanced a similar view when I'd gone to see him for a menopause check-up. Regarding the quality-of-life expectancy of a post-fertile woman, he had basically said our job was done and we might as well all just go ahead and die now.

I was loving being a grandmother-to-be and now that I was one, I saw it as a gift, a delightful role I'd been given to play without having to audition for the part. If truth be told, I couldn't pretend it didn't sometimes stir primal feelings, make me marvel at the endless intertwining and blossoming of the branches on the family tree. As Grandson grew, significant qualities and features he developed perfectly mimicked the qualities and features of various family members – the eyes, the expression, the humour; even his food preferences and aversions criss-crossed the gene pool in mysterious and fascinating ways. But I did not feel that being a grandmother defined me. And what about members of the female species who weren't grandmothers? How would they carry on living meaningful post-menopausal lives without a reproductive legacy? Did they worry about getting lonely in their old age, about being the last of their line, about not having grandchildren to grant them the milky warmth of a sleeping child against their shoulder, the knowledge that their genes would never go all the way to the deep end of the pool? Did they mind not having grandchildren to take foraging for sweets behind their parents' backs and remind them of the magic of Christmas?

Finally, I plucked up the cheek to ask one of my closest child-free friends. 'Do you regret not having children?'

When we'd first become friends, I had a one-year-old baby and she had a Roy Lichtenstein poster – the one of the woman with a teardrop trickling down her cheek and a thought bubble: 'I can't believe it, I forgot to have children!' The Lichtenstein poster always drew an ironic chuckle from the carefree, child-free young feminists in our circle. Child-Free friend kept her own hours, loved her work and never had to leave a party early for the babysitter. The question of whether or not to have children was the furthest thing from her mind. But as the hands on her biological clock nudged closer to striking the hour, she began to give the matter serious thought.

'Around the age of thirty-eight I started to feel quite panicky and thought, if I'm going to have children I have to do it now. I'd had an abortion so I knew that I could get pregnant. I played the whole movie in my head: I didn't have a partner at the time and there wasn't anyone on the horizon. I thought, well, I'd like to have a child with someone I want to be involved with, not just someone I'd be glued to for the rest of my life because we had a child. I thought about what being a single mother would be like: could I afford to raise a child? How would it work? How would *I* work?'

Then there were the external pressures: the dwindling hopes of her grandchildless parents, who, to be fair, tried not to let their disappointment show, and the casual assumptions of strangers.

It rankled when a man sitting next to her at a dinner asked how many children she had. When she replied that she didn't have any, 'he simply could not think of anything more to say to me'.

It rankled when someone interviewing her for a job remarked, 'Apparently you have no children?'

'Well, not any that I know about,' she said.

Yet as the biological possibility of having children faded, she was miserable, she had regrets; she knew that soon the choice would no longer be hers to make. Yes, she mourned the passing of her fertility. I had too, in spite of having had my full complement of children and not planning on any last-minute additions. Being fertile was about having a decision still within our grasp, a function of the body that we would all lose, whether we'd used it or not. The passing of fertility prefigured other losses, uneasily felt, if not yet experienced.

By the time she turned forty, Child-Free Friend had made up her mind.

'I thought, well, if you really wanted a child, you'd have one, but you can't have one now just in case you want one later.'

Her resolve briefly relapsed two years later when she fell in love and had an Oh. My. God. Lichtenstein moment. 'I thought, maybe we should have a child! Beat the clock while it's still ticking!'

But the moment passed and she decided that, after all, she'd rather have 'a nice relationship'.

'It was great just being together, doing what we wanted, when we wanted. It was then that I realised I was at peace with not having a child. It concluded things for me.

'At Christmas, I still think wouldn't it be nice to have some grandchildren around – it's fun having children around, I like children. But I haven't thought about any of that for a long time.'

Child-Free Friend hadn't forgotten to have children, quite the reverse: she'd put a lot of thought into it, which was more than you could say for some people who did have children.

*

While I was planning what a brilliant grandmother I was going to be to make up for having been a Balloon Parent, Son moved back home, into the spare room I was going to turn into a work-from-home office. He commandeered the only comfortable couch, took control of the TV remote and said 'better out than in' when he farted.

Overnight, our empty nest turned into a millennial case study. Feathers flew.

We were the generation who'd made the mistake of letting our children think we were their friends. We'd treated them as equals; they'd raided our wardrobes and smoked our weed; sometimes we even went to the same parties. Now one of our chickens had come home to roost.

Son's new job wouldn't have supported a hamster: like so many millennials, he couldn't afford to rent his own place and, frankly, he didn't show much enthusiasm for the idea anyway. Who could blame him? This way he got his laundry done, ate on the house and didn't have to tidy his room – he was too old to be grounded and I was too old to care about his room looking as if it had been ransacked by the CIA as long as he kept the door closed. Son came with a flotilla of trainers the size of jet skis which he left sweating on the windowsill after his daily two-hour sessions at the gym. He had a car, a bank account and a girlfriend. He had the freedom to come and go as he pleased. In other words, he had all the fun of the fair without paying the entrance fee.

At least he didn't ask for a hamster.

Still, I worried about how a twenty-five-year-old who didn't know how to iron a shirt would fare in the outside world. I worried about him settling down with a girl and raising a family in the back bedroom. In the wee hours, I worried about him turning into one of those forty-year-olds who lived with their mothers and slept in astronaut pyjamas.

Our new living arrangements took a while to adjust to, but as time went by I barely noticed Son's sweaty jet skis on the windowsill. I understood that when he said something was 'sick' he meant it was nice, and he introduced me to new music. Husband and I got used to squashing up to watch TV while Son sprawled on the only couch with springs. I caught myself behaving more and more like a … mother, a very indulgent mother. My determination to have an adult-to-adult relationship with Son finally cracked: I bought his toiletries and shopped for food that complied with his strict dietary requirements, which included extortionate grass-fed proteins. It was like old times.

It was my shot at redemption.

Neither Son's nor my regressive behaviour went unnoticed by Daughter. Having lived on her own since leaving school (correction, *boarding* school), she'd constructed a heart-rending narrative: basically, that she'd been tossed out of the nest and instructed to fly while mummy and daddy bird continued to feather the nest for Brother and pre-digest his worms.

Sometimes I had a sneaky feeling that I *was* overcompensating for missing his cow's-milk allergy and losing Harry Potter.

When Son eventually moved into his own place, I was surprised by how much I missed him, though admittedly getting the spare room back and turning it into a work-from-home office went some way to consoling me.

*

Now both well and truly launched into the wonderful world of mortgage repayments, Daughter and Son were the New Grown-Ups.

I could see a time when I would be consigned to the margins of their lives – if I was lucky, to a shed conversion at the bottom of the garden – a granny flat. Already they introduced me to their New Grown-Up friends as *my mum*, nothing that would identify me as an *individual in my own right*. I considered getting a name tag, like on the first day at big school.

Son-in-Law's mother – my delightful granny-in-law – became my mentor and guide in how to handle becoming an *un*grown-up. Being the proud custodian of several grandchildren already, she was further along in the granny game than I was.

'Watch out,' she warned me, 'soon you'll be buckled into the back seat of a people carrier with the kids, putting up your hand for a pee and a packet of crisps at the service station.'

Her rescue-chimp granny name was Mimi. Mimi looked nothing like a granny or, for that matter, a chimp: she had long blonde hair, wore an ankle chain and was spectacularly nimble. Once, when she locked herself out of her cottage, she'd vaulted in through a bathroom window the size of a letterbox. It was lucky I liked her. To make up for it, Mimi was a ditz: she lost keys and cell phones, she missed flights, drove over traffic cones and thought satnav was a free-to-air TV channel. Mimi made my own defective short-term memory and sense of spatial awareness look good, though admittedly the playing field was levelled when it came to trying to drive off in other people's cars. A disproportionate number of older women seemed to drive small white hatchbacks: they all looked the same, a further challenge when you had to look up your own number plate. Mimi and I both drove small white hatchbacks, occasionally into pillars. We knew the difference between our cars by the dents, thanks to our different parking techniques – I was a front-loader, she was a rear-ender.

Mimi was a ditz, alright, and everyone adored her. Even so, she could see a time when her general adorableness might be pronounced a liability by the New Grown-Ups. Already she was starting to get the feeling that her children felt more responsible for her than she did for them, that they were making decisions *for* her, discussing her *best interests* among themselves. I was beginning to feel it myself.

'We're not in our dotage yet,' said Mimi encouragingly. 'We must guard our independence for as long as possible.'

'When will I be old?' I asked Daughter.

'When you stop paying for dinner,' she replied.

Daughter already earned more money than I ever had, lived in a bigger house and drove a sexier car. Thanks to her I knew how to download apps and get the best shopping deals online. And now, here she was, a mother. One day I asked her what she wanted for Grandson, and she said, 'The happiest childhood I can give him.'

I wouldn't let her down. Everything I did with Grandson would be fun *and* educational. I would never say no if I was asked to babysit. I would never give advice. I would never encourage him to keep secrets from his parents except for the occasional tube of Smarties and how to blow smoke rings. This was my chance to give Daughter the support she needed as a new mum with a ten-hour-a-day job. This was my chance to atone for my own flawed parenting.

*

After my shaky entrance into Grannyland on the back of a sleeping pill on the night of Grandson's birth, I set out to show his parents that I could be trusted with his precious life. From the moment he came home I did what I was told. When I babysat, Daughter would leave me laminated and bound pages of typed notes – how to hold him, how to burp him, how to do the Heimlich manoeuvre, all with illustrations taken from textbooks. The notes were regularly updated to keep pace with Grandson's growth and development. They opened with a general introduction to childcare and a photo of Grandson looking like the last puppy in the window on Christmas Eve: he was sitting on the carpet in a little romper, straining towards the camera with his chubby arms in the 'uppie' pose; his eyes shone with trust, or were those tears? Either way, it was a picture calculated to concentrate my mind on the task at hand. While he napped I'd go outside for a smoke and carry on swotting-up the notes: I didn't feel patronised or indignant; I didn't think, *I've done all this before, Daughter – I was doing this when you were in nappies.* 'Before' was a very long time ago, and things had changed: back then there were no such things as Bluetooth security cameras that surveilled the nursery and remote-controlled musical rocking chairs and anatomically correct baby baths and Baltic amber teething necklaces. Best to follow the rules, best to get it right this time.

That Grandson was an exceptionally gifted child was clear from the start: you could tell he was having thoughts far in advance of his tender months from the way he lay in his cot chewing his fist and staring into space, doubtless pondering the nature of space itself. His grasp of language was equally precocious, and although Daughter didn't clap quite so loudly as Son-in-Law at his first word – 'dada' – we all agreed it would be best to alert Mensa. But soon after learning to speak, there came a moment when I wished Grandson had never opened his mouth.

Instead of calling me Coco, the stylish super-gran name I'd so carefully chosen, he called me *Toto*.

Husband said, 'Isn't that the name of the Lone Ranger's horse?'

Sister Four said, 'No, I think it's the name of Dorothy's dog in *The Wizard of Oz*.'

Daughter said she wouldn't be surprised, as Grandson's reading was very advanced and might well include books he hadn't read yet.

A French friend stopped laughing long enough to throw in her two centimes: in French, she said, holding her sides, Toto was slang for someone who was not quite *all there*.

Everyone agreed it served me right for being pretentious.

*

You never stop worrying about your children, whether they're four or thirty-four. Lurid nightmares involving boiling saucepans and paedophiles morph into worries about whether they're being bullied at school or overworked by psychotic bosses or trapped in unhappy relationships. When they're young you have to guess what's wrong because they can't tell you. When they're teenagers you have to guess what's wrong because they won't tell you. When they're grown-ups they just roll their eyes when you ask them if they're OK. I didn't see how showing maternal concern for their wellbeing could possibly be annoying, until the next time I spoke to my mother on the phone and realised what they meant.

'Hello, darling, how are you?'

'Fine, thanks, Mum.'

'You don't sound fine, I can tell by your voice.'

'Really, I'm fine.'

'Are you sure?'

'I'm sure.'

'You'd tell me if you weren't, wouldn't you?'

At this rate, probably not.

Little by little, I began to detect that there could be advantages to being the new *un*grown-up. Not being the designated person-in-charge of grave and stressful responsibilities would be a relief. I could take my foot off the pedal and collide with pillars in parking lots and claim diminished responsibility. I could stay in my room for days and sulk. I could play my music as loud as I liked and live on takeaways. I wouldn't have to make my bed, I'd just bloody well lie on it.

None of these *un*grown-up advantages would make leaving home any easier, but the die was cast: I was moving to France, or, perhaps more accurately, I was *semi*grating to France – hedging my bets, leaving the door open for Husband to join me if things worked out between us, committing to coming 'home' on a regular basis for family birthdays, Christmases and holidays. It had taken almost as long as Brexit for Husband and me to negotiate the terms of my exit from South Africa, a soft exit that offered our marriage a fighting chance: there was no turning back now.

I had long ago fallen out of love with my adopted country, a country that as I got older and my appetite for edginess faded, I found increasingly uncomfortable to navigate. Economic inequalities persisted and the race wounds of the past went too deep to see the bottom. It was clearer now than ever that the (shrinking) minority white population, who had ruled only by dominating the majority black population, would never really fit in. Most of us had retreated into suburban ghettos, barricaded inside by fear and our privilege. And there was plenty to fear, regardless of where you stood on the scale of poverty and wealth. No one could walk the city streets after dark without risking bodily harm. Society remained deeply patriarchal. Domestic violence and rape were rife. The elderly subsisted on meagre pensions that often had to stretch to feed their families too as unemployment ballooned. A restless movement of young black intellectuals wondered out loud: what was the point of whites? I did not want to grow old here. Husband did not want to grow old anywhere else.

Gradually these feelings, this low-grade civil war between Husband's needs and mine, had hardened into a cement of despair, anxiety and shame. Added to what was going on in my marriage and the confusions of my changing self, South Africa was not an environment conducive to reflection and healing, not to mine anyway.

Daughter and Son had their own lives and loves and dreams, all firmly rooted in the land of their birth. It was too late to make up their minds for them. Their feelings weren't my feelings; their choices were their choices. My needs were mine alone, the only ones I had any power to change or pursue. I reminded myself that I was more than the sum of my granny parts, that I didn't need to live in a shed conversion at the bottom of the garden to be a good one, that atonement was not a full-time occupation. Anyhow, it wasn't as if I was leaving forever, never to return. I nursed a private wish that, given time, I would convince them all to join me in my one-woman exodus. But I could not make them.

Could I really blame where I lived for being the final nail in my unhappiness? I had to keep an open mind; perhaps growing older somewhere gentler, somewhere closer to my mother as *she* grew older, wouldn't provide all the answers. But in my restless heart of hearts, I knew that it would help.

In my fever to be gone I had not taken much account of the fact that I was about to move to a country where I knew no one and my command of the language was more of a statement of intent.

But I had a journey to make, dragons to slay, demons to conquer. I had to guard my independence while I still had it. Get myself together. Follow my dreams. Trust my instincts. Suddenly, I was terrified. Was I an idiot? A selfish, spoiled fool, looking the gift of my family in the mouth, risking making Daughter and Son feel somehow abandoned again, turning my back on having a meaning-ful relationship with Grandson? Was I bound to repeat the mistakes of my father? It was too late to change my mind – I'd quit my job, my ticket was booked and a new home half a world away was waiting.

'You have to live your life,' said Son.

'You can't leave home,' said Daughter, 'you're the mum.'

Living the Dream

'Be careful what you wish for, lest it come true.'

— AESOP'S FABLES

Packing up my bags and plenty of baggage, I moved to France.

Some sage once said that running away wasn't the answer because you took yourself with you wherever you went. But to me this was the whole point – running away *with myself*! I preferred Audrey Hepburn's take on solitude: I don't want to be alone, she'd once said, I want to be left alone. Admittedly, I wasn't being chased down the street by baying fans whenever I ran out for a pint of milk in sunglasses, but the distinction she made between being alone and being left alone perfectly summed up my feelings. Audrey's smart little epigram spoke not only to a desire for privacy, but also to a craving for anonymity. Living in a place where I knew no one and no one knew me was both a daunting prospect and hugely appealing. I would be … nobody, and this would afford me the opportunity to just … *be*.

There was strong evidence to support the view that countless women had improved their lives by leaving them – lighting out for Bali with a copy of *Eat Pray Love*, searching for a way forward, or perhaps a way back. My quest was to find the meaning of life after youth in a place where I felt safe and free. And I had found my Bali.

My new home was a crumbly stone farmhouse in a rural corner of south-west France, a golden landscape of sunflowers and vines so closely resembling an Impressionist painting it appeared that life really was imitating art. It was the kind of place people came to on holiday and, after a few bottles of the local plonk and third-degree sunstroke, thought they wanted to live there. Just like me.

I couldn't wait to go to the local markets with my new basket and straw hat and pretend to be Juliette Binoche.

Since scraping through couples counselling, hammering out a Selfish-A-Type deal with Husband and embarking on a trial separation, he and I were getting along much better.

We'd travelled to France together, I on a one-way ticket, to sign the papers on the house, and had just two weeks to set everything up before Husband returned to South Africa. We spent the first evening assembling our DIY bed before we could lie on it (we needed separate continents, not separate beds).

Our mutual goodwill had even survived a trip to IKEA to buy the homeware essentials.

Despite IKEA's logo being visible from space, we managed to miss the turn-off, which we only realised when we saw a sign saying Next Exit Barcelona. We pulled into the emergency lane to have a row about whose fault it was. This was in the days when satnav was more likely to drive you into a brick wall than to your desired destination, and all we had to go on was the map drawn on a serviette by the kind owner of the B&B where we'd stayed while waiting to take occupation of the crumbly stone house. Eventually we pulled into IKEA's stadium-sized car park and joined the throngs of other couples in matching puffer jackets going through the revolving doors. In the mega-store's fabled canteen we broke Swedish meatballs together before entering the giant maze of showrooms to purchase exactly the same cushions and crockery as the rest of middle Europe. Going into friends' houses was like bumping into another woman wearing the same dress at a party: you just had to hope the Kivik rug looked better on your floor than hers.

Husband and I played house – arranging and rearranging furniture, rummaging for bits and pieces in second-hand markets, painting and scrubbing, shining up the place, making it home, a home we may or may not ever share on a permanent basis. I would come to think of the house as our late baby, that last-minute one couples had in an attempt to rescue a flagging relationship. We were building a new nest, but who were we building it for?

Soon it was time for Husband to leave, to return to the land he called home, to resuming gazing at the view he loved from the same old window, the window I had drawn a curtain over.

Parting was harder than I thought.

At the airport's ten-minute drop-off zone, Husband heaved his pink-and-white floral suitcase out of the boot – a birthday gift he'd once given me that I refused to have anything to do with. But Husband, a practical type, was not easily embarrassed.

A quick hard hug and he was gone, bustling off to Terminal D wheeling his silly pink suitcase, looking like Miss Venezuela.

At the entrance he turned and waved – not a romantic movie-farewell type wave, more of an urgent flapping.

Perhaps he'd changed his mind. Perhaps he was missing me already. Perhaps he wanted to stay. And in that moment, I'd have taken him and his pink suitcase back in a heartbeat.

I opened the car window. 'WHAT?'

'DON'T SMOKE IN THE CAR! OR THE HOUSE!'

With that he turned and disappeared inside the terminal. I couldn't wait to see the back of him.

It was dark by the time I got back to the crumbly stone house on a long and winding road through unfamiliar hamlets that briefly flared in the black emptiness of the surrounding countryside, past the undulating vineyards, along the twisty unlit lanes with their deep, invisible ditches and down the bumpy track that led to the house that I could not quite yet call home.

It was very quiet out there in the countryside: no cars whooshing by, no lights twinkling in the inky sky beyond the still curtain-less windows, no humans in sight or sound, just strange animal noises – an owl's hoot, a sudden scurry across the roof. I turned on the lamps and poured a whisky. I heated up a frozen pizza and ate my half. Then I remembered Husband was gone and ate his half. I sprawled on the couch and lit a cigarette.

At last, I was alone; at last, I'd been *left alone*. This was what I'd wanted, wasn't it?

It didn't take long to see that my new life was going to be somewhat different from how I'd imagined it – there were impediments I'd failed to consider, angles I'd over-looked. I'd never lived outside a city or done any gardening or lain awake at night worrying about the shrinking bee population. I'd only ever thought of nature, in so far as I thought of it at all, as something you had to drive through to get somewhere. I was scared of cows and anything that flapped, scuttled, buzzed, slithered or moved faster than me. This was most things, including a local farmer's ancient mother who'd come tearing past me in her battered matchbox car with no lights or side mirrors, accompanied by a miniature dog that seemed permanently stuck to the passenger window, probably by G-forces.

I bought an electric tennis racket for swatting things, which improved my backhand but had little effect on the fly population. When I was doing housework, I carried a can of spider killer in the pocket of the *Coronation Street* housecoat I'd bought in my local supermarket as a jokey conceit – I couldn't believe people still wore such get-ups *unironically.* As my urban life receded and I passed the days sweeping up builders' dust and beetles, the *Coronation Street* housecoat stopped being amusing and became the most indispensable garment in my wardrobe. When fired at point-blank range, the spider spray would blow back in my face, causing me to cough uncontrollably: it probably took five years off my life, never mind the planet's, but it was preferable to being set upon by giant furballs with legs. I didn't understand why seemingly intelligent people said dumb things like 'they're harmless' when spiders were a major cause of strokes and heart attacks, or 'they're more scared of you than you are of them'. How did they know? Had they *asked* a tarantula?

The countryside seethed with perils they never showed you in those romantic French period dramas in idyllic rustic settings. Nature was only there to provide atmosphere – a chocolate-box backdrop to the action, which generally revolved around sex and family feasts at long tables under plane trees with accordion music and a bit of slap and tickle under the table. Nobody in rustic French period dramas sat around furiously scratching mosquito bites in their nether regions. In rustic French period dramas when actresses in heaving bodices threw themselves down on the hay, the only thing likely to jump out at them was Johnny Depp.

One morning I woke up itching like a mad woman and looked down to see dozens of livid, suppurating bites all over my body. I went to see the village doctor, who took one look at these volcanic eruptions and asked if I'd been lying in any long grass lately. Clearly, he could not have mistaken me for a French actress. When I said I certainly had not been lying in long grass, he said, 'Well, anyway, you have *aoûtats*.' *Aoûtats*, I learned, were vicious little mites, invisible to the naked eye and very common around these parts in August. Mind you, he whistled, this was one of the worst cases he'd ever seen. He sent me on my way with a tube of cortisone cream and said, 'Are you sure you haven't been lying in long grass?'

Sometimes, my rustic paradise felt more like living in a David Attenborough documentary. I began to wonder whether nature and I would ever get along.

There were other obstacles I'd failed to properly consider in my hormonally charged haste to get away from my former life. For instance, it turned out I only thought I could speak French. The old-school phrase books I'd dusted off proved quite useless in twenty-first-century France, or twenty-first-century anywhere: 'Is this the smoking section of the aircraft?' 'Where is the public telephone?' 'Yugoslavia is a beautiful country.' 'I would like to send a telegram.'

I'd always loved French, a language that made everyone sound as if they were lying in bed smoking after mind-blowing sex. This, unfortunately, was not how I sounded. I developed a way of speaking fast, in a mash-up of tenses and made-up words, filling in the gaps with shrugs and grimaces I copied from real French people. But I had a good ear and could do a reasonable impersonation of a French accent; consequently, no one understood a thing I said, but they'd get a wary look, as if they might have missed something.

Without the benefit of pantomime shrugs and grimaces, phone calls were more challenging.

I'd leave messages on the electrician's answerphone: 'Salutations! The television cannot walk. Please come to watch it very soon. I embrace you!'

My new next-door neighbours embraced me with open arms, but let me get away with nothing. Monsieur C spoke reasonably good English, but Madame C, who had only learned schoolgirl English, which was about as effective as learning schoolgirl French, spoke none to speak of. Why would she? She was *French*, we were in *France*. It was funny how English-speakers appeared stunned when they found out that not all foreigners spoke English. I tried to imagine a French visitor to rural Wales being astounded to discover that not everyone in Tiddletown spoke French.

'You must learn to speak properly,' said Madame C. 'I'll help you.' She might have been a country woman, but she had a worldly sense of humour.

'Are you finished?' she'd say when my lips stopped moving. 'You're hurting my ears.' She'd clap her hands over her ears in case I hadn't understood, then make me conjugate *avoir* two hundred times.

Madame and Monsieur C took me under their wing: they introduced me to everyone who was anyone in the village, which, being a community of 149 registered voters, was pretty much everyone. They guided me through the Olympian paperwork the French excelled at and took over making phone calls on my behalf to builders and plumbers and the electrician – apparently by popular demand. They undertook my education in local customs, including how to stack four tonnes of wood by forming a human chain, how to serve dinner in the right order and how to exercise caution on the roads because French drivers were zippy and liked to be in front. One evening they took me to a raffle where the first prize was a donkey. I don't think I'd ever been so happy not to win anything in my life.

One morning Monsieur C called and said he was taking me to see the Tour de France. The legendary cycling race would be coming through a nearby village that afternoon. 'Bring a shopping bag,' he said mysteriously.

The peloton passed in a disappointing three-minute blur that blew my new straw hat into the road. But the real entertainment was the warm-up act – the *la caravane pub-licitaire*. This comprised a cavalcade of sponsors' trucks that thundered through the villages and towns ahead of the riders, flinging assorted freebies and foodstuffs into the cheering crowds lining the route. The *caravane* was a sort of French version of the Roman Games with salami sticks instead of slaves. It was, said Monsieur C, limbering up and snapping his shopping bag, by far the best part of the Tour. 'How else do you think they get so many people out on the streets for the TV cameras?' From my early observations of local life and culture, French people came out on the streets at the drop of a strike and hardly needed further encouragement. But as the noisy swell of onlookers jostled for the prime positions on the normally sleepy main street, I got quite caught up in all the excitement.

A current fizzed through the crowd as a van with a colossal *saucisson* on the roof came hurtling around the corner and invisible hands threw packets of mini sausages at us. People went crazy, shoving and scuffling for the little foil bags. Hard on the wheels of the sausage truck came a row of giant vegetables, a basket of dancing baguettes and a revolving milkshake the size of a small building. 'Nesquik!' yelled the man next to me as he launched himself at an airborne box of chocolate milk. A police van appeared, blue lights flashing. For a moment I thought the *gendarmerie* were about to do a bit of crowd control, but then they started throwing things at us as well. Fridge magnets bearing the national police logo rained down on our heads. People practically trampled the barricades to get at them. The freebies kept coming at us thick and fast – caps, keyrings, hard-boiled sweets, hotel pens. It was all quite shameless and totally exhilarating and eventually even I found myself in a tussle for a bottle of mineral water that had been launched like a missile from the Vittel truck. I spied Monsieur C coming up for air, clutching an armful of booty which we divided up between our shopping bags. As we inspected our bruises and the jewel in our crown, a giant foam hand, compliments of a local bookie, Monsieur C clicked his tongue: before the global economic crisis of 2008, he said, they gave away much better stuff; one year, someone got a racing bike.

Next year, I would wear a helmet.

In the beginning, I was busy: setting up house, meeting new people, driving on the wrong side of the road, finding my way around the exotically stocked supermarket and translating the labels. Just trying to work out the directions on the back of cleaning products could take up half a morning: *wipe with a damp sponge, mix one part detergent to three parts water, do not drink.* Following recipes was equally fascinating: *sprinkle, stir, beat, drizzle, soak.* I could even speak rudimentary Plumber: *leak, clog, drain.* I wrote everything down. My vocabulary grew.

*

Leaving South Africa had unshackled me from many unsettling feelings and things that I would not miss. Still, Daughter's words would haunt me.

You can't leave home, you're the mum.

But I was a daughter too, and for thirty years contact with my mother, my sisters and my whole bang-shoot family living six thousand miles away in England had been

sporadic, stuttering across continents and personal circumstances that were often straitened. My mother hadn't
made it to my wedding. I hadn't made it to my grandmother's funeral. Or the funerals of any of my three uncles. I
never got to take anyone a bunch of grapes in hospital.
Long before FaceTime and WhatsApp and Skype, the only
way to stay in touch was by prohibitively expensive phone
calls. On the rare occasions when we did call each other,
we spoke in breathless snatches, volleys of *how are you*s
and *we miss you*s before hanging up in a tearful flurry of
farewells, not much the wiser about how anyone was at all.

What I'd missed most of all living away from my mother
and sisters was being part of their everyday lives, the small
quotidian scenes my family were experts at working up
into gleeful tales: Mum's latest work drama, the funny
thing that happened to Auntie on the way to the supermarket, a disastrous date – in other words, the daily turnover
of gossip and pot-stirring that meant little if you weren't in
the pot. This was the connective tissue that bound families
together as tightly as any of the big milestones. When we
were all together – Mum's birthday, the occasional
Christmas, a summer holiday in South Africa – things
could get pretty intense: the anticipation would build up as
we ticked off the days and dreamed of the jolly times
ahead. For the first forty-eight hours after such reunions,
we'd all talk at the same time, marvelling at the changes
– in the children, in our hair and, occasionally, in our
partners. Sister Four would read our tarot cards and let us
start over if we got a bad hand. Sister Two would build
sand or snow sculptures with the children, depending on
which side of the hemisphere we were on. My mother was

always up for a game of Scrabble and another round of cake. After two days we'd collapse under the weight of all the excitement and have to retire – or be sent – to our rooms. Afternoon naps would resume; we'd curl up with books and have quiet time, or break up into small groups, or go off in pairs for walks and whispered one-on-ones. The next stage of these reunions was the part where we'd regress to our default sibling settings and start scrapping and ganging up and making jokes at each other's expense. This was when I'd know that everything was back to normal and all was right with the world. And then – too soon, always too soon! – it was time to part again in floods of tears and promises.

Sometimes years went by without seeing my mother. Privately, I was terrified that the next time I saw her she'd look older, no longer be recognisable as the mother whose picture I carried around in my head from the last time.

Now that I was in my fifties and she was in her seventies, it felt more pressing than ever to close the ocean between us. Living in France meant I could hop on a no-frills flight (what flight had frills any more?) and be sitting in her cosy flat in Devon drinking the first of many cups of tea a mere few hours later. Separated only by a sliver of channel, I could see her – and my sisters and cousins and aunts – pretty much whenever I liked.

*

Practically before I'd finished soaking the price stickers off the new IKEA crockery, Mum and Auntie were winging their way across the channel to visit me in the

new house. They came through Arrivals wearing blue
and white striped T-shirts with tight white jeans. Mum
was wearing espadrilles and Auntie had on a jaunty neck
scarf. They looked like gigolos. They were both gasping
for a cigarette.

'Can we smoke in your car, darling?'

I gave Auntie the thumbs up. 'We can do whatever the
hell we like.'

I closed the windows so their hair wouldn't get mussed
and we coughed all the way home.

After unpacking their modest hand luggage, which contained mostly make-up, my mother's rolling tobacco and
Auntie's thongs, I took them on a tour of the property.
They loved the place, but I could see that they were already
wilting in the searing southern heat. I'd given up dressing
in proper clothes: climate-change temperatures that could
rise to 40 degrees meant that anything that touched your
body stuck to it. I suggested that for a start they should
take off their tights, which they wore under their jeans to
hide their snowy British ankles. They were horrified. What
if people saw them?

'Look around,' I said. 'What people?'

They rolled up their sleeves and set about helping
me make my new home: they mopped up builders' dust
and starched sheets. Auntie got a crick in her neck from
sweeping the chimney, but staggered on with her head at a
sixty-degree angle. They were both obsessive-compulsive
cleaners and it was no good telling them to relax and enjoy
themselves: all I could do was hose them down when they
overheated and keep up their spirits with stiff cups of tea
and vodka.

In the end they were forced to peel off their jeans – it was either that or heatstroke. Auntie stripped down to her famous blue satin nightie (the one she'd had since the sixties and wore at home when no one was looking), and Mum borrowed a kaftan I'd bought at a market that didn't cling to anything, decidedly not to anything approaching style.

On day two Mum and Auntie set up camp in the garage. I found them sitting in deckchairs on a mouldy offcut of carpet with an ashtray on top of the washing machine.

'What are you doing in the garage?'

'Ooh, darling,' they said, 'it's so lovely and cool in here.'

The next morning my mother announced she was going to make her special red cabbage, the secret of which was to leave it outside to stew in natural sunlight. I had my doubts, but out came the pot, in went the cabbage and a few other mystery ingredients, and the whole mess was left outside the kitchen door on the moonscape of builders' rubble I hoped one day would become a shady jasmine-scented terrace brimming with red geraniums in terracotta pots.

'It's very quiet round here,' said Auntie. I could see they were itching to go somewhere, and I couldn't blame them: there was only so much you could do in a garage in a nightdress. They needed an outing. I offered to drop them off in the village (a two-mile hike that in the heat would have been like trying to cross the Gobi Desert). At least in the village they'd be able to take in some local colour and get a coffee and a croissant at the bar. They raced off to get changed, emerging half an hour later in lashings of mascara and pancake make-up that was already starting to trickle. Auntie had on her good Jaeger jacket. I'd given up trying to save them from boiling.

I decanted them into the village square with its obelisk-shaped war memorial: these memorials stood at the heart of every village, commemorating the local men – *boys* – who'd been killed in World War I. Some of the photographs, set in little cameos, were still faintly visible – a ghostly face, a smudge of moustache. Many of the family surnames were the same – brothers and sons and fathers who would never come home, leaving behind a tragically decimated generation. It was a sight that never failed to move me.

Mum and Auntie bolted out of the car. We agreed I'd pick them up in an hour. 'There's no rush, darling!'

It was a pretty village of ribboning cobbled lanes and medieval half-timbered houses. The intoxicating aroma of hot pastries wafted from the bakery; wisteria purpled the patio of the village's sole restaurant; old men in flat caps leaned from shuttered windows like film extras in one of those rustic French period dramas without mosquitos. The church, in contrast to its picturesque but humble surroundings, was lavish – vaulted, richly decorated ceilings, saints' tombs carved in their likenesses, glittering reliquaries and gold-leaf statues: in the middle ages even the poorest village bowed to the glory and might of the Catholic Church and coughed up their tithes.

The church was also the only sanctuary as cool as my garage. I'd suggested to Mum and Auntie that they might seek refuge from the heat in there if things got too steamy outside – an hour was a long time to spend in a place with six shops, one of which was for tractor repairs.

But I had not banked on their resourcefulness, or their steaminess.

When I went back to pick them up an hour later, I found them installed at a bistro table on the terrace outside the bar, surrounded by an animated group of weather-beaten men in espadrilles. They were drinking what looked like coffee but which turned out to be coffee laced with brandy. My mother didn't normally drink, but it was clear, even as I crossed the square towards their merry band, that she had drunk. She and Auntie were flirting like mad with the men in espadrilles, who were puffing out their chests and hailing the barman for more coffees.

When we got home I sent them to their room for a siesta. By the time they woke up, still glowing from their triumph, the pot of cabbage was bubbling away like a witch's brew and had a lizard in it. Later, my mother managed to set one of the new IKEA wicker chairs alight with a cigarette – in the parched heat it went up like tinder – and Auntie put out the flames with one of the new IKEA tea towels. We ate tomato sandwiches for supper and retired early: there had, we all agreed, been enough excitement for one day.

The following evening, we were invited round to the next-door neighbours' for an aperitif: I had not known Monsieur and Madame C long, but they had so gamely and generously thrown themselves into smoothing out the bumps of my transition to a new country, they already felt like family.

Like two tribes meeting for the first time, gifts were exchanged – a tin of Devonshire clotted cream toffees for a handsome box of marron glacé. If I thought my 1980s phrase-book French was out of date, my mother's French had last seen active service in 1953. 'I apologise for speaking French like a Spanish cow,' she said when I introduced her. Still, she was excellent at filling in the gaps in the conversation: she asked Madame C if she rode horses by yanking on imaginary reins and making clip-clop noises; she explained her bar job by pulling an imaginary pint and pointing at her chest. 'Your mother's very funny,' said Monsieur C. At least my mother had a grasp of the basics. Auntie only knew two foreign words and they were both Italian – *bellissima* and *bastardo* – words, she said, that had come in handy on a trip to Rome when she was a young woman.

It was time for Mum and Auntie to go home. It was the first time I didn't need to cry when we said goodbye because next time was just around the easyJet corner.

They called from the airport to report good news and bad news: the good news was that the crick in Auntie's neck from sweeping the chimney had been miraculously fixed when a rugby ball that two *bastardo*s were tossing around Departures hit her in the head. The bad news was that their flight had been cancelled, but not to worry because easyJet was putting them up at the Holiday Inn, which was very comfortable and had air-conditioning. When I offered to fetch them and bring them back to the house, my mother said hastily, 'No, *no*, darling, we've put you to quite enough trouble already.' I understood: they'd certainly earned the right to take the weight off their aching feet and order room service in an air-conditioned room that didn't double as a garage. They needed a holiday. Closing the geographic gap had made us a normal family again; no one had to stand on ceremony, and no one did.

One by one, my sisters came to stay.

Sister Four, my go-to buddy in beauty emergencies, arrived bearing charcoal face masks, sonic exfoliators and snake oil serum. In between perfecting her tan, she spent hours mixing up crunchy pastes which either she rubbed on her décolletage or ate. Sister Three, the artist of the family, came to stay and painted a lovely picture of the living room which I hung in the living room. Sister Two, the animal whisperer, came to stay and tried to talk the toad that had taken up residence outside the back door into going in peace. Every evening as the sun went down it plopped on the mat like a curse, forcing me to Riverdance around it every time I went out to empty the trash. Sister Two gently picked it up with her bare hands, coaxed it into a bucket and released it into the wild of the next-door farmer's field. 'It'll probably find its way back,' she said. 'Toads have a homing instinct, you know.' No, I didn't know. The next night it was back on the doormat.

*

Starting up a new life in a new place had been all-consuming, but the novelties were starting to wear off. In many ways this was a relief: I no longer had to ask directions to get to the pharmacy; I spoke enough French to be broadly understood, even if Madame C did still flinch when I opened my mouth; the mayor and I were on cheek-pecking terms. But when all was said and done, there was only so much time you could spend admiring another spectacular sunset and congratulating yourself on finding a tile cleaner that really worked.

The sumptuous view from my window – the gold and green parcels of land, the handsome row of oaks rising on an azure blue horizon – was indeed sumptuous, and entirely devoid of humans. There was all the time in the world for the reflection I had craved.

So. Much. Time.

I had a recurring nightmare about Son. In my dream he was very young and in mortal danger: he teetered at the edge of deep pools or sometimes at the side of a vast glassy lake. There were always other people around, but they went about their business and paid no attention; I was the only one who could see the danger he was in, and only I could save him. But he was so hard to reach. The dream always ended with me managing to scoop him out of the water just as he began to sink beneath the cold, silent surface. I would wake with a gasp in a bottomless pool of sweaty dread.

I started a blog. I recorded my radio shows for WRP from under the duvet. I drank alone. Weekends went on forever. Instead of probing the uncharted nooks and crannies of my inner life, finding new purpose and practising mindfulness, I watched back-to-back reruns of the French versions of *Come Dine with Me* and *House Hunters*. I told myself I was expanding my knowledge of French culture and vocabulary – *undercooked, fixer-upper* – but mostly it was because I'd run out of better things to do and there were still hours to kill before I could take a sleeping pill and go to bed. In hindsight, it looked a lot like depression.

I seldom shopped at the markets for fresh produce any more. I'd done the rounds of all the local ones at least twice, and it was wasn't much fun going alone. I needed so little anyway – a couple of tomatoes, a lump of cheese, a baguette that if not consumed immediately would turn into a baseball bat by nightfall. These pitiful purchases marked me out as someone with no family or friends to break bread with. My provisions looked so meagre compared to the other jolly panniers bursting with seasonal fruits and fish and wheels of brioche, no doubt destined for a feast at a long table under a plane tree with accordions. Anyway, I couldn't be bothered to cook – all that chopping and washing-up for a meal that would take five minutes to polish off in front of *Don't Tell the Bride*. My freezer filled up with Dr Oetker pizzas and meals-for-one from Picard, a popular French purveyor of flash-frozen cuisine.

Mostly I shopped at a hypermarket the size of an aircraft hangar on the outskirts of town where you could find tomatoes, Toilet Duck and toasters under the same roof. It saved a lot of time, even if I didn't always know what to do with it.

I began to miss my family in unexpected ways.

To be fair, Husband and the children tried to include me in their family get-togethers from across the other side of the world. Around Sunday lunchtime I'd get put on FaceTime and propped up on the kitchen counter. Husband would be in his apron seasoning a chicken; Son, who went to chef school, would be telling him he was doing it all wrong. Daughter would be trying to prise Grandson off the dog he was love-strangling, and I would catch the odd glimpse of the back of Son-in-Law's head as he tried to duck out of the frame. I'd drink in these homey scenes, the chatter and steaming pans. I'd try not to mind that Husband had changed the cushions around and the house plants were going yellow. Then everyone would be called to the table and I'd be clicked off in a clatter of cutlery, mid-argument about whose turn it was to get the parson's nose. 'Bye, Mum! *Byeeee!*'

What had I expected? Naturally their lives went on without me.

Husband called to say he'd subscribed to Apple Music Family Sharing. It covered four users – one each for Daughter and Son and one for me. I couldn't get mine to work so I called the Apple Music Family Sharing helpline. They explained that my share in the Apple Music Family could not be activated because I was *in the wrong territory.*

'You're always in the wrong territory,' said Husband.

In spite of the isolation, the sense of freedom and safety I felt in my bucolic little corner of France was very real, and I did feel it as a kind of healing.

The last break-in in the village had happened two years before I arrived and was still talked about. When the homeowners interrupted the housebreakers at their work, the burglars had knocked over furniture in their scramble to get away. As far as I could tell, French burglars tended not to barge in when they knew you'd be at home, press a gun to your stomach and threaten to hurt your children if you didn't tell them where the safe was. By all accounts, French burglars, at least the type of French burglars who worked our patch of the provinces, were generally not inclined to tie you up and make you lie on the carpet with your nose pressed against the nap and say they were going to shoot you if you looked at them. The modus operandi of small-town French burglaries was really quite different from the way in which crimes were executed in South

Africa. When it was my family's turn – in Johannesburg everyone got a turn – I remember lying face down on the carpet next to Son and dreamily wondering how I'd missed the giant dust bunnies hanging off the underside of the sofa as the gunman tugged off my wedding ring. Afterwards, the trauma counsellor said we were lucky they hadn't shot the dogs, which, she said, was usually the first thing they did. Everyone – including us – said how lucky we'd been because we hadn't got shot and, well, in a town like this, it could always be worse.

In Johannesburg these were called *home invasions*, which made them sound like those TV makeover shows where two fops came into your house and made statements with flock wallpaper and wittily oversized lightbulbs.

Mind you, there *was* an outside chance of getting shot in my bucolic little corner of France – the hunting season was another hazard of country life I hadn't factored in. Every year several people were killed or injured by a stray hunter's bullet. Once, not far from our village, a stag being chased by the hounds had crashed through the double-glazed patio doors of a house and collapsed on the kitchen table where the family was eating breakfast. Terrifying and gory though such incidents were, they generally happened by accident, not on purpose, which, to me, made an important psychological difference.

*

The first time the children came to visit, they went off to explore the property they might inherit one day if they played their cards right. Daughter instantly fell in love with everything and Son-in-Law, who grew up on a farm, got a faraway light in his eye, imagining the crops he could plant, the chickens he could raise: he even decided to learn French and looked very pleased with himself when he asked a waiter to bring him the *jour du day*, more commonly known in French as the *plat du jour*. Son, on the other hand, didn't like getting his hands or his white Adidas trainers dirty and preferred his cows to come on the T-bone. My little apple hadn't fallen far. By day three, Son had glazed over. Staring sightlessly at the unchanging oaks on the horizon, the great canopy of cloudless sky, he turned to me and said, 'Don't you get bored?'

It was the question I'd hardly dared to ask myself.

Considering all the fuss I'd kicked up about coming here, I felt contractually obliged to be happy forever and ever, Amen. I'd got what I'd wanted: a Shangri-La-cum-rehab where, in the fullness of time, my inner truth would be revealed, though I didn't think I'd ever achieve the advanced consciousness it would require to care about treading on ants.

But what had it all been for if I was going to nod off every time I tried to meditate on infinity, on how those handsome oaks would still be holding up the horizon long after I was compost? What was it all for when I had tired of my own company, when I was no longer sure I wished to find myself so much as get over myself, when uncomfortable memories buzzed around my head like the ever-present flies? Was the only party I'd ever get invited to again a pity party?

Having been emptied of worldly distractions, my mind filled up with thoughts that had nowhere else to go. I missed the noise and distractions of the city: mad people on trains and deadlines and proper clothes and shopping on Sundays and Uber Eats. I missed Husband.

*

I was lonely, but I was not alone. I had Monsieur and Madame C next door and a community that had warmly welcomed me to its ranks: at the traditional Easter Omelette in the village hall – a meal that consisted exclusively of omelettes – they even made me a separate meal because, unbidden, Madame C had notified them that I didn't eat eggs. There are no secrets in a village, which made me wonder how it could possibly take a whole episode of *Midsomer Murders* to work out whodunnit. In my village we knew who-was-even-thinking-about-doing-it – buying a car, seeing the podiatrist, renovating their kitchen.

I'd made new friends. M, the one with holes in her tights who'd been cavorting all summer with an attractive young man in his thirties, introduced me to her eclectic circle of friends – musicians and carers, a DJ deliciously named Zaza, a former skater with Ice Capades and a woman we called the Commandant, who cleaned houses to fund her annual backpacking adventures to Africa to hang out with silverback gorillas and other elusive species. The Commandant was a bit like Madame C – she helped me with my French but, as her nickname implied, she was no pushover. That was the thing about living in small, out of the way places – all sorts of interesting people were thrown together. There was no point judging books by their covers: you had to read at least a few pages before making up your mind about whether you were going to get into their story. Being on the same page was about shared values and sensibilities, humour and tastes in movies and music: it had little – nothing, in fact – to do with what anyone did for a living.

The only snob in the ointment was me: from the outset I was determined to avoid falling in with the Anglo ex-pat tribe, easily identified by the Labrador drool on their Barbour jackets and the fact that so few of them seemed to have any French friends. With immaculate good taste, they restored neglected, falling-down country houses purchased at extortionate prices during the *Place in the Sun* boom set off by Peter Mayle's *A Year in Provence* when the pound was mightier than the euro. Cow sheds were turned into wow-factor kitchens; muddy fields were transformed into rose gardens; rusty hoes and old plough handles profitably abandoned by the farmer were recast as statement pieces and mounted on walls.

Not that I hadn't been guilty of this sort of behaviour myself – I had an authentic French rustic kitchen with hi-spec German appliances – it was just that I didn't see the point of moving to France to hang out with English people and moan about how plumbers never came when they said they would.

But as I was to discover, they weren't all like that, and equally there seemed little point (other than to make a point) in refusing to be friends with someone you liked just because they were English. I never did become part of the ex-pat crowd, but I did make one or two good friends among them, including one who called animals 'people' and made her own elderflower cordials, and another who wore a crested pinkie ring and had a good seat on a horse. On paper, neither of them was exactly my cup of sister, but then, neither was I theirs. That was the beauty of being outside your comfort zone. If you just listened hard enough, the countryside hummed with a rich variety of human species, which went some way to making up for the rich variety of animal species against which I kept up a low-grade war.

*

Things were going well with Husband: living six thousand miles apart seemed to be working for us. Now that the festering resentments about the big things were out of the way (indeed, a hemisphere out of the way), romance was rekindled. He found new ways to work that meant being able to spend more time in France. I looked forward to his visits; I was happy to see him come trundling through Arrivals with his silly pink suitcase. For a day or two it would be all violins and rosé. But I could set my Fitbit by us having a row on day three – one of those couple's rows that's like a boil you don't have time to lance until you're on holiday and can at last relax over a jug of sangria with bouzouki music loud enough to cover the hissing.

Once Husband and I stopped gazing into each other's eyes, we'd start to notice other things. Where were his gargoyles? he'd want to know (a hideous sketch by a local artist that I'd stuffed in a cupboard when he'd left the last time). And why was the car's front bumper hanging off? (He should have seen the other guy's.) And I'd remember that he never picked up shoes and always set his ringtone at a volume that could be heard in the next village.

It took time getting used to being around each other again, readjusting to each other's annoying little ways. Luckily we still had lots in common, and we both still snored. It was fun going to the markets together, taking turns to carry our brimming basket, meeting up with my new friends who became our new friends, driving to Barcelona for the weekend and tooting the horn as we whizzed confidently past the exit to IKEA. Over time, we turned the crumbly stone farmhouse into a self-catering holiday house and the barn into our home.

And then he'd be gone. In the days leading up to Husband's departure my emotions were mixed: I'd feel anxious (about being alone again), a little bit sad (I'd miss him) and a little bit happy (about being alone again).

*

People looked at me pityingly when I told them I was finding it hard to handle the summers: the merciless sun that beat down with retina-damaging, wrinkle-deepening, bristle-magnifying, hot-flush-fanning intensity.

Hot flushes made everything hotter. Suddenly, with no warning, I would turn the colour of my mother's witch brew cabbage and sweat would pour off me. These 'episodes' could go on for hours. Hot flushes were old standards in the repertoire of menopause jokes: a meno-pausal woman walks into a bar and forgets why she's there; where are my reading glasses? Oops! They're on my head. God forbid we should lose our sense of humour on top of everything else. But really, they weren't funny at all.

I tried to stay out of the sun. The cloudless, bottomless days and clammy nights that reminded most normal people why they were happy to be alive, left me feeling listless and whiny. In August I'd decamp to the garage on the bit of old carpet Mum and Auntie had thrown on the chilly cement and scratch my *aoûtats* until someone said, 'You can come out now, it's autumn.'

Husband and I played tag. He spent as much time as possible in France during the summer, which was my cue to fly back to Johannesburg and the southern hemisphere's winter. I'd return to France only when Husband reported that it was too cold to swim and everyone in the village was wearing fleeces. September to June were safe months, during which we were free to overlap.

All this back and forth had earned us silver status on Air France. It still meant being shoehorned into the back of the plane with a plastic fork and a stale bread roll, but we were allowed to take extra luggage. I gave Husband a smart new navy suitcase for his birthday that he refused to have anything to do with.

Over the years, our lifestyle – together and apart, a few months here, a few months there – became routine.

I was in South Africa more often than I'd imagined I ever would be again when I'd first semigrated to France. But everything was different now. I was different now. Instead of feeling trapped when I went there, I felt like a tourist on a three-month visa.

It even felt good to be back in Johannesburg, a hustling, bustling metropolis of mingled tongues and excellent coffee, bookshops and buskers and an ever-revolving kaleidoscope of people to watch. A skyline of neon-lit office blocks, street lights, cosy domestic dioramas illuminated by amber squares of window in the surrounding blocks of flats – the night was never completely dark. These were my stars, and I fell asleep to the distant whoosh of cars on the freeway. Johannesburg was a tough-love old mining town with a rich seam of warmth and humour running through it that now I could appreciate through a softer lens, from another angle, through an outlier's eyes. It was not all sad and bad, but then, I was no longer so sad and bad myself.

Ten years had gone by, and I knew that this city would be mine for as long as my children and grandchildren lived there, so we might as well be friends.

But I never stayed long enough to wish I hadn't.

There always came a point when I knew it was time to leave again, to pack up my bags (and somewhat less baggage) and return to my other world, because the one could not thrive without the other.

Home came to mean many things. Home was with Husband and children and grandchildren. Home was with my mother and aunts and sisters. Home was wherever I was. I tried to make sure I was always in the right territory when it mattered – births and birthdays, Christmases and crises, and my family on both sides of the ocean would loyally shuffle up to make space for me.

Would Husband and I ever live together permanently? Barring something unforeseen happening, I didn't see why we'd need to: we had found a way to be happy, just the way we were.

I imagined the couples counsellor turning in his tree-house.

Soon I would be sixty. I can't say I was looking forward to it: squirming through kindly meant speeches about my lifetime achievements and wondering if I'd used up my quota of lifetime achievements. Some of the sixtieth birthdays I'd been to were a bit like that – a faithful plod through the chronology of the birthday person's life, wit and wisdom. Sixtieth birthdays were retrospectives, because who knew? The next time anyone made a flattering speech about you it might be at your funeral.

But Husband was planning a very special celebration, one that would turn out to be more of a surprise than either of us – any of us – could possibly have foreseen.

Sixty

'One day I literally woke up and thought, My God, these knees have been with me for 60 years. I've had these elbows for 60 years. My heart has been beating for 60 years. The feet I stand on have carried me for 60 years. And when you think about it that way, you can be nothing but grateful.'

— OPRAH WINFREY

It was all arranged: the plane tickets were booked, the surprise Nick Cave concert tickets bought, my Botox topped up. The crumbly stone farmhouse in the French countryside would be turned over to a week-long house party to see in my sixtieth birthday, the one I'd made up my mind to enjoy as if I was actually happy about it.

As final preparations for the party and our joint exit from South Africa were laid, Husband and I were sojourning together in Johannesburg. It was one of our marital open seasons: autumn in South Africa and spring in France, and we were spending as much time as possible with Grandson and the newest addition to the family, his adorable baby sister. Over the years parting had become almost routine, though Grandson would always ask me, 'How long will you be in France, Toto?' Which would bring a lump to my throat because it was an impossible question to answer in a way that would make sense to him: 'France' was simply a name that meant 'going away'. But grandmothers were nice-to-haves, cherries on top of the parents. Leaving Grandson and, later, Granddaughter, for months at a time did not make me feel guilty: I was able to be with them more often than many other grandmothers who lived far away were – certainly more often than my own mother had been able to be with my children – and when we were together we made every moment count.

The South African side of the family would not be there for my big Six-Oh-Dear party, but the Brit contingent would be credibly represented. All my sisters and their partners were coming. Lifelong friends from London were coming. Disappointingly, Mum and Auntie weren't coming – their travelling days, they declared, were over. They couldn't be doing with the obstacle course at the airport, having to take off your clothes while being man-handled by bored security staff flirting with each other while running their hand up your leg. Then there was the two-mile hike to the boarding gate, and they certainly were not about to join the special assistance crowd and be *wheeled* onto the plane. Auntie said she was never going further than Aldi again.

As things turned out, none of us were.

Four days before Husband and I were due to fly back to France to get the house ready for the party, the world went into lockdown in the grip of a deadly new virus called Corona, which made it sound vaguely festive, like a royal investiture where everyone gets the day off or a fancy dress party. Flights were cancelled, borders were closed, impassable chasms opened between continents, countries and neighbours: no one was going anywhere, possibly ever again. Disappointment about my cancelled party was rapidly overtaken by far graver events.

After the work I'd done on myself in the last decade – asking the universe and Gwyneth Paltrow to guide me, making peace with my people, finding myself ... in fact, my whole midlife fucking existential journey had just gone up the spout. In the light of hitherto unimaginable circumstances, it was a piffling, pitiful, meaningless *shambles*.

There was a war on.

Now in their eighties, my mother and Auntie were prime candidates for the virus and had been ordered to stay indoors along with millions of other seemingly indestructible old people who, thanks to medical advances, had turned into Night Walkers and now threatened all our lives. What if Mum and Auntie got it? What if I never saw them again? But when I called her, Mum said not to worry because she'd already had it. 'Remember that terrible cough I had in January that made the downstairs neighbours bang on my ceiling with a broom? That must have been the virus, darling.'

She was threatening to ask her local health authority for a certificate of immunity so that she could join the frontlines and run errands for other old people in her block. In the war she'd been too young to join the doughty ranks of the WI, but now she could make up for it by being of service to others in the Covid crisis. Sister Two and I worked out that if indeed she'd had the virus in January, she was probably Patient Zero in North Devon. We insisted that she'd done quite enough for her community already and suggested that she might try just doing what she was told for a change.

'I'm not afraid to die,' she replied defiantly.

Sister Two and I took a dim view. 'Look, Mum, *you* might not mind popping off; you've had a long and fruitful life. What about the rest of us? If you get it, anyone who comes near you will be in danger. Auntie won't be able to come around for *Strictly* and canasta. Sister Four won't be able to pop in after work. You won't be able to go to the shops. The dog won't get walked. Come to think of it, you might end up having to eat the dog.'

Sister Four was the only one of us who lived close enough to Mum to see her regularly. She warned her that from now on she'd only communicate with her through the letterbox.

Seemingly unperturbed, Mum and Auntie formed their own support bubble and carried on killing each other at cards.

*

In the space of a few days, a world that had come to seem so small and navigable was suddenly as vast and impenetrable as it would have been before oars were invented. Like everyone else on the planet, I was in a state of stupefaction: what had just happened? What would happen next? There must be some mistake – in a few weeks we'd all be back to normal. It would take time for the shock of the new to settle into despair.

Worried as I was about being cut off from Mum, I was relieved that Husband and I were on the same side of the planet and in the same town as the children and grandchildren. And I was immensely relieved that Son had moved into his own flat a month before lockdown: it was going to be hard enough living with Husband for an *indeterminate period of time* in our compact Johannesburg apartment, the one the estate agent had described as a 'perfect lock-up-and-go for empty nesters'. The agent never said anything about what it would be like if you locked down and didn't go anywhere. Living apart had proved key to our sustainability as a married couple; now we were stuck together like cell mates in a correctional facility: how would Husband and I get along now? Would we work together to tunnel our way to freedom with teaspoons, or whittle them into murder weapons? You couldn't eat a packet of crisps without the crunch reverberating around the apartment like an imploding building. 'I can hear you *crunching*,' Husband would call from the bathroom. And he was hard of hearing, though not as hard as he was of listening.

In the beginning, lockdown was weirdly exhilarating: while the virus raged in terrifying earnest through Europe, it had yet to reach Africa in a way that caused significant worry; infections were still in the tens and there had been no deaths. It was like a phony war we had to be prepared for even though nothing bad had happened yet. I joined the national stampede to the shops for surgical masks, hand sanitiser and toilet paper, now scarcer than a first edition of *Harry Potter*. My morale was high and I'd had the foresight to get my hair and nails done. There were no errands to run, no admin clogging up my inbox, no frantic juggling of appointments, no social obligations, no more test cricket on TV. My sagging jawline disappeared behind the mask I'd scrounged off the nail technician.

Residents in our block of flats rallied to the cause. We set up a WhatsApp group and shared intel, rumours and baseless predictions about symptoms to watch out for and emergency numbers; loaves of banana bread were left on doorsteps; people posted amusing viral memes, back when the idea of pouring wine on your breakfast cereal still seemed funny. On the dot of 7 p.m. every evening we leaned out of our windows and banged pots in solidarity with the frontline health workers, including one of our very own, a nurse who lived in the flat next door. Like little drummer boys leading the troops into battle, we beat out rousing tattoos with wooden spoons on our pots until the nurse next door suggested that the best way to show our support when he came off a twelve-hour shift would be to shut the fuck up and let him get some sleep.

Husband signed up for an online yoga class. The instructor – Adriana was her name – had the body of a Russian trapeze artist and never said things like 'it's your turn to hang up the washing'. Other than that, I didn't see what she had that I didn't. But Husband seemed bewitched, flapping me away if I got in the way of the laptop when they were gazing into each other's groins and doing the Downward Dog. Adriana this, Adriana that; Adriana was becoming a royal pain in my flabby butt.

Three weeks into lockdown, on the eve of my sixtieth birthday, the South African government announced that everyone aged sixty and older would no longer be allowed outside *at all*. There was no point pretending any more: sixty was old, officially. Instead of spending my birthday singing along to Nick Cave throat-slashers and waving my lighter in time to 'The Ship Song' (I was already too old to remember I had a cell-phone torch), I'd be locked indoors with all the other old people. I consoled myself with the thought that Nick Cave would be too. In a further shock, the government announced that alcohol and tobacco sales would be banned from midnight. This was intended to keep the population at a sober social distance from one another and free up hospital beds for Covid patients instead of the usual Friday-night intake of drunks with axes in their heads.

Here was my chance to manage my lifestyle while I still had one. What better moment, what brighter lining in the cloud hanging over us, than to give up bad old habits and come through this crisis a thinner, better person *with no effort on my part*?

After giving this opportunity serious consideration, I concluded that we were all going to die anyway and I'd rather go out on a gin sling than ginseng and a nicotine patch. With eight hours left before prohibition, I raced to the off-licence and joined the crush of other semi-hysterical middle-aged women in Birkenstocks waiting for Jumbo Wine & Spirits to open. It was like a Lionel Ritchie concert. Security guards in visors and latex gloves took up position in a kettling formation. It was not a morning to browse the shelves for fruity top notes and fair-trade labels. By the time I got to the whisky aisle there were only seven bottles left. I took six, my never-take-the-last-biscuit-on-the-plate upbringing trumping good sense. Smoking proved more challenging, as the cigarette shelves at the off-licence had already been stripped, but in the following weeks ever-resourceful smokers set up underground networks, taking it in turns to make runs to the fake cigarette dealers in the seedier parts of town while dodging the stop-and-search police roadblocks. I was on the frontlines.

*

The Big Birthday dawned. Carefully unrolling myself out of bed, I just had time to do my stretches and make an espresso before my mother's traditional birthday call, which I knew from fifty-nine years of experience would be the first. No one else would be awake, and anyhow, the memory of a birth day was of far greater significance to a mother. She was the only one who actually remembered it – the pain and the pleasure, the bitch of a nun who told her to put out her cigarette in between contractions.

'Happy birthday, oh best beloved, my firstborn! How does it feel to be sixty?'

Having hated turning sixty herself, she sounded far more chipper about my joining the ranks of sexagenarians (a tragically misleading word that made being in your sixties sound quite racy).

'It's the new forty!' she said.

I sincerely hoped it wasn't as it would mean starting my midlife crisis all over again, like a mistrial.

'Listen, you have beautiful children and grandchildren, wonderful friends and a loving husband. You have your health.'

Of course, she was right: as the earth wobbled on its

axis, it was a good day to count my blessings. I had shelter and warmth and, thanks to the lockdown home-baking craze, a small plantation's worth of banana bread. On Maslow's hierarchy of needs, I was among the lucky ones. No one I knew personally had the virus and my birthday wish – for a pre-loved Prada bag that everyone would chip in for – now seemed shallow and pointless: we were all going to run out of money and it probably wouldn't go with my pyjamas. My revised sixtieth birthday wish was simply that my family and friends would be safe, and that I'd be lucky enough to grow old.

It was about the best birthday I'd ever had: throughout the day gifts arrived on the doorstep, though sadly without their givers. Son made me a charcoal drawing of the crumbly stone farmhouse in the countryside; Daughter produced a YouTube video of messages she'd spent weeks gathering from family and friends around the world; a friend who lived down the road (which might as well have been in Bermuda) dropped off a dress of hers I'd once admired. At sundown two of my neighbours leaned out of their window and performed 'Happy Birthday' in Morse code with pashminas. Husband announced that he and Adriana were taking a break. Such gifts could not be bought for money.

In Daughter's 'Happy Birthday' video, Sister Two sat at her kitchen table with a large, exciting-looking parcel in front of her. It looked vaguely … *bag-shaped*. I didn't want to get my hopes up, which was just as well because they were dashed as soon as Sister Two unwrapped my present to reveal a nylon backpack with a pick hanging off it.

'It's a pre-loved Bear Grylls bag!' she said, looking extremely pleased with herself.

Sister Two had been on a Bear Grylls survival weekend which involved swimming across a freezing river and spending the night on a bed of pine needles in wet underwear. She had been in training for the apocalypse for years, and now that it was here, she was going to make the most of it.

One by one, a magician pulling scarves out of a hat, she pulled objects out of the Bear Grylls bag and held them up to the camera with a flourish.

'Here's a thermal blanket for when you're homeless. Here are water-purifying tablets for when the sewerage system breaks down. Here's a Swiss Army knife for self-protection. Oh, and this is my favourite – a catapult to kill your own food!'

'You said you wanted a bag.'

Though Sister Two couldn't see my face, she knew the effect her gift would have on me – the desired one. I was forced to admit that, while a Bear Grylls survival kit might not have been what I'd always wanted, under the circumstances it could be exactly what I needed, though seeing as there were no more planes, I'd have to swim across a shark-infested Atlantic smeared in whale blubber to get it. Idly I wondered how Bear Grylls was getting on in lockdown – rappelling down the staircase, ziplining around the kitchen, foraging for baked beans? Probably not very well, I thought happily.

The planet breathed a sigh as pollution-choked skies cleared and the leatherback turtles returned to pristine beaches. The planet was rebooting; the planet was getting *my* makeover.

Sixty

*

When I'd first mentioned to Husband that I was thinking of writing about my experiences through the minefield of midlife, he said, 'Well, you'd better hurry up – menopause won't last forever.' I wasn't sure how to take this; was it a thought I could draw hope from (thank God, it would pass) or just deeply unsettling (once it had passed, I'd be past it)?

The wheels of menopause turn slowly, but we get plenty of warning. It begins with a far-off rumble of thunder on your way out the door, so you take an umbrella, just in case. Gradually the rumble gets louder and the sky lowers, spitting out ominous drops. Up goes the umbrella – mind the hair! – and you wish you'd thought to bring a raincoat, because now the sky is black and throwing down cannon-balls. Lightning forks and thunder claps; the wind whips and tears at the shreds of your umbrella and blows your hair inside out.

But, like all storms, eventually it passes: the rain clouds move on to piss on someone else's parade, a watery sun comes out, the puddles dry up. If you're lucky and have kept up your pelvic floor exercises, you might even see a rainbow, or at the very least, a silver lining.

*

My big fat funny scary odyssey through midlife was coming to an end. I'd certainly given the girl who'd once been me a rowdy send-off. Now it was time to let her go, to pick up my heels and walk briskly towards the rest of my life.

I've never understood what people mean when they said they feel 'young at heart', as if feeling 'old at heart' is the only alternative. It seems to me to be just another way of saying that nothing will ever be as good again. And wouldn't that be sad? It's true that nothing will ever be the *same* again, because life is not static; it changes all the time, it changes with us, we change with it. This is life's gift and its pleasure, its pain and its sorrow. At a time when life has never been less certain, it is all the more precious. And there can be no more deferments.

These days when I look into my Wicked Queen mirror, the woman I see reflected back at me does not make me want to jump for joy. I can't pretend that each new knock on the door doesn't give me a small fright: a face that after years of age-denying injectables doesn't quite match the rest of me; just the other day I noticed my palms were starting to look as if I'd been in the bath too long. I don't consider these noble scars, memorialising the joys and struggles I've experienced on the battlefield of life – that's desperate talk. I learn to live with my blotches and splotches because I must.

I don't think being older has miraculously turned me into a Wise Owl – anyhow, I'm not sure that's the look I'm going for. I may never grow out my greys or take up gardening or climb a mountain for charity or stick to a diet. I still do things sensible women wouldn't do or have long ago stopped doing. I still get by with a little help from my allopathic friends. The Ecstasy tablet remains sealed in its envelope in the drawer of my bedside table: I'm saving it for a rainy day, because there will always be rainy days.

Sixty

I don't think of my heart as young or old – it beats in the now, because where the hell else would it beat? I don't feel sixteen, I feel my age. After all, it's the only one I've got, and I will keep on coming of age until there is no age left to come of. I'm learning to embrace the things I have and let go of things I will never have again: I've even started to use words like *embrace* without sticking my finger down my throat. I hope I'm all done gazing at my navel because there are so many more interesting things to gaze at. I've made new connections and unearthed buried passions. I am grateful for the never-ending gift of my children and grandchildren, and for rediscovering the love that was hiding in plain sight. I suspect that Husband and I will grow old together, as long as we spend enough time apart. I'd like that.

The rest of my life has arrived, and I'm still in one piece, just put back together in new and interesting ways. And I have things to do, so many more things I want to do.

By any means necessary.

Epiphanies

Epiphany is a big word. Certainly, I didn't think I was having anything so grand while I was crawling through the debris of my youth crying out for diazepam. But here are a few things I've learned, things I know to be simple and true, the values I strive to live by, even when I don't succeed.

- I've forgiven myself for most, if not all, of my trespasses, and worked out which ones weren't really trespasses in the first place.

- I've learned how to live with my contradictions, though I try not to let them confuse other people.

- I've learned to live with other people's contradictions, because they're what make us imperfect in interesting ways.

- I've come to appreciate the relief of shaking out uncomfortable truths and exposing them to the light.

- Becoming a better person is hard work, but you have to show up, even if you're late.

- It's impossible to be happy all the time, which puts the bad days in perspective.

- Compassion and kindness are sacred, but they take practice.

- Laughter is essential, preferably at one's own expense.

- Faith is good; doubt is unavoidable.

- Learning never ends until we do.

The Fuck-It List

Every woman over fifty needs a Fuck-It list because WE'RE STILL TOO YOUNG FOR A BUCKET LIST!

Compiling my own list of Fuck Its has been incredibly liberating – a sort of manifesto-in-progress of all the things I don't want to do, probably never wanted to do and refuse to ever do again: obligations that are a complete waste of time that I'll never get back; people and places I have absolutely no desire to visit before I die. My Fuck-It list grows as it goes. I asked my friends to share their own Fuck-It lists with me, and I've been inspired by the range of objectives they've come up with, objectives I might not have thought of myself but which are totally worth copying. Here are a few of the things we variously voted as being critical to the advance of Fuck-It-ism.

Girls, this is the 'No' list we've always wanted, and there's nothing to lose except trouble.

- We won't stay up till midnight on New Year's Eve or go to anything that starts after 8 p.m. when we could be in bed with a pill and a Greggs sausage roll.

- We won't make small talk with taxi drivers.

- We won't spend more than one minute in a museum speculating about whether a fragment of Stone Age rock was used as a paring knife.

- We won't spend more than one minute at an art exhibition pretending to be fascinated by a burst bin liner and wondering if the artist is as big a disappointment to his parents.

- We won't answer the phone or the doorbell just because it rings.

- We won't go to India just because everyone says it's a deeply spiritual experience.

- We won't let bigoted/racist/sexist/bullying behaviour go unchallenged out of politeness.

- We won't put up with loud-mouth bores at bus stops out of politeness.

- We won't let teenage beauty therapists tell us that we've been using the wrong moisturiser for forty years.

- We won't finish a book just because we started it.

- We won't take nutritional advice from anorexic celebrities.

- We won't flog dead relationships.

- We won't make fake friends at networking sessions with people we normally wouldn't let pat the dog and who won't give us the job anyway.

- We won't accept invitations from people we have nothing in common with just because we can't think up a good excuse in time.

- We won't apologise for ourselves before we even open our mouths.

Try it – once you start, you won't want to stop.

Acknowledgements

With thanks to everyone who contributed to making this book.

The women who shared their stories with me over countless conversations, whose bold hearts, empathy and humour informed and inspired all that I wrote, and others, who supported me in their own unique and generous ways:

Monica Albonico, Christa Bauer, Ruth Becker, Debbie Bell, Ariane Bonzon, Christine Chapman, Keith Coleman, Bernard Corneil, Françoise Corneil, Maggie Davey, Helena Dolny, Karen Dys, Cathy Fisher, Dugan Fraser, Hugh Fraser, Bridget Impey, Emma Gilbey Keller, Nathalie Göbbels, Jane Gregory, Janice Honeyman, Alex Katz, Julia Keller, Liza Key, Shuna le Moine, Sylvie Manigot, Irwin Manoim, Dolly Matsubukanye, Chris McGreal, Juliet Mellish, Flo Millet, Mary Msibi, Charmain Naidoo, Samkeli Ngulube, Debbie Norval, Crispian Olver, John Perlman, Isabelle Zaza Place, Robbie Potenza, Janine Rauch, Margie Ross, Lomin Saayman, Melinda Silverman, Anne Stanwix, Miriam Wheeldon, Ben Willis, David Wright, Martine Zambon, Bryna Zasman.

My brilliant, beady-eyed friends Lauren Jacobson, Michele Magwood and Tanya Pampalone, whose input helped me carve ideas out of clay, and my sister Belinda

Bauer, who showed me the ropes and made sure I never had enough to hang myself.

The big swinging pros: super scout Rebecca Servadio, who appeared at just the right moment; my publisher Karen Duffy who took a chance on me and elegantly steered this book all the way to the shelf; the unflappable Kate Ballard, for waving her wand over successive drafts, Emma Dunne, who winkled out the devils in the detail, and all at Atlantic Books who put thought, time and skills into getting the book out there – a far cry from the days when I sat at home alone in my PJs, doubting that it would ever happen.

My irrepressible agent, Judith Murray, who breathed life into my writing and never rested – never let me rest! – until I brought her a better book than the one we started with. Judith, you are the biz.

The wonderful women in my family: my extraordinary sisters, Belinda, Katy and Lizzie, who stopped being annoying in time to become my best friends; my half-sister Lisa, who isn't old enough yet to have to get over being young; my cousin, Angela, the big sister I always wanted; my auntie Gila, a constant light in my life, and my mother-in-law, June, with whom I formed a close bond over the years and I think has forgiven me for not being Jewish.

My rebels-in-chief: my mother, Gilly, and auntie Sue, for trusting me to throw them under the right bus, for being unputdownable storytellers who manage to spin gold from life's lemons, for growing old with style, gusto and guts. You are the stars of this show.

My beautiful children, Nandi and Samuel, the bright shining New Grown-Ups who have taught me so much about ways of loving. My darlings, I hope I haven't embarrassed you any more than I absolutely had to, and that you'll let me keep my car keys until I start knocking down traffic lights. My perfect son-in-law, Brett, and my beloved grandchildren, Jackson and Madeline, who are making their own stories and shaping mine in ways I could once barely have imagined.

Deep gratitude and respect to my husband, Clive, who encouraged me to write my truth, even when it didn't quite accord with his version of events. Husband, you've been with me all the way, even when we were continents apart – sometimes for better, sometimes for worse, but always, in the end, for the best. You have my Selfish A-type heart.